HOW TO SELL YOUR HOME
In Good or Bad Times

Michael C. Murphy

 Sterling Publishing Co., Inc.   New York

Library of Congress Cataloging-in-Publication Data

Murphy, Michael C. (Michael Charles), 1950–
   How to sell your home in good or bad times / by Michael C. Murphy.
      p.   cm.
   Includes index.
   ISBN 0-8069-7366-8
   1. House selling.   2. Real estate business.   I. Title.
  HD1379.M835   1991
  333.33'8—dc20   91-22130
                                         CIP

10 9 8 7 6 5 4 3 2 1

Published in 1991 by Sterling Publishing Company, Inc.
387 Park Avenue South, New York, N.Y. 10016
© 1991 by Michael C. Murphy
Distributed in Canada by Sterling Publishing
c/o Canadian Manda Group, P.O. Box 920, Station U
Toronto, Ontario, Canada M8Z 5P9
Distributed in Great Britain and Europe by Cassell PLC
Villiers House, 41/47 Strand, London WC2N 5JE, England
Distributed in Australia by Capricorn Link Ltd.
P.O. Box 665, Lane Cove, NSW 2066
Manufactured in the United States of America
All rights reserved

Sterling ISBN 0-8069-7366-8

Contents

Acknowledgments

Many people have contributed their time and expertise in making this book. Rich Gradel, attorney and CPA, provided the special tax information in Chapter 14. Bill Biros and supersalesman Brian Boles of Biros Realtors on Chicago's South Side supplied advice and forms. Thanks also to mortgage banker T.C. Blair, attorney and broker Kevin J. Murphy, Joy Collett at the IRS, appraiser Doug Embrey, and Bo Kaczmarek for the mortgage tables. Art Moher and Richard Sherman of Golden Dome Realty, Laughlin Consulting Group, Jim Morgan and Jenny Wolf at West Coast Properties, and Jeff Jeffers at WNDU–TV provided valuable information.

The following fellow attorneys confabulated and assisted with various topics: Geoffrey P. Norton, Robert Scott, Robert Galgan, Beth Farrell, Mary Wafer, Timothy P. Murphy, Leslie Coulson, Jan Rewers, Elio Polselli, Carol Stanton, William A. McCummiskey, Rennard Strickland, James O'Neill, and Larry Dudus. Colleagues at the University Center at Tulsa have helped, especially Greg Marshall, Steve Ward, Beth Snyder, Diana Sharp, Calvin Hall, Doug Woodall, and Paulette Gauger. Diane Lowrey and LaTonya Phillips were responsible for manuscript preparation. Sterling Publishing Company's Senior Vice President Charles G. Nurnberg has provided the author with unerring guidance for a decade, and editor Claire Wilson has been a valued collaborator. Finally, the author is most grateful to his nine brothers and sisters and to his parents, Mary Jane and Jerome Murphy. Their loyalty, support, confidence, and love help to surmount the vicissitudes of life.

Preface

Congratulations for having the wisdom to invest in yourself by purchasing this book. When you put your home on the market, it will be competing with many others for the attention and affection of a buyer. The ideas in this book can help you get a competitive edge. Many sellers make little effort to inform themselves before jumping into one of the biggest financial transactions of their lives. Whether you are using an agent or selling your home by yourself, understanding the process will save you marketing time and help you get top dollar for your home.

This book is crammed full of tips, features, and ideas that a home seller can use. Some of these concepts include: working with agents and lawyers; special chapters aimed at For-Sale-By-Owner (FISBO) sellers; pricing your home right; comprehensive marketing plans; how to handle negotiations; tips on preparing your home for sale and how to show your home; tax consequences of the sale of your home; successful open-house strategies; creative seller financing; selling in soft or depressed markets; understanding contracts and legal forms; becoming familiar with real estate forms; and debunking the real estate collapse scenario. Checklists, forms, tips, and mortgage tables are provided for your use.

Michael C. Murphy is the author of *How to Buy a Home While You Can Still Afford to* (Sterling). Almost 50,000 readers have profited from his advice and achieved a big part of their own American dream. Like you, they are moving up and ready to reach for bigger dreams. The spirit of your dreams is captured in the guidance of these pages.

1
The 1990s: A Decade of Falling Home Prices?

The decade of the 1990s was ushered in with predictions aplenty. Prognosticators made headlines with forecasts covering a wide variety of subjects: war in the Middle East could send the price of oil skyrocketing to more than $100 per barrel; a massive earthquake will probably rock the central USA, and California will probably suffer the "big one" before 2000; Fidel Castro might jam television signals in the southeastern USA; but the Soviet and European communists were convinced of their past errors, and their reforms might earn them a Nobel Peace Prize.

Business and economic forecasters warned of more failing thrifts and banks; accelerated inflation; more rapid gyrations in the stock market, exacerbated by programmed trading; more budget deficits and higher taxes; and a recession to start the decade.

A Grim Outlook for Housing?

In the housing sector, most forecasts were of the usual vanilla variety. A handful of forecasts were downright shocking and predicted a collapse in single-family home prices in the 1990s. The media jumped on this, and the public couldn't get enough of it. Homeowners wondered if they were next while viewing television stories about various depressed markets. The shakeout in the oil patch in the mid-80s left the housing markets in Texas, Oklahoma, and Louisiana reeling for five years. As the decade began, most markets in the northeastern USA were soft. Some neighborhoods in the

Boston, Hartford, New York City, and northern New Jersey areas experienced 20% declines in values. Foreclosures and HUD-owned, repossessed homes helped glut the supply of homes for sale in some areas. Beleaguered sellers were even resorting to the auction method of selling their homes when creative financing failed to generate a sale.

Was all this gloom and malaise in some housing markets a preview of the decade to come? Let's examine the argument by those who believe housing prices will decline sharply in the 1990s. Proponents of the housing bust theory focus upon first-time homebuyers and the role they play in housing markets. First-time homebuyers are usually 25-34 years old. They typically account for 30% of all buyers and purchase an existing home from homeowners in the 35-54 year old age group that has been dubbed the "move-up" (or "Trade-Up") segment of the housing market. Those homeowners over age 55 are usually referred to as "empty-nesters." The first-time homebuyers may be the key to the fate of the move-up buyers. The move-up buyer has built up equity in his home over the years by paying down his mortgage loan balance and benefitting from appreciating values. (Your equity is the difference between the current market value of your home and your remaining loan balance.) The move-up homeowner wants to sell his "starter" home and use the proceeds (or profit) from that sale to make a down payment on a bigger and more expensive "Luxury" or "Executive" home. The move-up owner depends upon the first-time buyer to convert that paper equity to cold cash. Thus, the first-time buyer is the key performer in the chain of events. If the first-time buyer does *not* buy from the move-up owner, the move-up owner will not be able to buy from the empty-nesters or new home builders.

The central argument made by housing bust proponents is that there will be *fewer* first-time homebuyers in the decade of the 1990s and that they will find it more difficult than their predecessors did in the 1970s and 1980s to *afford* a starter home. Demographic studies of population growth support the argument that first-time buyers will be fewer in number. The huge number of baby-boomers born from 1945 to 1965 are aging and passing through the first-time buyer stage. In 1970 there were 16 million households headed by those under age 35; in 1980 the total swelled to 25 million; and in 1990 it levelled off at 26 million. By the year 2000, demographers believe there will be only 21 to 22 million households in the under-age-35 category. From 2000 to 2010 there will be even fewer younger households. The baby boom was followed by the "baby bust." Zero population growth (ZPG) and the birth-death rates of the 1970s make those forecasts very plausible.

Will these fewer first-time buyers be able to afford to buy a starter home? Will they have the cash necessary to make a downpayment and to meet closing/settlement costs? Will they have income levels necessary to qualify for a loan? The affordability question is hard to answer because the major variable is the interest rate, and it fluctuates. Inflation drives interest rates, and the two move in the same direction over time because lenders seek an inflation-adjusted real rate of return.

Interest Rates and Inflation

Let's spend a minute on the concept of "real" interest rates. In 1990, inflation was 6.1%, as measured by the Consumer Price Index. Suppose you lent your friend $1 on January 1, 1990, and your friend agreed to pay you 5% interest, and to return your dollar on December 31, 1990. You would receive $1.05 on December 31, 1990, but because your dollar's purchasing power had depreciated 6.1% due to inflation, what cost you $1.00 to buy a year ago when the loan was made now costs you $1.06 to buy. You are a loser! You lost the use of your money for a year, you assumed the risk that the borrower would not go bankrupt or fail to repay the entire loan amount, and you made a loan at 5% when inflation was 6%. If the loan was repaid in full on the due date, you lost 1.1% in the transaction. (Actually you would lose more after you pay taxes on that income!)

Just to break even on a loan before-tax terms, the lender must charge an interest rate equal to the actual rate of inflation for the loan period. But why would a lender want to break even and give loans for free? Lenders have overhead costs to pay and also assume the risk that the loan will be repaid. Lenders want an inflation-adjusted ("real") rate of return that is usually 2%–4% more than the expected rate of inflation. With 6.1% inflation in 1990, it was not surprising to see short term interest rates around 8% and long term interest rates on 30-year home loans around 10%.

It is virtually impossible to predict interest rates for the decade. Forecasters give it a try, and the consensus is that inflation will average 5% annually in the 1990s, and 30-year home loans will be made at 9% rates.

My Forecast is Rosier

Forecasting is a difficult process because unknown variables surface and known variables can change in unpredictable ways. However, you bought this book and are entitled to my best guesses on the decades of the 1990s. Here's my best shot—take it with a grain of salt. I do *not* hold the opinion that housing prices will collapse nationwide. National statistics are almost meaningless to me, because housing is not a portable consumer good. (You do not pick up your home and move it with you!) Because real estate markets are local in nature, a different set of supply-and-demand factors are at work in each city or area. The interplay of these supply and demand factors is what determines housing prices. On the demand side, the gloomsters are correct in saying that net household formation will decline among the under-35 age group. Relatively slower growth in real disposable income for this group may also slow demand for single-family starter homes. Problems with the banking and thrift institutions may lead to higher downpayments, mortgage insurance fees, and other initial cost. These expenses could dampen buyer enthusiasm. On the other hand, lower inflation and interest rates could increase demand and solve the affordability problem and unleash the pent-up demand of the 35-age group that rented in the 1980s.

On the supply side, I expect labor and material costs to continue to increase at a rate equal to that of inflation, as measured by the consumer price index. These construction costs affect the price of *new* homes. The price of land will rise at twice the rate of inflation. Zoning, restrictive covenants, environmental and land use ordinances, and limited growth philosophies will continue to add 25%–30% to the cost of building a new home. Statistical models of housing markets also fail to consider the desirability of some of the existing housing stock. There may be plenty of modestly priced homes in older neighborhoods in some of our big cities, yet few buyers of any ethnicity or culture want to live there because of crime, drugs, and a poor quality of life. If first-time buyers will not live there, they must bid up the prices for starter homes in desirable areas, or pay more for a newly constructed home.

In the 1990s, I believe that market segmentation will become even more pronounced and visible. The move-up markets should be hot, as the aging baby boomers reach their peak earning years and have increased real disposable personal income. Most new construction will probably be of the luxury home variety—not the starter home type. In the 1970s, the value of a median *new* home increased at a *real* rate of 3.3%. In the 1980s, that figure was 2.1%. Expect more of the same for the 1990s.

Existing home prices should be treated as a separate segment. Their prices increased at a real (inflation adjusted) rate of 3.1% in the 1970s, but just 0.1% in the 1980s. Stated another way, the prices of existing homes in the 1980s just kept pace with inflation. In the 1990s, I expect the prices of existing homes nationwide to increase at a rate slightly *below* the rate of inflation.

The big question you are concerned about, and rightfully so, is how is the housing market in *my* area going to do in the 1990s? I can give only one general answer to fit the tens of thousands of local real estate markets. Keep your eyes on one statistic: employment growth for your area. If your growth rate is close to the national average, expect housing prices to generally move in line with inflation over time. If your growth rate is less than average, prices will probably not keep pace with inflation. Those areas experiencing job growth rates above the national average will probably also experience rising home prices at a rate above the inflation rate.

2
Why Are You Selling?

You have bought this book because you are seriously considering selling your home. *Why* are you selling your home? What is the *reason* for your decision to sell? What needs are not fulfilled by your present home?

Your reason or "motivation" for selling affects your bargaining position and could mean the difference in thousands of dollars at closing to you! How so? Your motivation may compress your time frame to make a decision, and force you to accept a low offer to meet some closing deadline that you have set or that circumstances have forced upon you. Would you like to be a buyer negotiating with a seller that has to be in Chicago to start a new job in 3 weeks? Would you like to be a buyer negotiating with sellers who have to make two mortgage payments until they sell their home? Of course you would—buyers dream of finding motivated sellers! Remember, buyers ask two basic questions initially: first, what is the asking price?, and second, why are they selling? As a seller, your objective is to maximize your financial gain on the sale of your home. The right *timing* of your marketing plans can be crucial.

Seller's Reasons Vary

Have *you* evaluated your reason for selling? Some of the most common reasons why people sell their homes follow. The need for *more space* may precipitate a home sale and move to larger housing. A new addition to the family or growing children can put a premium on existing space. Elderly or infirm relatives may become part of your household and add to the space crunch. For some sellers, *too much space* is motivation to sell. The "empty nest" effect takes hold when the last child leaves homes. Divorce, death or illness may also cause individuals to seek smaller housing units. Powerful emotions may surface in the decision-making process sellers face, and these unhappy events can trigger pressures to sell rapidly.

The *quality of life* in your neighborhood may be your primary motivation for selling. Drugs and thugs may be taking over in your schools, parks, and shops. Air and noise pollution in the environment may be increasing to disturbing levels. Demographic trends may disturb you. Vacancy rates in residential and commercial real estate may signal hard times ahead for your area. Unemployment trends may alarm you. Statistics aside, perceptions that residents have of their own neighborhood are very important. Behavior usually follows belief, so gut feelings that the neighborhood is going downhill and the grass is greener elsewhere may eventually lead to a decision to move.

Financial considerations motivate many sellers. Firings, layoffs, reduced work hours, and emergency expenditures can play havoc with a family budget. Monthly mortgage payments may be too high. Utilities may be too high. The costs of commuting to work may be too high. Even with a revamped budget and debt rescheduling, some households may have to sell their home. The financial changes in your life may be pleasant ones, and a pay raise or second income may lead to thoughts of *moving up* to a more prestigious neighborhood. Some sellers implement a long-term *trade-up* strategy, and plan to live in 6 or 7 homes before they settle into their dream home. They plan to live in a home for 2 or 3 years, build up their equity, sell their home and then use the equity to buy a more expensive home. They repeat this process until they have their "perfect" home. *Transfers* and *job-related moves* may motivate sellers. (Some corporations have relocation and buy-out programs. If you are selling for this reason, check this out!)

Adding-On Versus Selling

Occasionally, homeowners who want more space consider adding-on to their present home as an alternative to moving. You may really love your neighborhood! The schools, parks, shopping, transportation, your children's friends, and your friends are perfect! You have spent lots of energy and money on your color schemes, landscaping and other features of your home. Why not add-on? Some economic realities may be sobering. It can be unwise to upgrade the value of your home total price level above those of surrounding homes. If you live in a neighborhood of homes that are valued in the $80,000–$90,000 price range, your upgraded home will be hard to sell at $120,000. Remember: $1 spent on add-ons will rarely increase your equity by $1. (You may recoup only 50 cents for each dollar spent!) Add-ons can diminish a home's usefulness. A two bedroom home may have one bathroom and a modest sized kitchen. If two more bedrooms are added on, the additional residents may cause a traffic jam in the bathroom and congest the kitchen area. Poorly designed add-ons may look amateurish and clumsy and add little to your home's value.

Consider these economic realities, but who says economics must rule your decision-making process? If you are sure that you'll be in your house for another 20 years, a $30,000 add-on may still be right for you. It really depends upon your values, and whether you view housing as an investment or a consumer good or some combination of the two.

3
Sprucing Up for a Date with a Buyer

Are you ready for some news that will wrinkle your brows? The odds are high that you are going to have to spend some time, energy, and money sprucing up your home to prepare it for sale. I can already hear you grumbling . . . "Why me? My house is in great shape now!". . . . "Not me! I'm not the one who is gung-ho on selling, my spouse is, and he/she will do the work". . . . or "We can't afford to" . . .

The condition of your property and home will become *very* important to you, starting right now! The condition of your home affects the number of lookers you will get, and then the number of serious offers you will get. Ultimately, the condition of your home affects the price you will receive for your home. How important is the condition of your home? That depends on the dynamics of your local housing market at the time you sell. In a buyer's market, things can be tough on sellers because there is a surplus of homes for sale, and there are fewer buyers. In such a buyer's market, home condition becomes a bigger factor as buyers compare properties. In a seller's market, the importance of condition is diminished somewhat. In a *really* hot seller's market, an oversized doghouse or Cub Scout pup tent could sell!

Curb Appeal and Psychology

A "For Sale" sign attracts all sorts of attention from nosey neighbors, gawkers, bicyclists, walkers, Sunday drivers, and honest-to-goodness prospective buyers. These prospects may be in their own cars, or they may be riding with an agent. Your home and property must have enough curb appeal to at least get those buyers out of the car to take a look inside. What percentage of prospects never even get out of the car and cross over the curb? Estimates suggest that 50% of the prospects never see the inside because something about the outside turns them off. Can you afford to lose these prospects?

Consumer behaviorists and real estate professionals offer several explanations and views of the buyer's psychological framework. First impressions are very important in meeting people or products. Did you spend a little extra time on your appearance and makeup before that first date with Mr. Special? Guys, how about the last time you had to meet with someone important? Do sellers of used cars spruce up the product before sale? Does your local grocer oil and shine the cucumbers? Do consumer products companies spend millions of dollars on package-design research before a product hits the shelves? Does virtually every candidate at the big job interview have on a dark suit?

What typical conclusions might a buyer draw if your home lacks curb appeal? "If the outside looks shabby, so does the inside." "If the owners didn't pay attention to such a simple thing as peeling paint, they probably neglected a lot of big problems, too. We just spent two months and $2,000 fixing up our place to sell, we don't want to buy another experience like that. We just want to relax a bit." "I don't want to spend my weekends up on a ladder. There's got to be some better houses out there, let's drive on. We can always come back."

Guess what? There are better houses out there, because other sellers and their agents realize that people don't buy houses—they buy dreams, emotions, feelings, and impressions. They are buying a bundle of attributes that will yield some expectations beyond shelter. Now that you realize this, you can cash in on it. Let me suggest some ways to make you an efficient market researcher.

Raising Your Consciousness

For one week, I want you to play the Curb Appeal Game. Every time you drive somewhere, look carefully at the outside of every home and the property. What makes one home more appealing than another? Take a notebook with you and jot down the features and touches that you reacted positively to. Look at different types of homes all over town, whether they are for sale or not. The kids, your spouse, your parents, and your friends can play too. At the end of the week, review your notes and summarize them.

The next week, you should begin to play the Buyer Game. If you haven't yet done so, go shopping inside homes for sale for ideas. There may be open houses galore this weekend that you can visit without appointments. If you are already working with an agent, he or she may arrange a tour of your competition. Take your notebook. What did you like or dislike about each home? How did the house show? What was your first impression? What were your final impressions and why?

Now its time to turn a critical eye upon your own home and property. Your agent can be most helpful in this task, and so can your friends, neighbors, and relatives. Invite them over to play the Buyer Game at your house. Be sure to invite the cranky and very picky relatives you have. You want critical analysis, not soothing jibberish from "yes men." Everyone can write down his or her impressions and ideas and reconvene in the kitchen for some of your world famous whatever. You can conduct a focus group session and hone in on specific problem areas. After everyone leaves, organize your notes.

By now, you have been bombarded with ideas. Some suggestions frightened your socks off, such as "get new carpeting," "get a new roof," or "sod your entire lawn." Other suggestions were aimed at minor problems, such as "put a new washer in the bathroom faucet," or "mop the basement floor." Your mood was upbeat last week, and you were excited about your upcoming move. Now you feel a little bit run down and wonder if anyone in their right mind will buy this rundown lemon you are trying to sell. Sure they will! Remember, you are not selling a new home, you are selling a used, lived-in, pre-owned (yes, go ahead and say it) old home! Buyers don't expect *perfection* in existing homes. If they want perfection they can pay $30 per square foot more and buy a new home. Most buyers want a sound house that looks well-cared for, and that is what you will give them. Right?! Hey, things don't look so dreary after all! Go out for a pizza or some ice cream, and we'll tackle that work list tomorrow.

Winning the War Against Clutter

OK, where do you start? There is much work to be done, and it must be assigned priority ranking. To prioritize these tasks, you must remember that the buyer is buying a bundle of attributes in your home. The most important attribute for most buyers is space. Let's start there.

Your objective is to re-arrange your furnishings in such a manner that your living space appears to be large, spacious, uncluttered, and ultimately roomy enough to accommodate all the belongings of a prospective buyer. The first places to attack are the attic, basement, garage, and storage shed. There are two good reasons to begin with these spots: first, they are already the final resting spot for many discarded and seldom used items; and second, when they are cleaned out it will create additional space for storing more important items that you will be boxing up shortly.

Throwing out items can be hard. It goes against some of our habits (thrift, wasteful behavior is sinful, etc.) and our emotions (that was junior's first toy). My great Aunt Irma's basement contained cancelled checks from the 1930s and enough old empty candy boxes from 1960 to supply the city of Chicago with toffee for 10 years. We chuckle, but there is a little bit of Aunt Irma in all of us. How do you decide what to keep and what to part with? Here are a few questions to ask yourself.

· How useful is this item?

· Who uses it?

· How often is it used?

· When was used last?

· Is the item worth repairing?—Why haven't I done so?

- How many of these do we already have?
- Is it really valuable?
- If so, would I be willing to pay $$ to put it in a mini-storage place?

Many people consider several alternatives to the garbage dump. One popular option is the garage sale. Some people swear by them, some people swear at or about them. For some it is an exciting adventure to hold a garage sale, to others it isn't worth the $15 an hour to put up with 6:00 A.M. early-birds ringing the bell. If you aren't real excited about hosting a garage sale, all is not lost. Odds are good that there is *somebody* on your block that is, and would love to have your stuff as part of a giant blockwide sale. Let them orchestrate the affair, give them the headaches, and share the loot.

You can also donate the items to your local church's rummage sale, Goodwill Industries, the Salvation Army, Amvets, or whoever. You might feel good and get a tax deduction. Some for-profit resale shops buy clothes and other stuff by the pound. Check your phone books. Many people hold a garage sale and donate the nonsellers to a charitable organization.

Creating an Impression of Spaciousness

Now that the biggest storage spots are free of clutter, turn your attention to all the rooms people live and relax in. Remember, you are trying to create the impression of spaciousness. The "right" amount of space cannot be calculated precisely by formulas, but people know when a room "feels" too small. Let's examine two extremes. First, consider a vacant house with no furnishings in it. Plenty of open space is evident to the eye, but the eye has no reference points to focus upon, such as furniture, beds, pictures, etc. The critical eye will wander, and focus upon anything it spots, be it nail holes in the wall, chipped paint, worn spots in the carpet, etc. Without reference points, the buyers perceptions of habitability and satisfaction can become distorted. Not convinced?! OK, take a trip to a new housing development in your area. Notice that the model home unit is furnished, and buyers can mentally "see" themselves living there. They want to buy the model unit, not the vacant or not yet built units. While you are visiting the model home, get a feeling for space. How much furniture is there, and how is it arranged?

The opposite of a vacant house is a cluttered house. Have you ever been in a house that is so crowded with furnishings that you feel like you are trapped in an obstacle course or a fun house at the amusement park? Houses with too much furniture, oversized furniture, too many paintings, decorations, and knicknacks show poorly. They appear to be too small, and prospective buyers have a hard time imagining themselves and their belongings fitting comfortably into the house.

Your objective is to find a happy medium between the vacant house and the cluttered house. You solve the clutter problem one room at a time.

Take a critical look at your home. Let's use the living room as an example. Is the furniture arranged around the perimeter of the room, creating an airy, open feeling? Maybe you should think about storing some of those oversized pieces in the attic, basement or garage (now that you cleaned those areas first!). Is that coffee table too large? How about the cabinet? Maybe a chair or two should be removed, and the paintings or wall hangings can contribute to the cluttered feeling also. One note of caution about removing wall hangings; the paint behind them is usually a different (cleaner, lighter) shade than the rest of the wall and there may be nail holes.

You may be able to wash the walls, spackle the holes and touch them up with a dab of the original paint (if you have the paint!). Or, you may have to repaint the room. If you choose to repaint the room, remember, you want to create the feeling of space. Select a ceiling white color, and paint the walls with a bright color (in other words, pick a neutral, basic—some may say bland—color). Woodwork should be done in a semi-gloss enamel finish because it wears well and cleans best over the years. Again, don't get too artistic in selecting colors. Bold woodwork colors that contrast with light wall and ceiling colors can make the room seem smaller. Your best bet is to pick a trim color that is similar to the color of the walls.

Cabinets and shelves may be stuffed and cluttered. It's time to box up some of those items, label them and store them in the attic or basement. Don't feel bad—you are moving soon, and will have to box it up shortly, so do it now.

You can apply the same space-creating principles to the other rooms of the house. Each room may offer different problems. Closets are usually a big challenge for the clutter killers. It is absolutely essential that you clean and organize your closets in such a manner to emphasize space. Prospective buyers want storage space! What can you do about your closets? Out of season clothes should be removed and stored. What about those shoes? Are you planning to open up a store with Mrs. Marcos? Why not store those shoes you will not wear over the next few months while you are selling your home? Organizing the space you have can be a big help. Discount stores sell closet organizers. Take a look at them, even if you aren't going to buy one, you'll get some useful ideas to help you remodel or re-arrange your closet space. Sometimes a simple change, such as raising or lowering the height of the clothes rack or bar can create additional space to add shelves or compartments. Closets should be well lit and painted with light colors. You must force yourself to create closet space. A good rule of thumb is this: if there is the slightest doubt—take it out!!

Tone Down Your Turf

Its important to remember that prospective buyers are thinking about how *their* belongings would look in the space you call home. Their minds are already making changes in the layout and decoration of your space. You are proud of your furnishings and decorative scheme (you spent hours on that wallpaper!). Buyers may think your taste is terrible. Buyers can also be put off by a house that is imbued with too much of your personality. Buyers are strangers entering your turf, and are apprehensive about entering your lair. After all, they aren't shopping for new friends, they are shopping for a home of their dreams, that fits their lifestyle and personalities. If you de-emphasize your personality, it makes it easier for them to imagine themselves living in your home. You can tone down your personality by removing items that stress your personality. Some of these items may be family photos, collectibles, magazines, hobby-related items, sports mementos, and posters in the children's room. Pack away these items so that your personality becomes neutralized and the buyers can concentrate on the attributes of your home, not the people who live there.

Houses and rooms can have distinctive odors that turn off prospective buyers. Haven't you been in other houses that smell different than what you are used to? Does your house smell? Because you live there, you may not even notice any odors. You may have to ask a friend, neighbor, or relative for an unbiased opinion. You may not notice pet odors. Musty-smelling basements scare buyers because they think you may have problems with the foundation or plumbing system. Closets should appear to be spacious, light and airy. Bathrooms can be a haven for a variety of odors, and you must eliminate them. Garbage cans and areas are prime offenders.

Tour Your Own Home as a Buyer

Let's put ourselves in the position of the prospective buyer, and take a tour of your home. At the end of this chapter is an extensive checklist of items that will help you spruce up your property. For now, you want to see things and develop impressions as a buyer would.

As a buyer views your home from the street, what is the impression your home gives? Should the buyer get out of the car, or drive on? Is the yard neat and trim? How about the exterior of the home? Peeling paint, damaged siding, wood, or masonry, cracked windows, loose shingles on the roof, and any glaring defect may keep a buyer in the car. Aesthetically, does the style and colors of your home fit the character of the neighborhood? Light color makes a home look larger. If you have too many windows that make the home appear smaller, paint the window frames the same color as the rest of the house or wall.

The exterior of a home can be jazzed up a bit with window shutters, awnings, and flowers. Flower beds add color, as do window planter boxes and flower pots on the front steps and porch.

The prospective buyer is still sitting in the car, looking at your home. Is your driveway in good shape or is it cracked and full of holes? Cosmetic repairs may help. One of the best touches you can add to an asphalt driveway is a fresh coat of blacktop sealer. The task of resurfacing is simple enough to do yourself (Wear your worst pair of shoes, because odds are you'll get some stains on them.) The buyer is eyeballing your fence now, how does it look? The garage looks good from a distance, and the buyer's interest is raised. The buyer makes the move, and gets out of the car.

The front steps and entrance now become the focus of the buyer's attention and help create powerful first impressions. Small details can attract attention. Rips in screen doors, cracks in the windows, and loose hardware take on added importance because the buyer has nothing else to focus upon. Give him or her perfect minor details, and throw in a little pizzazz, too. Maybe some paint would really do wonders, or maybe some really sharp house numerals, or maybe some classy door hardware, or maybe a new mailbox, or maybe. . . .

Inside the House

The buyer is inside your front door now, standing in your entrance hall, anxiously looking around and barely paying attention to the introductions. A well lit area that is bright and cheerful makes a nice greeting. Mirrors may make the room appear larger. Throw rugs and curtains add color.

Living rooms and dining rooms are the usual first stops for buyers. Any obvious defects such as cracks in the walls or ceilings must be remedied (the same is true for all rooms in the home). An uncluttered room shows best and allows for traffic to flow freely. Clean, natural walls help create a spacious feeling. A well-lit room and natural light coming in the windows give an up-tempo feel to the rooms. Buyers mentally wonder, can I picture myself in this room? Will my belongings fit and look good here?

Bedrooms must appear large enough for the buyer's furniture and needs. Reorganize and rearrange. Remove extra furniture. Store as much as possible, be it clothing, grooming aids, or whatever. Clear the dresser tops. Try to neutralize your personality. Closet space is a big attention getter. Children's bedrooms should be free of clutter and odors. Take down those posters of the new turtles on the block. Emphasize space, and ease of care.

The buyer pays particular attention to bathrooms. The plumbing must work perfectly with no problems or leaks. Temperamental toilets that require a little trick to flush and refill properly signal trouble to buyers. The bathroom should be spotless, period. $10 for a new shower curtain may be the best investment you made this week. Bathroom odors must be eliminated. Colors should be light and bright.

Will Your Kitchen Kill the Sale?

The most important room in the house is probably the kitchen. For most buyers, the kitchen is the heart of the home. Sellers should devote extraordinary attention to this room. Buyers will scrutinize this room and be very picky. Remember—buyers are looking for space, and you must accentuate all that you have. Buyers want working space on the counter tops, so you must clear the counters of all small appliances, containers, dishes, cleaning gear, and whatever you and the family have put there. Try storing these items somewhere handy (maybe the basement?). Emphasize your shelf space, drawer space, cabinet space, pantry space, and closet space by thinning out the contents of these storage areas and organizing them. Box up everything you don't plan on using the next 6–8 weeks. Why keep 3 sets of salt & pepper shakers or 20 coffee cups? Can you add hooks or shelves to expand existing space? How about hanging pot racks?

Kitchen walls and ceilings take a daily dose of grease, grime, food stains, and scuffs. Perhaps yours are in need of more than mere cleaning. Paint and wallpaper for the kitchen are almost always "sure-to-recoup" costs. Select light and bright color schemes to make the room seem larger. Yellow has been a favorite kitchen color for years, because it connotes sunlight and airiness. Be sure you clean the grease spots, and seal both them and water stains before painting. Enamel paint wears best, and reflect light well to make the room appear larger. Your local hardware store will have several primer/sealer products you can choose from.

Your kitchen cabinets may be eyesores. What can you do? Consider either sanding and staining them, or painting them. Use light colors unless you are a professional decorator. Consider also replacing the knobs and handles. You'd be amazed how much younger and modern cabinets look with updated hardware. You'll also be pleasantly surprised at the low cost of quality hardware.

Whether your major appliances stay with the house, or go with you, or may be bargaining chips, you must keep them *spotless*. They reflect upon your housekeeping habits, and buyers extrapolate hypotheses about the condition of the whole house from their observations of pieces of the house. The same applies to the sink. It should be spotless and free of leaks and drips.

Your kitchen floor takes more pounding and shows wear faster than any other floor. Trouble spots are the high traffic areas, such as the floor areas in front of the sink, stove, and refrigerator; and the floor area under the kitchen table chairs. Sometimes repairs can be as simple as replacing a section of tile. This works best with darker tiles. Lighter colors become shaded with time, and a new or replacement tile sticks out. In this case, replacing the entire floor may be in order. Doing the job yourself is easiest with some of the self-stick vinyl tiles on the market. Quiet and neutral colors are your best bet. If you have hardwood floors underneath your carpet or tile or linoleum, you should consider stripping off the floor covering and sanding and staining the wood. Lighter stains make the room appear larger, while darker stains add a formal touch. If you don't want to tackle the job, many local handymen can help.

How Much Will It Cost?

By now you are wondering, "How much money should I spend on repairs and renovations?" Here are some tips to keep in mind.

1. If your house is in very poor condition, you may consider selling it "as is." A small percentage of house hunters are looking for a "handyman's special" or "fixer-upper."

2. If you are trying to sell your home in a buyer's market, expect to make price concessions or incur redecorating and repair costs.

3. Sellers typically recover only about 60% of what they spend on redecorating/remodeling. Studies show that the best odds of recovering your costs are: money spent on paint; money spent in the kitchen; and money spent on the bathroom.

4. Prioritize your expenditures. Priority one should be correcting any defects in the electrical, mechanical, or plumbing components of your house. The next priority should be the most obvious flaws and problems.

5. Do not replace old carpeting unless it is a really tough buyer's market. Even then, be careful in color selection. Your best bet is to let the prospective buyers know that there is a "carpet allowance," and you will pay for the new carpeting of the buyer's choice.

Pre-Sale Preparation Checklist

Lawn

In good shape?
Any thin or bare spots?
Needs seed or sod?
Will fertilizer help?
Does sprinkler system work properly?
(Spring) Does lawn need mowing?
(Summer) Does lawn need mowing?
(Fall) Leaves raked?
(Winter) Snow shovelled?
　　Patches of ice salted?

Weed-Eater and Edger Work

Sidewalks edged?

Driveway edged?
Curbs edged?
Fence growth trimmed?
Tree-base growth trimmed?

Trees
Any low-hanging branches to prune?
Dead branches to prune?
Dead trees to remove?
Stumps to dig out?

Flowers and Shrubs
Need to weed flowerbeds?
Plant more flowers?
Bushes and shrubs pruned?
Remove dead shrubs/bushes?
Replace dead shrubs/bushes?

Fences
Each slat/section in good shape?
Paint or replacement needed?
Holes in wire need repair?
Poles solidified in ground?
Retaining walls in good shape?
Sidewalks in good condition?

Gates
Do they latch properly?
Hinges secure and functional?
Slats/panels/wire need repair or paint?

Storage Sheds
Need paint or repairs?
Organized to emphasize space & features?

Garbage
Cans/receptacles in right spot?

Boxes, bags, lawn clutter removed?
Eyesores removed? (car parts, old toys, etc . . .)

Lawn Furniture, Swing-Sets, Etc.
Working properly?
Need paint?
Dog dirt cleaned up?

Patios and Decks
Any signs of water damage/does wood need to be replaced?
Painted? Stained? Water Sealed?
Deck furniture in good shape?
Arranged attractively?
Any cracks in cement?
Loose tiles, bricks?
Standing water removed?
Musty odor eliminated?
Barbecue grill cleaned & operational?

Garage/Carport
Need paint or exterior repairs?
Is each door operating smoothly?
Is the garage floor swept or hosed down?
Do the windows open easily?
Any cracked window panes?
Are the screens in good repair?
Do electrical outlets and switches work?
Tools stored neatly?
Garden tools and shovels hung up?
Clutter removed?
Light fixtures working?
Workbench organized?
Shelves organized?

Driveway
Do cracks need repair?
Should asphalt be sealed?
Any chugholes need patching?

Stone or gravel need levelling?
Weeds removed?
Standing water removed?

Roofs and Gutters

Do gutters leak?
Are gutters cleaned?
Do gutters need paint?
Downspouts in good shape?
Are the eaves OK?
Any decayed wood needing replacement?
Any damaged or missing shingles?
Are vents, turban fans, etc., flashed and
   waterproofed.

Exterior Walls

Any cracks in masonry?
Do walls need paint?
Any decayed wood needing replacement?
Any missing bricks?
Any loose or damaged siding?
Are windows caulked?
Outside windows cleaned?
Cracked windows repaired?
Screens in good shape?
Awnings in good shape?
Exterior faucets and outlets operational?
Outside lighting operational?
Any foundation wall cracks?

Front Entrance (outside)

Steps in good repair?
Handrail secure?
Handrail need paint?
Doormat look sharp?
Flowers in place?
Light fixture looks good?
Light bulbs replaced?
Doorbell operational?
All glass and windows cleaned?
Smudges and paw prints cleaned?
Brass and hardware polished?
Mailbox looks sharp?
House numbers easily visible?

House numbers need to be replaced?
Front door operate smoothly?
Front door hardware looks attractive?
Door need paint or repair?
Hinges need lubrication?
Chairs on porch in good shape?
Storm door and screens in good shape?

Front Entrance Hall

Door hardware clean and operational?
Floor cleaned?
Carpet cleaned?
Throw rugs cleaned?
Closet door operates properly?
Closet(s) free of clutter?
Closet light working?
Curtains cheerful and clean?
Windows washed?
Walls cleaned/papered/painted?
Wall and ceiling cracks/holes fixed?
Will mirror help?
Mirror(s) clean?
Adequate lighting?
Will replacing light fixture help?
Will flowers help?
Smoke alarm working?

Living and Dining Rooms

Any cracks in ceiling or walls?
Nail holes in walls?
Furniture marks and scuffs on walls?
Water stains on ceiling?
Does ceiling need a light color of paint?
Walls need cleaning? Paint?
Wallpaper in good shape?
Windows operate easily and properly?
Window locks operate properly?
Window panes in perfect condition?
Window glazing OK?
Windows washed?
Blinds clean and operational?
Curtains/drapes/dressings clean?
Curtain rods/hardware secure and
   operational?
Window sills and woodwork cleaned?
Holes in woodwork filled?
Does woodwork need paint?

Baseboards/trim clean? Need paint?
Floor cleaned/waxed?
Carpet cleaned?
Doors cleaned?
Door hardware operational?
Closet free of clutter?
Closet organized to show space?
Closet well lit?
Shelves clean and organized?
Electrical outlets in good shape?
Light switches in good shape?
Light fixtures work? Look good? Clean?
Smoke detector working?
Has room been depersonalized?
Furniture cleaned/polished?
Need to re-arranged furniture to look
    spacious?
Need to remove some furniture from
    room?
Room odors eliminated?
Dining room table legs secure?
Table polished?
Tablecloth washed?
Will flowers or ornamentation help?
Table, chairs sturdy and clean?

Family Room/Den/Study

Any cracks in ceiling or walls?
Nail holes in walls?
Furniture marks and scuffs on walls?
Water stains on ceiling?
Does ceiling need a light color of paint?
Walls need cleaning? Paint?
Wallpaper in good shape?
Windows operate easily and properly?
Window locks operate properly?
Window panes in perfect condition?
Window glazing OK?
Windows washed?
Blinds clean and operational?
Curtains/drapes/dressings clean?
Curtain rods/hardware secure and
    operational?
Window sills and woodwork cleaned?
Holes in woodwork filled?
Does woodwork need paint?
Baseboards/trim clean? Need paint?
Floor cleaned/waxed?

Carpet cleaned?
Doors cleaned?
Door hardware operational?
Closet free of clutter?
Closet organized to show space?
Closet well lit?
Shelves clean and organized?
Electrical outlets in good shape?
Light switches in good shape?
Light fixtures work? Look good? Clean?
Smoke detector working?
Has room been depersonalized?
Furniture cleaned/polished?
Need to re-arrange furniture to look
    spacious?
Need to remove some furniture from
    room?
Room odors eliminated?
Toys, games and booby traps off the
    floor?
Stereo wires, cable wires secured?

Bedrooms

Any cracks in ceiling or walls?
Nail holes in walls?
Furniture marks and scuffs on walls?
Water stains on ceiling?
Does ceiling need a light color of paint?
Walls need cleaning? Paint?
Wallpaper in good shape?
Windows operate easily and properly?
Window locks operate properly?
Window panes in perfect condition?
Window glazing OK?
Windows washed?
Blinds clean and operational?
Curtains/drapes/dressings clean?
Curtain rods/hardware secure and
    operational?
Window sills and woodwork cleaned?
Holes in woodwork filled?
Does woodwork need paint?
Baseboards/trim clean? Need paint?
Floor cleaned/waxed?
Carpet cleaned?
Doors cleaned?
Door hardware operational?

Closet free of clutter?
Closet organized to show space?
Closet well lit?
Shelves clean and operational?
Light switches in good shape?
Light fixtures work? Look good? Clean?
Smoke detector working?
Has room been depersonalized?
Furniture cleaned/polished?
Need to re-arrange furniture to look spacious?
Need to remove some furniture from room?
Room odors eliminated?
Clothes picked up and stored?
Dirty laundry removed?
Bedspread look good? Clean?
Nightstand/table clean? Organized?

Kitchen

Sinks cleaned? Stains removed?
Any leaks or drips?
Range/Stove/Ovens spotless?
Refrigerator clean? Defrosted?
Dishwasher clean?
Garbage disposal working?
Appliances clean? Working order?
Counters cleared and cleaned?
Cabinets organized and arranged?
Cabinet hardware operational?
Would new hardware and paint help?
Exhaust fan clean and operational?
Any loose legs on tables/chairs?
Would flowers help?
Any cracks in ceiling or walls?
Nail holes in walls?
Furniture marks and scuffs on walls?
Water stains on ceiling?
Does ceiling need a light color of paint?
Walls need cleaning? Paint?
Wallpaper in good shape?
Windows operate easily and properly?
Window locks operate properly?
Window panes in perfect condition?
Window glazing OK?
Windows washed?
Blinds clean and operational?
Curtains/drapes/dressings clean?

Curtain rods/hardware secure and operational?
Window sills and woodwork cleaned?
Holes in woodwork filled?
Does woodwork need paint?
Baseboards/trim clean? Need paint?
Floor cleaned/waxed?
Carpet cleaned?
Doors cleaned?
Door hardware operational?
Closet free of clutter?
Closet organized to show space?
Closet well lit?
Shelves clean and organized?
Electrical outlets in good shape?
Light switches in good shape?
Light fixtures work? Look good? Clean?
Smoke detector working?
Has room been depersonalized?
Furniture cleaned/polished?
Need to re-arrange furniture to look spacious?
Need to remove some furniture from room?
Room odors eliminated?
Is kitchen floor too worn?
Can it be replaced?

Bathrooms

Does the toilet flush and fill properly?
Would a new toilet seat help?
Is the toilet spotless?
Is the sink clean? Stains removed?
Any drips or leaks in the sink?
Is the bathtub clean?
Any drips or leaks in tub?
Would a new tub mat help?
Does the shower operate properly?
Any drips or leaks?
Would a new shower head help?
Is bathroom tile clean?
Do tiles need repair?
Tile grout cleaned?
Appropriate caulking? Sealing?
Shower curtain cleaned?
Would a new shower curtain help?
Cabinets clean and organized?
Mirrors clean?

Cracks and holes in walls/ceiling
repaired?
Would paint help?
Is wallpaper in good shape?
Windows clean and in good shape?
Blinds clean and operational?
Window dressings and hardware
operational?
Would new curtains help?
Woodwork and trim clean?
Would paint help?
Doors and hardware operational?
Floor clean?
Rugs clean?
Electrical outlets and switches OK?
Light fixtures look good?
Room odors eliminated?

Attic

Light fixtures working?
Steps/stairway clear?
Junk and clutter removed?
Box up loose items?
Any water stains on roof?
Any water stains around vents?
Attic fan operating?
Vents clear?
Clean cobwebs?
Clean floors?
Windows clean and operational?

Basement

Door and hardware operate properly?

Stairs free and clear of obstacles?
Handrail secure?
Light fixtures operational?
Clutter removed?
Stored items boxed neatly?
Any cracks in foundation?
Any cracks in floor?
Any damp spots?
Any leaky pipes?
Sweaty pipes wrapped?
Laundry area look good?
Any leaks in laundry area?
Need a dehumidifier for dampness?
Pet and musty odors eliminated?
All drains run freely?
Windows clean and operational?
Floor cleaned?
Furnace area clean?
Workbench area organized?

Forget-Me-Nots

Smoke detectors operating?
Telephone outlets/jacks operating?
Burglar alarm/Security system
operational?
Hallways clean?
Special features in good shape? (pool,
saunas, hot tubs, etc.)

Others? . . .

4
Selecting an Agent

The biggest mistake sellers can make is picking the wrong agent to list their home with. If you use an agent to sell your home—and 80% + of all sellers do—the selection of the right agent is the most crucial decision you will make. Unfortunately, the vast majority of sellers give the matter little thought. Typical scenarios unfold like this: "let's call Aunt Yvette. Her daughter Colleen is in real estate. They'll be mad if we don't give the business to the family." "I'll call my hairdresser, she's in real estate part-time and knows everybody!" "I think this guy I played golf with is in real estate. Lemme see, what the hell is his name?" "Call the lady that sold us this house." These scenarios are prescriptions for a six-month headache. Let's get on the right track by reviewing the basics.

Who's Who in the Professional Lineup?

Anyone can buy or sell real property *for himself*, but if you want to sell or buy property on behalf of someone else, you must be licensed by the state to act as an agent for another. To obtain a license to act as a real estate agent, an individual must pass an exam. These are two types of real estate agents: the salesperson and the broker.

To become a sales agent, an individual must pass a state examination. The subjects covered on the exam usually encompass concepts of agency law, real property, and ethics. Each state has its own exam. Once a sales agent passes the state exam, she or he becomes associated with a real estate broker and works under the supervision and auspices of that broker. The broker will be responsible for training the salesperson, and brokers usually handle and disperse all funds during escrow. Brokers typically must have several years of experience and continuing education course work before they can sit for the state licensing exam to become a broker. The exam is much more detailed and difficult than the sales agent exam.

When agents become associated with brokers, the most common legal relationship between the parties is that of independent contractors. As independent contractors, agents do not receive a salary or retirement benefits from the broker. An agent is responsible for paying her own federal, state, and local income taxes as well as social security contributions. Agents earn commissions when they produce buyers for homes, and also when they (on behalf of their broker) contract with a seller to market the seller's home and to produce a ready, willing, and able buyer. Brokers and agents will agree upon a shared division of commission fees, with a 50%/50% split being the most common. The broker is rewarded for providing the agent with expertise, training, supervision, office space and office expenses, advertising budgets, etc. Are agents less knowledgeable or capable than brokers? Not necessarily! Many agents have no desire to take on the risks of operating their own office and supervising tens or hundreds of agents.

Many brokers become associated with the National Association of Realtors®, which is a private professional organization that promulgates codes of ethical conduct and provides many educational and business aids. A broker who joins is called a Realtor, whereas sales agents are designated as Realtor Associates. The NAR sponsors many local Board of Realtors chapters in which members participate actively. These local boards usually sponsor a multiple listing service (MLS) that is a very powerful selling tool (more on this later).

Find a Good Firm First

Let's suppose you have decided that you do not want to sell your house on your own. How do you find a good agent to work with you? Begin your search by concentrating on the brokerage firm, not on an individual agent. Because real estate markets are local in nature, you should find a firm that specializes in your immediate neighborhood. You can employ several search techniques to help you find out which firms dominate the market in your neighborhood. One easy method is to check the real estate ads in the weekend newspapers. Which firm names pop-up most often in ads for your area? You can also conduct a visual survey in your neighborhood by noting the firm name on the various "For Sale" signs. Jot down those addresses and firm names. You may later decide to visit with the homeowner/seller to ask them how they like the service that they are receiving from Company X or Agent Z.

After noticing one or more firms that specialize in your area, you can check out each brokerage firm's reputation in the local real estate community. Local lenders, lawyers, title companies, and escrow/closing services are sources for reference. You may also check with local better business bureaus, the chamber of commerce, former clients, neighbors, and the local real estate boards.

Once you have selected one or more firms, make an appointment to meet with the managing broker. In your meeting with the broker, you want to find out as much as you can about the operation of his or her business. Do they specialize in residential real estate? It is important that they do. Firms that devote most of their attention to commercial sales and leasing, vacant land, or farm land are not for you. They tend to shortchange residential sellers and buyers with less expertise and knowledge, less effective advertising, and less enthusiasm by agents who are more interested in selling a $2 million dollar office building than selling your $100,000 home.

Ask the managing broker about typical marketing strategies for homes like yours. How often are ads run? How often is an open house held? Who handles phone calls that come in to the office asking about your home? Ask to see the persons on phone duty or floor duty. Talk with them and observe their telephone manner and professionalism. Does the firm have secretarial help for the agents? How many agents does the firm have? Are they part-time or full-time agents? Does the firm belong to a multiple listing service? Is the firm part of a referral system that helps relocate buyers and sellers from all over the nation?

THE CLOSER THE BETTER

You should look for a firm that is located reasonably close to your home, because the quality of service you receive from a brokerage firm is often correlated positively with the distance of the property for sale from the firm's office location. Suppose your agent is unavailable, and a telephone inquiry comes in to the broker's office about your house that is for sale. How will the office handle the call? If the buyers on the phone are hot prospects, they want to view your house right now. If the broker's office is close to your home, it is easier for one of two things to happen. First, the prospects can come in to the office, be financially qualified, and the agent on floor duty can alert you that prospective buyers are coming over, and that you should prepare for them. Second, if the prospects want to meet the agent at your house immediately, the agent can get there swiftly and doesn't feel bad about closing the office for a short time while the phone is answered by a service or machine.

Sometimes prospective buyers visit brokerage offices just to browse through the for-sale listings. If your home is close by, the odds are better that the prospects may drive by or even ask for a showing. Agents showing other homes are also more likely to include yours on a showing list if your location is close by. Let's face it, the laws of human nature apply to agents, too. If your home is far away, it takes more time and gas to get to you. If prospects are running late, guess which house for sale gets dropped from the list of homes to visit?! Right—yours!!

After you have selected a firm that you feel will be best for you, ask the broker to recommend three of his top agents to you so that you can inter-view each of them. (More on how to handle these interviews shortly!)

ALTERNATE APPROACHES

Although I highly recommend the approach I have just outlined, others prefer different methods. An obvious selection would be the agent that helped sell you the house you currently live in. If you were pleased with the service, consider inviting him or her to make a presentation to you. Remember, you are still looking for those services and qualities that their *firm* should offer, as previously noted.

Some sellers try this approach: put a "For Sale by Owner" sign in your yard, but wait to place an ad in the newspaper. Try this for a week. The agents that are most likely to knock on your door are those who specialize in your neighborhood, have a good network in your neighborhood, and keep a constant eye on your neighborhood. In week two, you can run a newspaper ad, and the buyers and agents should respond en masse. Who knows, you may even sell the house! Even if you do not, you will meet the most confident agents and can select the top ones to interview.

If your company is transferring you to a different town, your company may recommend that you work with a certain agent or firm. Companies may direct a large volume of business to certain firms and receive a discount in the commission. Your company may also have a plan to buy your home if it doesn't sell in X months, and may insist that you use a certain firm or agent.

Another approach to meeting agents is to visit the open houses that are being held in your neighborhood. You can get a look at your competition if the homes are comparable in price to yours, and meet the agents that may specialize in your area. At the open house you can size up the agents—as they try to size *you* up!! If you are impressed with their knowledge, interpersonal skills, marketing techniques and conduct, you may invite several to make a presentation to you.

List or Die

The term "listing" refers to a property that is being sold by a broker. Listings are the lifeblood of each brokerage firm, even though brokers make money by selling other brokers' listings. If a broker has no listings, it is difficult to develop prestige and expand his or her customer base. Without listings, a broker has no inventory to sell, and therefore nothing to advertise in the big Sunday newspaper real estate section. Without listings, the broker cannot put up those classy signs in yards of sellers. If the walls of a broker's office have no pretty pictures of current listings, walk-in prospects may decide to walk elsewhere. Listing is the name of the game in real estate. You list . . . or you die.

Because listing is so important to the firm, agents are trained extensively in how to give a listing presentation. Typical training techniques include extensive study of audio and video tapes; practice presentations with emphasis on overcoming seller objections; gaining familiarity with contracts and Multiple Listing Service (MLS) documents; and accompanying experienced agents on actual listing visits. Words and actions are carefully scripted by experts in consumer behavior, and then rehearsed and memorized by agents. Want a sample? The word "contract" scares people, so agents are taught to use the word "agreement." Agents don't ask you to "sign" documents, they ask you to "O.K." things. The word "cost" is negative, whereas the use of the word "investment" is encouraged. Agents are coached on things as detailed as the proper way to ring a doorbell! (Ring once; step back 5 or 6 feet; turn your body and face at a 45 degree angle to the door; appear as if you are looking down the street; whistle or smile so as to appear nonthreatening; and when the door is answered, spew out the predetermined formula of words.)

Agents are coached on everything from body language to the effective use of silence, and to maneuvering sellers to the kitchen table to "OK some paperwork." Some agents show mini-movies on portable viewing devices, some prefer the VCR and videotape approach. Almost all will have a presentation book that shows you pictures of their firm, lots of pictures of happy sellers they have served, a few testimonial letters or notes, pictures of themselves with awards, and an outline of their marketing strategy, complete with sample advertisement and open house paraphernalia. There may be some complicated and lengthy sample financial and legal forms in the presentation book that aid the agent in convincing you that they have the expertise that you are lacking.

This tiny glimpse into the world of listing should not shock or surprise you. The professional sales arena is very competitive and is becoming more sophisticated daily, whether the product being sold is soup, insurance, tires, or real estate. Remember the day you had to sell yourself to your spouse's relatives for the first time? Were you careful to use the right words and actions?

What to Look for in an Agent

Now that you have selected three professional real estate agents to interview, how do you handle yourself at their separate auditions? What are you looking for in an agent? In broad terms, you are seeking an agent who can demonstrate professional knowledge and competence about your neighborhood, current market conditions, current financing trends, and a solid marketing plan for your specific home. You are also seeking someone with the right personal chemistry to work with you during one of the biggest financial transactions in your life.

What words and actions of the agent exemplify those characteristics you are looking for? Is the agent well-prepared when she or he meets with you? Besides the competitive market analysis (CMA), (see page 60), does the agent have data about his or her firm and its performance in your neighborhood? Has the agent done her or his homework on your property taxes, loan balance, lot size, etc? Is the agent courteous yet persistent in asking you about personal matters and your financial situation? Questions such as "Why are you selling?" "Do you need your equity from this house to buy your next home?" and "Can you afford to make two mortgage payments?" need to be answered. If the agent is persistent with you, that is a good sign because she or he can handle prospective buyers with the same skill. How else can financially qualified buyers be screened from the wishers and gawkers who waste your time?!

Is the agent enthused about your property? Sales agents who believe in what they are selling import this sense of enthusiasm, pride, and value to prospective buyers. The great agents realize value in a variety of price ranges and understand target marketing. Whether they are selling a Donald Trump-like mansion to a millionaire, or a starter home to a 22-year-old couple, the great agents believe in their product's ability to meet the buyer's needs. When they speak with you about listing, they ask detailed questions about your home and your neighborhood.

I suggest that when each of the three agents arrive, you let them take charge and direct the conversation and interview. They will probably tour the home and property first, with clipboard and measuring tape in hand. After looking over the home, their listing presentation should follow. Each presentation will vary, and the following checklist will serve as a reminder of important items to cover, just in case the presentation was not aimed at certain topics.

Interview Checklist

Performance and Track Record

- Tell me about your experience in real estate sales.
- What types of properties and neighborhoods do you specialize in?
- Tell me about your last three sales. (Are those sales in the neighborhood the agent claims to specialize in?)
- Do you have any homes in my neighborhood for sale right now? If so, may I have the names of the owners so I can ask them about your service so far?
- How many homes have you sold in this neighborhood in the past 12 months?
- May I have the names and addresses of those people who have employed you to sell their homes in the last 12 months, so I can ask about your service?

Personal Knowledge

- Tell me about your educational background.
- What kind of seminars do you attend? What topics are covered?
- Do you hold any special professional designations?
- Can you recommend three or four good books to me about selling my house? Can I borrow your copy tomorrow?
- Will you work up a "Net to Seller" estimate for me based upon a sales price of $X; a commission of Z%; and several different types of buyer financing? (See page 147)
- Tell me what the differences are between various types of listing agreements.

Marketing Strategy

- Please give me a detailed Comparative Market Analysis (CMA).
- What do I need to do to make my house more marketable? Do you recommend specific repairs, remodeling, or decorating?
- How fast will I sell my house at your suggested price?
- When does your firm negotiate on the commission?
- Will I receive a written marketing campaign from you?
- How many ads will be run? In what media? How often?
- Will my home appear on the Multiple Listing Service (MLS)?
- How are your commissions split? How are commissions split on MLS sales?
- Does your firm reduce its commission for in-house sales or other special circumstances?

Personal References and Contacts

- Can you give me the names of several real estate attorneys you work with? May I call them for a reference?
- Can you give me the names of several lenders or mortgage brokers you deal with? I want to call them for a reference.
- Can you give me the names of agents from different firms that dealt with you on your last three co-brokered sales, so that I can phone them about your service?

Do Your Follow-Up Homework

After you have interviewed the three agents, you probably have a gut feeling about which one you prefer. Start with your top choice, and check out her or his references, beginning with the sellers who listed with that agent in the past 12 months. Ask those sellers if their home sold at listing price. If not, what was the sales price? How long was the home on the market? Was any seller financing involved? How often did they see or talk to their agent during the listing and up to closing/settlement? What headaches did they have in the whole process? Was the agent's firm of any help in the selling process? Were they happy with agent X? Would they employ agent X again?

Next, phone those references that currently have their homes for sale with agent X. What are they happy or unhappy with so far? How long have the houses been on the market? Finally, contact the attorneys, lenders, and other agents to ask about agent X's level of performance and professionalism.

A final note of caution: taking a shortcut is tempting. Don't do it! Check those references carefully. Failure to do so may give you six months of headaches and dent your bank account. Crow and humble pie taste particularly bad when you are making double mortgage payments.

5
Listing Contracts and Forms

The listing agreement is a contract between the sellers of real estate and the real estate broker who agrees to perform certain services in return for a specified commission paid by the seller. Generally, the broker agrees to produce a ready, willing, and able buyer who will buy the property at the specified price and meet any other requirements the seller specified in the listing agreement. As long as the broker produces a buyer on the terms noted, the broker is entitled to the commission, even if the sale is never consummated. Because the broker or his representatives drafted the contract, it is favorable to the broker. We'll discuss the contract in detail shortly.

Contracts for the sale of real estate must be in writing to be enforceable by virtue of state laws called the statute of frauds. However, a contract to hire a broker need *not* be in writing in roughly half of the states in the USA. Stated another way, an oral listing agreement may be valid and enforceable in your state. If in doubt, seek competent legal advice.

"Exclusive Right to Sell" Listing

The most prevalent type of listing that is used is the "Exclusive Right to Sell." The salient feature of this type of listing is that the broker is entitled to his commission, regardless of whether you sell the home or the broker does. If your cousin calls you, never talks to the broker, and contracts to buy your home, you still owe the commission. Brokers justify these terms with the following rationale: If we are going to spend time and money promoting your home, we don't want to compete with you. If our ads generate prospects who knock on your door, we don't think the commission is rightfully yours. Another point of interest: most local multiple listing services (MLS) will only accept the "Exclusive Right to Sell" form of listing for inclusion in the MLS system.

Virtually all agents who make listing presentations to you will want you to sign this type of agreement. Remember to interview at least three agents so that you guard against broker breaches of fiduciary responsibilities and the dangers of highball or lowball pricing.

Rosetta
REALTORS

9501 South Street • Oxford, MS • (601) 422-0011

EXCLUSIVE AUTHORIZATION AND RIGHT TO SELL

IN CONSIDERATION of the services of the firm of ROSETTA REALTORS, herein called Broker, I hereby employ Broker, exclusively and irrevocably, for the period beginning _____ _____, 199__ and ending midnight _____, 199__ to sell the property situated at _____ _____; and grant Broker the exclusive and irrevocable right to sell said property within said time for the sum of $_____ dollars and to accept a deposit thereon in the amount of $_____ .
      I HEREBY agree to pay Broker as commission ____per cent of the selling price if said property is sold during the term hereof or any extension thereof by Broker or by me or by another broker or through any source. If said property is withdrawn from sale, transferred, or leased during the term hereof or any extension thereof, I agree to pay Broker said per cent of the above listed price. Broker agrees to use his best efforts to secure a purchaser for the property. Broker's commission shall be paid no later than closing and Seller authorizes the Broker to apply the earnest money to his commission and authorizes the purchasers or their agent to pay any balance due on said commission directly to Broker at closing.
      If a sale, lease, or other transfer of said property is made within three (3) months after this authorization or any extension thereof terminates to parties with whom Broker negotiates during the term or any extension thereof, then I agree to pay said commission to Broker.
      If deposits or amounts paid on account of purchase price are forfeited, Broker shall be entitled to one half thereof, but not to exceed the amount of the commission.
      It is illegal to refuse to sell or show property to any person because of race, color, religion, national origin, sex or physical disability.
      I hereby agree to the foregoing and acknowledge receipt of a copy hereof.

Dated _____, 199__

_____

_____ Owner(s)

ROSETTA REALTORS

_____ Broker

Exclusive Agency Listing

Under an "exclusive agency" listing agreement, the broker is granted the right to act as your only *agent,* and is entitled to a commission if he produces a buyer through *his* efforts. If you find a buyer through your efforts, you owe no commission. Again, brokers frown upon competing with their own seller, and some MLS systems will not list these agreements.

Open Listings

The "open listing" is used in some commercial real estate transactions, and in residential sales in small towns and rural areas that do not have multiple listing systems for economic reasons. With an "open listing," the first person (be she agent #7 or yourself) to produce a buyer gets the commission. Have you ever seen a vacant parcel of land or a farm on the outskirts of town and several different real estate broker's for sale signs posted? This signals an open listing. Because agents have no assurances in this competitive environment, they are not likely to spend a lot of time or advertising dollars on properties under "open listing" agreements. Realizing that, sellers typically offer a commission in the 3% to 4% range, which is roughly half the normal rate. Sellers know that they will incur most of the promotional and marketing expenses themselves. MLS services, almost without exception, will not accept "open listings" for inclusion in the system. Although an oral "open listing" is valid in about half of our states, I urge you to avoid them.

For all practical purposes, if you sell your home using an agent you will rarely deal with an open listing. If you choose the For-Sale-By-Owner (FISBO) path, the open listing may be of use to you. I'll teach you more about that in Chapter 4.

Discount Brokers

Most areas of significant population are served by one or more "discount brokers." Unlike full-service brokers, discount brokers provide sellers with fewer services and at a reduced commission rate. Usually they assist you with paperwork, give you a sign, advertise in a limited manner, and have someone answer the telephone when you cannot. Normally, showing the property is the owner's responsibility. Rarely are they participants in the MLS. How do you find these brokers? Watch for their ads in the Sunday real estate section or in the yellow pages. They often use words like "Sell-it-yourself," "Show-it-yourself," "Sold by owner," "discount-commission real estate broker," and similar phrases.

An In-Depth Look at a Listing Contract

Now that you understand the basics about different types of listing agreements, let's take a detailed look at the most common type—the "exclusive right to sell listing." This is the type of listing you will probably encounter, so pay attention! A sample listing contract is reproduced on page 35. Take a few minutes to look it over now.

Like so many so-called "standard forms" (including the ones you may use at work), these documents are drafted to serve the best interests of the one who paid to have them drafted. Their format and content are not mandated by state law, although a clause or two may be. What this means to you is that much of the language and terms are negotiable.

Commission Fees

Let's begin by looking at commission rates. You may hear that the "customary" or "standard" commission in your area is 6% or 7% for residential sales. Commission rates can always be negotiated, and rates are not set by professional groups or boards. (If they were, the Federal Trade Commission, the Attorney General, and a host of State's Attorneys would charge them with violating various anti-trust laws.) This does not mean that a given broker must negotiate with you over commission. Each broker faces a different cash-flow situation and break-even point. Expenses vary among brokers, and so do revenues. Each broker is free to charge whatever he deems appropriate, be it 1% or 25%.

Let's look at an example to better understand how brokers and agents split commissions. Suppose Chuck Heron is a broker in Honolulu. Laura Ashe is a sales agent working for the Heron agency. She lists a $300,000 home, and two days later another Heron agent, Shelley Snow, produces a buyer. After the sale is completed, how do those three people split the 6% commission that the seller paid the Heron Agency? That depends on what the broker Chuck Heron agreed to with each of the agents when they independently contracted to work as his agents. Suppose Heron agreed to the following: if the house is "in-house," and a Heron agent (Shelley Snow) sells a listing procured by another Heron agent (Laura Ashe), then the listing agent shall receive 33⅓% of the commission fee paid, the selling agent shall receive 33⅓% of the commission fee paid, and the broker shall receive 33⅓% of the commission fee paid. If the seller paid a full 6% commission on $300,000, the commission paid would total $18,000. As per their agreement, Chuck the broker would receive $6,000; and Laura the listing agent would receive $6,000; and Shelley the selling agent would receive $6,000.

Suppose that the same house that was listed by Laura was sold via the multiple listing service (MLS) by another brokerage firm owned by broker

Steve Sewell. One of Steve's agents, Shannon Stubbs, found a buyer. How would the $18,000 commission be split? First of all, both brokers Chuck and Steve belong to a local MLS system that determines that the listing broker and selling broker will split the commission 50%/50%, and share the fee paid equally. Each broker would then pay the listing agent (Laura), and the selling agent (Shannon) according to the terms of their contract to hire and serve as the broker's agents. Let's suppose each agent's agreement contained the following language: if the listing is co-brokered via the MLS system and a sale results, the listing agent or the selling agent shall receive 25% of the commission fee paid. Under this co-brokered sale, the commission would be split as follows: The listing broker Chuck gets $4,500; the listing agent Laura gets $4,500; the selling broker Steve gets $4,500; and the selling agent Shannon gets $4,500.

The previous examples featured common commission splits. Note the financial incentives to sell your own listing, or to keep the sale within the firm (in-house). A seller could attempt to negotiate for the following clause in a listing agreement: "if the listing agent or another agent from the listing broker's firm produces a buyer, then the commission shall be reduced from 6% to 5%."

Such a clause will enable you to take advantage of an in-house sale that gives the house what is happily referred to in the brokerage business as a "double score" or "twin killing." What other bargaining chips do you have in negotiating the broker's commission? Here are some possibilities:

- Market conditions: Your local market may be a bullish seller's market where buyers exceed sellers. Homes sell within 7 days at or above listing price. (In a market like this, an old barn could sell in 5 days if it was zoned residential!) The broker can smell a quick kill and maybe even a twin killing. This situation puts you in a strong bargaining position.

- Reduced services: In return for a reduction in services (ads, open houses, showings, etc.) to you the seller, the broker will reduce the commission. Get it in writing, and be sure the services to be rendered are specifically noted. Do *not* give up the MLS!

- The double play ploy: If the broker will reduce the commission on the sale of your present home, you promise in writing to utilize the same brokerage firm to help you buy your next home.

- The agent already has a buyer: If the agent has a ready buyer, the broker will not have to spend a dime on marketing or tie up anyone's time on tours or open houses or phone lines. The sale will be in-house!

If the broker or seller thinks the agent with the alleged buyer is just bluffing to get a listing, the listing can specifically mention the buyer's name and the duration of the listing can be a few days.

- You may have more real estate to list: If you have several properties to list, the broker is more likely to give you a reduced commission.

- The sale is collapsing: If the sale is in jeopardy, brokers often reduce their commissions. For example, the FHA tells the seller he will have to make repairs that would cost $1,200. The contract of sale only obligates the seller to spend $200, and if the estimated value of repairs exceeds $200, the seller can cancel the sale. Rather than lose $5,000 in commission, the broker(s) may offer to reduce the commission(s) by $1,000.

Length of the Listing

What should the duration of your listing agreement be? The not-so-standard listing form that the broker or agent will want you to sign may have six months written neatly in the text. The two polar views can be summarized in this way: the buyer thinks one month is long enough to see some action or hire another broker who can deliver some buyers; while the broker thinks six months is a "fair" period of time to reap some benefits from all the dollars spent on advertisements, multiple listing, and office overhead. Who's right? Maybe both, maybe neither. The best way to determine a fair duration for the listing is to check the average number of days on market for recent sales of comparable homes.

The agent's Comparative Market Analysis (CMA) or Competitive Market Analysis will give you this data. If the average time on the market has been 23 days, why does a broker need 6 months to sell your house? Give him a maximum of 90 days, and that is generous! Your listing agreement should contain a specific expiration date, and should *not* contain a clause that automatically extends the agreement upon expiration or buyer's remorse. You should consider a cancellation or withdrawal clause that allows you to rescind the contract upon certain conditions (death, illness, your purchase of a new home falls through, the new job falls through, the school will not accept Junior, etc.). Watch out for cancellation penalties and fees!

Carryover Clauses

Your listing contract will contain a clause that states if anyone to whom the agent has shown the property to or negotiated with concerning the property prior to the expiration date buys the property within X days after the listing expires, the agent shall be due the commission. This "protection clause" or "holdover clause" protects the agent from losing buyers to you. (Some sellers and prospective buyers have been known to privately say: "Let's get together after the listing expires and cut out the middleman. We can save $9,000 on the commission and reduce the asking price by that amount.") Brokers and agents devoted financial and human resources to getting these two together, and this clause will protect them. (Common law and case precedence will, too.) I have no gripes with these clauses, as long as they are reasonable in time. (60 days is customary.) These clauses should also require the agent to provide the seller with a written list of names that the agent has or is working with before or on the expiration date. Fair is fair!

Corporate Buy-Out Clause

Some sellers are transferred to another town by their employer. These sellers are called "corporate relos," short for corporate relocations. Many companies offer to buy the employee's home as part of the transfer agreement. Before taking the company offer, relo sellers may test the market to see if they can get a better offer than the price offered by the company. The sellers may list the property, yet decide to take the company offer before the listing expires. With the listing still in force, if the seller sells to the company, the seller owes the broker the commission *unless* the listing contains a "corporate purchase" clause. These clauses usually provide that the seller can sell to the company anytime during the listing period without incurring liability, provided that the property is relisted by the company with the same broker.

Information Requested on Listing Forms

Most listing contracts incorporate or include blank spaces that ask the seller for a wide variety of specific information. Usually the type of information requested and the format in which it is requested are determined by a local board that your broker is a member of and in whose multiple listing service (MLS) he or she participates. Each area uses different forms. (See page 41 for an example.)

It is absolutely essential that you provide accurate information on the listing and ancillary forms. I repeat, you *must* provide true and accurate information!! If you fail to provide accurate and truthful information, you could wind up with two big, big problems.

Headache Number One: You and your agent may be legally liable for misrepresentation and certain omissions.

Headache Number Two: Your marketing efforts can be seriously weakened by inaccurate information.

Financial Terms

One type of information that is typically requested on various listing forms is that involving *financial terms*. You may have to provide the name of your lender that holds your current note and mortgage, the approximate loan balance, the number of years left on the loan/note, your present monthly

SOUTHWEST SUBURBAN BOARD OF REALTORS
MULTIPLE LISTING SERVICE

REALTOR: SELLER:

_____   _____

_____   _____

_____   _____

In consideration of the following services performed and to be performed by Realtor: (1) Study of subject property and of the area surrounding the subject property and comparable locations, (2) Study of sales and offerings of comparable properties; (3) Listing of subject property and agreement to submit the listing information to prospective purchasers, and submission of the listing information to the SOUTHWEST SUBURBAN BOARD OF REALTORS MULTPLE LISTING SERVICE, of which Realtor is a member for transmittal to Realtor firms, Seller agrees that Realtor shall have the exclusive right to sell the property described herein until its termination date.

PROPERTY ADDRESS: _____

PRICE: $_____ or any sum Seller agrees to accept.

TERMS OF SALE: Cash, or such other terms as Seller agrees to accept: _____
_____
_____

This sale shall include all permanent fixtures and the following items of personal property: _____
_____
_____
_____

REAL ESTATE TAXES: (19___) $_____.   Homestead Exemption: Yes ___ No ___.

Approx. Lot Size:_____ x _____ x _____ x _____.   POSSESSION:_____

Seller agrees to pay Realtor a commission in the amount of _____ % of the sale price if Realtor procures a buyer, if the property is sold within said time by Seller or any other person, or is sold within _____ days from the expiration date hereof to any prospect to whom the said listing information was submitted during the term of this exclusive agreement. However, Seller shall not be obligated to pay said commission if a valid listing agreement is entered into during the term of said protection period with another broker and the sale of the property is made during the term of the subsequent listing agreement.

Seller agrees to pay advertising in the amount of _____ % of the sale price if sale is made.

Seller agrees to pay a discount of not more than ____ % of the amount of the purchaser's loan if property sold with F.H.A. or V.A. Financing. (Said amount to be deducted from the proceeds of the sale at the time of closing.)

THIS AGREEMENT SHALL TERMINATE 12:01 A. M. _____ _____ _____
                                                                          Month   Day   Year

Title to subject property is presently in the name of _____

_____

and the undersigned are authorized to sign this agreement.

No amendments or alterations to this agreement are valid or binding unless made in writing and signed by the parties. This agreement shall be binding upon and inure to the benefit of the heirs, executors, administrators, trustees and assignees of the parties hereto.

The General provisions on the reverse hereof are incorporated herein by reference.

DATED AT _____   THIS _____ DAY OF _____ 19 ___

_____   _____
Realtor   Seller

_____   _____
Realtor Associate   Seller

               SELLER'S PHONE: _____

REV. 3/86

Listing Contracts and Forms **41**

payments, your annual ad valorem taxes (property taxes), and what type of loan you have (see Chapter 18). The form may ask you what terms you will accept. Most people will accept only cash at closing, and may so note on the form with words such as "all cash" or "cash only." If your home sells in the FHA price ranges, it is wise to let everyone know that you "will go FHA or VA." If your original note is assumable, by all means say "nonqualifying assumption" or "assumable upon buyer qualification." If you are willing to help with financing by taking back a note for some of your equity, write "owner will carry" in the appropriate space on the forms. Anytime a seller is willing to sell without receiving all cash at closing/settlement, this signals to buyers and their agents that the seller is willing to consider creative financing. This provides a marketing boost to the sale of your property because it increases the potential number of prospective buyers by alerting a particular market segment (those with little cash for big down payments) that you may negotiate with them. (Chapters 12 and 17 cover financing.)

Info about Your Home and Neighborhood

Another type of information usually requested deals with the physical characteristics of your property and home. What are the dimensions of your property? Your survey will show your lot size. Your exact legal description (not your street address) may be requested. Your deed should contain this information. Some forms want to know the square footage of your home. Measurement customs can vary from area to area. Some measure the outside of the home. Some count only living space inside the home, and eliminate from their calculations the inclusion of space attributable to porches, basements, attics, etc.

Forms may also want you to supply information such as how old is your home, utility costs, type of electrical, mechanical, and plumbing systems, school districts, and the nearest major cross street. The listing forms may contain space to give the dimensions of each of your rooms. If it does, be sure to fill in the measurements. It is of importance to agents and buyers looking for something specific such as a small extra bedroom to use as a home office, or a large den or a family room, etc. (If the listing forms do not request such data, you can provide it to prospects via the "information sheet" that I will describe shortly when we discuss your marketing plan.)

Showing Information

The forms want to know how the property is to be shown. Can other MLS brokers show the property if they phone you first for an appointment? Or,

Rosetta **REALTORS**
Commercial • Residential

9501 South Street
Oxford, MS
(601) 422-0011

$82,000.00

FIRST FLOOR: Living/Dining room combination (27' x 16½') with
large picture window and dining area window; nice, 1½-year-old
mauve carpeting with hardwood floors underneath. Kitchen (16½'
x 8' in eating area; 16½' x 12' in cooking area) has all appliances
included. Two bedrooms (@ 11' x 12' each) each with two windows
and a closet. Hardwood floors. Bathroom with sink, toilet, shower
and bathtub, and closet.

SECOND FLOOR: Bedroom (16' x 15½') has hardwood floors and two
closets. Second bedroom (16' x 12') also has hardwood floors and
closet. Bathroom has sink, toilet, shower and bathtub, and closet.

BASEMENT: Finished with tile floor and panelling; sewer windows;
laundry room with washer and dryer; refrigerator; General Electric
furnace (8 years old); large hot water heater.

MISCELLANEOUS: Two-car garage with automatic (Genie) opener.
Schools nearby, including St. Cajetan and Clissold grammar schools
and Morgan Park, Marist, Brother Rice, and Mother McAuley high schools.
Home is approximately 35 years old and has gas heat and central air.

do you want them to make appointments only through the listing broker? Do you want 24 hours notice before showing? How does an agent get into the home? Do they have to go to the listing broker's office to get the key? Many locales use what is called a "keybox" or a "lockbox." The keybox is a small, metal, box-like device that is screwed into the woodwork by your door. The keys to your house fit inside the keybox. To get into the keybox, you must have a special key that is usually given only to members of the local MLS system. If the home is vacant, a keybox is very helpful and you should use it. If you are still living in your home, the keybox may or may not be for you. It makes showings easier for brokers and agents, but may give you less privacy and security worries. Your agent can advise you about local custom as well as the security issues. Thieves can pry a keybox off the woodwork with a crowbar, or even a hammer if the screws are small. They can take the box home, cut it open, and have your housekeys. As noted above, you will get more lookers and more exposure using a keybox. Are your comparable competitors using keyboxes? You must weigh the tradeoffs after getting all the input from your agent.

Other showing information can be noted on the forms. Perhaps you have a day sleeper. Not that, and write "no showing between 7 A.M. and 4 P.M.—day sleeper." Or maybe you don't want showings after 7 P.M. If you have pets, let the MLS agents know that, and tell them where the pets are. For example, "dog on chain SW corner of yard." "Cat in basement, don't let him out."

A final word about showing restrictions. The more restrictive your showing arrangements are, the fewer the lookers you will attract, and the opportunities to sell will diminish. If you are in a seller's market, restrictions may not hurt you as much. If you are in a buyer's market, the fewer restrictions for showing the better are your chances of selling. Showing is discussed in greater detail in Chapters 8, 9, and 18.

Being Fussy about Details

MLS property information forms should be carefully checked for accuracy of all types of information, especially the phone number and address of the property. If the area is hard to find for outsiders, are directions to the home clearly given on the listing forms? Many MLS services publish a photo of your home along with all the information I am describing. Be sure your agent submits a flattering photo! You'd be surprised how many agents and prospective buyers decide what properties to show and view based upon these pictures. A picture may be worth 10,000 words, so be picky and insist upon a good one! You should also insist upon reviewing the published MLS information on your property when it comes out. Also, review the brokerage firm's in-house information sheets (listing sheets) to check for errors and omissions. (See page 43 for an example.) Errors and mistakes can be costly.

Fixtures or Personal Property?

Your listing forms should also spell out which items of personal property are part of the sale and "go with the house," or will not be part of the sale. Fixtures are defined as personal property that has become affixed to real property with the intent that it become permanently part of the real property. Fixtures are part of the sale, and "go with the property." Disagreements over what "stays with the house" can bog down a deal in escrow or even kill a closing. That expensive chandelier Grandma gave you for your wedding was personal property when it was sitting in the box. After installation, it probably became a fixture, and would go with the sale unless it was specifically excluded by contract.

Let's review some of the most commonly disputed items. Appliances are normally personal property that the seller may take with him. Some examples of appliances are washers, dryers, microwave ovens, refrigerators, freezers, and free-standing ovens and ranges. But if the appliances are built-in or custom-made, they are usually deemed to be fixtures as are cabinets, shelves, and built-in (not free-standing) bookcases are considered fixtures.

Window dressings can be items of dispute. Blinds, shades, draperies, curtain rods and hardware, and valances are usually *not* considered fixtures unless they are tailor-made custom-size items. Light fixtures are generally considered to be fixtures. Built-in mirrors are fixtures, wall-to-wall hanging mirrors are not. Carpeting that is attached is a fixture, but other types of carpeting (throw rugs, etc.) are not. Security systems and alarms, as well as smoke detectors are fixtures. Furniture is personal property. Television antennas, satellite dishes, cable TV hookups, and telephone wiring and jacks have been held by courts to be fixtures.

Items outside your home may also be fixtures. Disputes arise over gas barbecue units, basketball backboards, awnings, storm windows, screens, and even rosebushes. All of these items are usually fixtures.

On the other hand, picnic tables, patio and deck furnishings, potted plants, and window air-conditioning units are usually deemed personal property.

Legal Tests

If you wind up in court over some of these disputed items, the court will apply three basic tests of a fixture. Test one is the method of attachment. Can the item be removed without damaging the real property it is attached to? Test two is the beneficial use/adaptability test. For example, a screen door or a gas hot water heater can easily be removed without damaging anything, but they are items that are ordinarily used and necessary to enjoy living in the house. Test three is the contractual relationship of the litigants. All things being equal, courts tend to favor buyers over sellers, and tenants

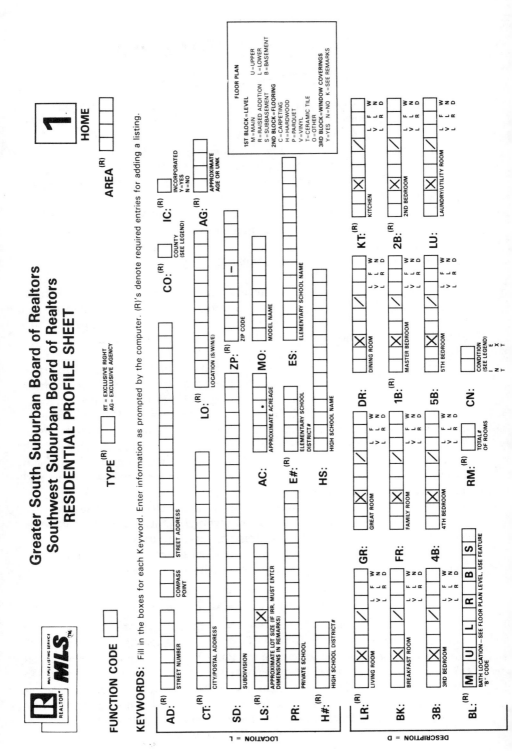

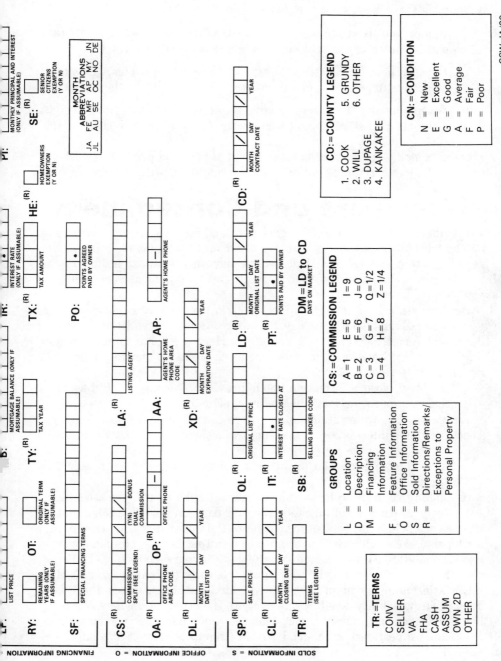

FINANCING INFORMATION = F

LP: LIST PRICE

RY: REMAINING YEARS (ONLY IF ASSUMABLE)

OT: ORIGINAL TERM (ONLY IF ASSUMABLE)

B: MORTGAGE BALANCE (ONLY IF ASSUMABLE)

IR: INTEREST RATE (ONLY IF ASSUMABLE)

PI: MONTHLY PRINCIPAL AND INTEREST (ONLY IF ASSUMABLE)

SF: SPECIAL FINANCING TERMS

TY:(R) TAX YEAR

TX:(R) TAX AMOUNT

HE:(R) HOMEOWNERS EXEMPTION (Y OR N)

SE:(R) SENIOR CITIZENS EXEMPTION (Y OR N)

MONTH ABBREVIATIONS
JA FE MR AP MY JN
JL AU SE OC NO DE

OFFICE INFORMATION = O

CS:(R) COMMISSION SPLIT (SEE LEGEND) / (Y/N) DUAL COMMISSION / BONUS

LA:(R) LISTING AGENT

PO: POINTS AGREED PAID BY OWNER

OA:(R) OFFICE PHONE AREA CODE

OP:(R) OFFICE PHONE

AA: AGENT'S HOME PHONE AREA CODE

AP: AGENT'S HOME PHONE

DL:(R) MONTH / DAY / YEAR DATE LISTED

XD:(R) MONTH / DAY / YEAR EXPIRATION DATE

SOLD INFORMATION = S

SP:(R) SALE PRICE

OL:(R) ORIGINAL LIST PRICE

LD:(R) MONTH / DAY / YEAR ORIGINAL LIST DATE

CD:(R) MONTH / DAY / YEAR CONTRACT DATE

CL:(R) MONTH / DAY / YEAR CLOSING DATE

IT:(R) INTEREST RATE CLOSED AT

PT:(R) POINTS PAID BY OWNER

TR:(R) TERMS (SEE LEGEND)

SB: SELLING BROKER CODE

DM=LD to CD DAYS ON MARKET

TR:=TERMS
CONV
SELLER
VA
FHA
CASH
ASSUM
OWN 2D
OTHER

GROUPS
L = Location
D = Description
M = Financing Information
F = Feature Information
O = Office Information
S = Sold Information
R = Directions/Remarks/ Exceptions to Personal Property

CS:=COMMISSION LEGEND
A=1   E=5   I=9
B=2   F=6   J=0
C=3   G=7   Q=1/2
D=4   H=8   Z=1/4

CO:=COUNTY LEGEND
1. COOK   5. GRUNDY
2. WILL   6. OTHER
3. DUPAGE
4. KANKAKEE

CN:=CONDITION
N = New
E = Excellent
G = Good
A = Average
F = Fair
P = Poor

GSW JA/90

over landlords. Courts do not have to give equal consideration to these tests when trying to determine the intent of the annexor.

The obvious lesson is to avoid problems and stay out of court. How do you accomplish this objective? I suggest you do three things.

1. Before you list your home or FISBO (For-Sale-By-Owner) it, take careful inventory of all items you are concerned about.

2. Discuss these items with your agent before you sign a listing contract or with your attorney before you put your FISBO on the market.

3. When showing the home, remove the items (such as Grandma's gift chandelier) that you plan to take with you, and replace these items.

Finally, remember that you may use items of personal property (washers, dryers, etc.) as bargaining chips when you negotiate with buyers.

Disclosure and Concealment

If the information on the listing agreement and forms is wrong, inaccurate, or not truthful, a buyer may sue the seller and his agent in fraud or misrepresentation. Sellers and their agents may also be under a duty to *volunteer* certain information to buyers in the listing forms and before a contract to purchase is signed.

Because state laws impose different disclosure requirements on sellers, you should consult your attorney for advice. Some states have developed disclosure forms, others do not use them. Here are some samples of non-disclosure of information that made a seller liable to a buyer for damages or recision of the sales contract:

failure to disclose information about previous flooding in the basement
concealment of fire damage behind new panelling
concealment of water stains and damage caused by leaky roof
not providing information on non-conforming zoning uses that could not be ascertained by county records
not providing information about encroachment disputes with adjoining property owners
and failing to disclose local code violations, such as using plastic pipes.

In Reed vs. King, an often cited 1983 case from California, a seller and his agent were held liable for not disclosing to the buyer that ten years earlier a woman and her children were murdered in that house. The memories of and stigma attached to the incident affected the market value of the house. Case law from many jurisdictions imposes a duty to volunteer or disclose information under some of the following circumstances: where there is fiduciary responsibility owed by one party to the other, and where one party had knowledge of a material fact that the other party cannot find out by reasonable investigation. A good rule of thumb is this: If in doubt, disclose it!!

6
Do I Need a Lawyer?

How involved are attorneys in a typical residential real estate transaction? That depends upon where you live and the local customs regarding the role of the attorney, the broker, the title company, the escrow agent, and other providers of real estate services. As this book explains, there are many functions and services that must be performed in order to transfer real property to a buyer. Among these functions are: signing a listing contract with a broker (for those who choose to sell via an agent); setting an asking price; showing the home; negotiating with prospective buyers; choosing or drafting the contract or offer forms; satisfying contractual contingencies (such as inspections, providing good title, arranging for and getting the proper financing for the buyer; etc); monitoring the progress of the deal after contract and before closing/settlement; preparing the deed and various affidavits and paperwork for closing; and conducting the actual closing/settlement.

If you live in the northeast United States, attorneys customarily are involved in all of the above services, except showing the house and perhaps picking a broker and setting an asking price. In the Great Lakes area, it is often title companies and lenders who play the largest roles in the transaction after a contract is signed. In the western United States, escrow agents play significant roles. Brokers and lenders may dominate the process in some southern states. If you are a For-Sale-By-Owner your attorney may advise you about more functions than if you were utilizing a broker's services.

Do you need a lawyer? Yes, you do! Which functions/services will she or he provide? That is something for you to discuss with your attorney, and the answer will be dictated by local custom as well as by your individual needs and wants. When should you hire an attorney? The sooner the better! Do it before you list your home with an agent or before you make any moves to market your home FISBO. If you wait until you have signed contracts with brokers or buyers, it may be too late for your lawyer to best protect your interests.

CHOOSING A REAL ESTATE LAWYER

Lawyers specialize in one or several areas of practice. Bob, who lives down the block, may be a corporate counsel for the Big Widget Company. The odds are good that Bob has not handled a sale of a home transaction in years. Erin may be a patent lawyer, but she has little knowledge in the area of residential real estate transactions. Sam may have done a great job in handling your divorce, but real estate is not his specialty. So where do you find a real estate attorney? If you used an attorney when you purchased your home, by all means use that attorney again if you were satisfied with the service you received.

If you do not have a real estate attorney, how do you find one? Ask local lenders, brokers, title companies and local attorneys to refer you to a good, experienced real estate attorney. Ask your co-workers, business associates, friends, relatives, and neighbors for recommendations. Accountants may also be of help in providing you with a name. Once you get a few names, schedule a meeting with one or more lawyers to discuss possible representation. What should you discuss?

1) Experience/Qualifications

Approximately what percent of the lawyer's business is real estate related? How long has he or she been in practice? Has the attorney represented any FISBO sellers recently? Does the attorney handle your affair personally, or is it farmed out to junior associates or paralegals? About how many real estate deals does he/she work on each month?

2) Services to Be Rendered

Let the lawyer explain to you his or her role in the transaction, from start to finish. Remember, customs vary nationwide. If you are a FISBO seller, do you want your attorney to assist with any of your business or marketing decisions? Can you call the lawyer after office hours, if need be? Will the attorney provide you with all the necessary offer and binder forms if you are a FISBO?

3) Former Clients as References

Would your prospective attorney give you the names of a few former real estate sellers that he or she has represented? You can later talk with these clients to determine if they were satisfied with the service and fees. What did they like or dislike about their experience with the lawyer? Would they hire the lawyer again?

4) Fee Arrangement

Does the attorney charge a flat fee, a percentage fee based upon the sales price of the home, or an hourly rate? What complications might arise, how likely are they, and what would it cost to straighten them out? If need be, you could compare the fees and services to be rendered with those a lender or closing service tells you to expect an attorney to charge. Of course you can compare the fees of one attorney versus others. Ask the attorney if he/she itemizes bills and if you could see a sample bill for a similar transaction. Would your contract for services with them be in writing; if so could you see a sample?

When choosing a real estate attorney, don't forget the interpersonal skills that it takes to get along with other participants and service providers. Pick someone you can get along with and work with. A good attorney can save you time, money, and stress.

On occasion, an attorney may represent both parties in a transaction. (This occurs more in small towns or isolated areas.) There is no ethical violation in this situation as long as the attorney reveals this fact to both parties and they consent to it. It is probably best to have your own attorney who is concerned only with representing you and your best interests.

7
Pricing Your Home

Setting the asking price for your home is a crucial decision. More than any other factor, price determines how long your house will be on the market. Price and marketing time are highly correlated. Excessive marketing time can cost you dollars if you are committed to buying another home and will close that purchase on a certain date. Nobody wants to make two different mortgage payments. Excessive marketing time can also have psychological costs to you. If you don't believe me, ask someone who has tried for six months or more to sell a home. As your house just sits there on the market, you feel helpless. You worry a lot, lose some sleep, and get crabby with others. Because your plans and dreams hinge upon the sale of your home, anxiety takes its toll. You can reduce your chances of suffering financial and psychic stress by setting the right asking price.

Underpricing the Home

Sellers always fear underpricing their home, selling it below market, and missing out on thousands of dollars that should have been in their pocket. On a very few occasions, this happens because the seller, agent, or appraiser makes a mistake in judgment. How do you know if your price is too low? Your phone will ring constantly, your doorbell will chime often, and the home will be shown immediately to many prospective buyers. You may receive several offers immediately after the listing.

Overpricing Is More Common

In practice, the more common error is overpricing your home. How does this happen? On occasion, an agent that is competing with other agents to list your home may promise that she or he can get you more money for your home by selling it at higher price than that proposed by other prospective listing agents. The agent who "highballs" you knows that the price she or he lists your home at is too high, but plans to drop the price later when you realize nobody is negotiating with you.

Another common scenario that leads to overpricing is the tendency of homeowners to over-value repairs and improvements made to the home. Buyers don't care that you just paid $3,500 for a new roof or $1,500 to repair the furnace. They expect to get a house with components that function reasonably well—something that every other seller is offering them. Buyers may not care that you added an outdoor deck for $3,000. In fact, some buyers hate decks and may want to rip it down and replace it with lawn. To such a buyer, the deck is just another expense. What will it cost to tear it down and truck the lumber and cement to the dump? What will it cost to put in a nice lawn?

Overpricing can also be caused by a lack of accurate data or a lack of information about current market conditions. Your home may be insured for $100,000. That figure may be the replacement or reproduction cost of your home, but it is rarely related to the current market value of your home. Remember, you are also selling the land that goes with the home, too. Perhaps the reproduction cost is fairly accurate if your home has just been constructed. Another source of data is the property value set by the county assessor's office for purposes of determining your property taxes. Normally, this figure is not current, and is not much help in setting a good asking price. Neighborhood scuttlebutt can be inaccurate. The Smiths, who live five houses down the block, allegedly listed their home at $105,000.00 and got full price. Who says they got full price? Did you see the contract? Did the seller help finance the sale? Were there any concessions for redecorating? Was any personal property (washer, dryer, microwave, furniture) thrown in on the deal?

Another reason people overprice is because they hope to sell their home to some "out of town buyer" or some ill-informed local buyer who hasn't done his homework and shopped the market. (You've never won the lottery, but maybe you'll get lucky and find a stupid buyer.)

OVERPRICING CAN BE COSTLY

What happens when you have overpriced your home? If you have it listed with an agent, his or her company will have a preview tour for all the agents working for the company. The agents will not be too enthusiastic about an overpriced house and will probably not bring you any prospects. If you have an open house, an overpriced home will generate less traffic and fewer word-of-mouth referrals from neighbors and casual lookers. An advertisement for an overpriced home draws fewer phone calls. In many respects, selling your home is a numbers game. You may get ten phone calls from buyers, six of those ten callers may drive by, and three may get out of the car to look inside. Overpricing stacks the numbers against you and is a risky game to play.

Suppose you have listed your home at $115,000 instead of the $100,000 figure it was appraised at. You wait six to eight weeks and decide to reduce the price $2,000 every month until it sells. Have you lost anything besides time? Maybe. When you first marketed your home, there may have been 1,000 qualified buyers in your area looking for $100,000 homes. Many of these buyers have bought homes. Are these buyers being replaced by new-comers to the pool of qualified buyers? Maybe yes, maybe no. Variables that influence the demand side of residential real estate markets change constantly. Interest rates can rise, and the buyers pool may decrease. If interest rates fall, the pool may increase.

Shocks to the supply side of residential real estate could occur. A plant closing may add a new crop of $100,000 homes to the market. A new development featuring homes in the $100,00 range may begin construction. On a pleasant note, perhaps a business relocates in your area, and 300 of its employees will be moving to your town.

Even if you are in no rush to sell and have the time to play the price reduction game, you still may encounter some obstacles. Whenever a property is listed for a long time, buyers become very wary. What's wrong with that house (besides being overpriced previously)? Are there some hidden defects that other buyers discovered that I don't see? (Did the basement flood this spring when we had heavy rains?) Buyers become suspicious of properties that have been on the market too long. Your home develops a reputation as a loser. Buyers may decide to wait for a better crop of new listings.

If you plan to sell your house in a leisurely manner, where are you going to move to when you sell? If you are buying another home, perhaps prices of homes in that range have gone up. Can you still qualify for a home loan of that amount?

Another problem with an overpriced house is that most buyers seek institutional financing, and when the lender has an appraisal done, your house will not appraise at the selling price that an ill-informed buyer agreed to. Then what? Can the buyer still qualify for the loan? Can the buyer put more money down? Do you reduce your price? Does the buyer back out of the sale? You may have lost six to eight weeks of time that your home could have been on the market.

Now that you have been slapped in the face with some sobering thoughts on pricing, let's look at some strategies for setting the asking price.

A Do-It-Yourself Approach to Pricing

If you plan to set the asking price for your home without paying a professional for advice, there are several ways you can gather information. You will need to know the general price ranges that homes in your neighborhood have recently sold for, and also what price homes comparable to yours have sold for. The comparables should be as close to your exact location as possible. You should try to find at least three comparables, and take up to ten if you can. You may know of several sales in the past year of homes on your block or blocks close by. If you are lucky, one of these homes may be the exact twin or double of yours in style and size. Walk down the block, introduce yourself as a neighbor, and have a chat with the homeowner. Compliment them on their purchase and sing the praises of the neighborhood. Tell them you are going to sell your home soon due to X reason, and you sure will miss the neighborhood. Ask them what price they paid for their home, and if the financing was conventional or other. You may ask them what amenities or factors led them to choose this particular house over others they looked at. Just before you leave, thank them sincerely, remind them that you will be selling soon. Leave them with this thought: maybe they know a family member, associate at work, or friend from the old neighborhood that wants to buy in this neighborhood. Tell them you'll stop by in a couple of weeks and drop off a fact sheet and/or open house information.

If you personally can't recall who has moved in recently, ask the block's chief information sources. Each block usually has one or more people who know just about everybody. You can also go to your local library and dust off old back issues of your local paper. (There may not be any dust on microfilm or microfiche!) Papers from three to twelve months ago will give you some leads to follow up on. While at the library, ask the reference librarian for assistance. Tell her or him exactly what you are looking for. They may lead you to a source you never knew existed, such as a local business journal that gives weekly reports on all the local real estate transactions that were recorded at the county courthouse!

Check the Legal Records

The county courthouse is a great source of real estate information. Once you have the addresses of properties that have sold within the last 12 months, you can get a very good idea of the sales price via the documentary stamps affixed to deeds and instruments affecting title. Be sure to ask for help at the courthouse. Someone will show you how to look up the legal descriptions of these properties that you have only street addresses for; they will show you how the books are filed and which book you need to look in; and they will explain to you how documentary stamps tell you how many thousands of dollars were involved in the sale. These records are public information that you are entitled to, and courteous help is available. They are happy to assist you, and help newcomers especially—so that they don't misfile documents.

Get Help from the Pros

You can also get some data from lenders, title companies, and escrow companies. Because these entities are in the real estate business, they have the experience and access to information that you need. They hope you use their title company or escrow agency to close the deal; and they hope your buyer finances the purchase with them, and that you also consider them when you buy another home. These professional sources can give you information about past sales and current market conditions.

Perhaps the easiest task is finding the asking prices of homes that are currently for sale. You can ride through your neighborhood and see all the For Sale signs, jot down the addresses and phone numbers, and give them a call. Your local newspapers also carry real estate ads that are very useful. Look for open house signs or ads and visit your competition. Some sellers pose as buyers and have a real estate agent drive them around to all the competition. I don't think telling a lie is the right thing to do. Tell the truth, and a few confident agents will assist you. They hope that you will list with them if your for-sale-by-owner strategy fails.

What about Professional Appraisals?

You may want to hire an independent fee appraiser to give you some guidance in selecting the right asking price. This professional will give you an independent, unbiased, objective assessment of the fair market value of your property and home. Fair market value has been defined in several ways. Some define it as the probable price that a property will bring. Others refer to it as the lowest price a ready, willing, and able seller will take and the highest price a ready, willing, and able buyer will pay for a specific property.

It is the job of the appraiser to determine what fair market value should be in dollar terms. You want to hire an appraiser that is experienced in *residential* real estate and familiar with your area. How do you find one? The yellow pages may be the fastest way, but it can be a shot in the dark. You can ask some real estate professionals for the names of good appraisers. Ask your mortgage lenders, local real estate attorneys, real estate agents, bankers, title company officers, and others for recommendations. There are several trade and professional organizations for appraisers that offer designations that can be earned through continuing education and exams. These professional groups also promulgate standards of practice and codes of conduct. Estimates suggest that only one in ten appraisers belongs to a professional group such as the American Institute of Real Estate Appraisers, the American Society of Appraisers, or the National Association of Independent Fee Appraisers.

APPRAISAL METHODS

Appraisers commonly use three methods of determining value. Rental property is usually evaluated using the income approach. In this method, the appraiser capitalizes the property's net income at a rate of return consistent with prevailing market conditions to arrive at fair market value. In rental properties, it is ultimately the earning power of the property that determines value.

Two other methods are employed when appraising residential property. The cost approach (also called the replacement or reproduction method) focuses upon how much it would cost to replace the structures and improvements (house, garage, etc.) upon the land. A figure to allow for age, wear and tear, and depreciation is subtracted from the reproduction cost. Finally, the value of the land is added to determine fair market value. The cost method is usually employed for insurance purposes.

The most common appraisal method for evaluating residential housing is the market value approach. The appraiser gathers information about comparable homes ("COMPS") in your immediate area that have either sold or have been offered for sale within the last 12 months. The appraiser tries to find homes that are very similar to yours in terms of number of bedrooms, square feet of living space, number of bathrooms, age and condition of the house, and lot size. The appraiser also notes how long the home was on the market, what the asking price and final sale prices were, what terms and financing were utilized, what special features a property had and any other distinguishing features. Comparable properties that are currently for sale, together with the above noted salient features, are also listed in the appraisal. Your property is compared to these other similar properties, and the appraiser makes a judgment as to the fair market value of your property. Appraising is part science and part art, and it ultimately is the opinion of one expert. For an example of an appraisal, see page 58.

APPRAISALS CAN BE USEFUL

Should you get an appraisal? Are they worth $250 to $350? If you choose the For-Sale-By-Owner marketing approach, an appraisal is usually well worth the money. You may not have the time or inclination to hunt down the requisite data. If you are engaging the services of a real estate agent, an appraisal can also be helpful. If you and your agent disagree over a good listing price, an appraisal may be most helpful. It can help you determine if prospective agents are trying to "highball" you by telling you that they can sell your home for a much higher price just to get the listing. It can also be a safeguard against "lowball" underpricing. Whether you use an agent to sell your home or not, prospective buyers are impressed with appraisals done by independent experts. Buyers place more credence in the written word than the spoken word. Buyers feel secure in knowing that the odds are very high that should they put in a contract to buy your home that the financing will not fall through because the home and property failed to appraise at a value high enough to satisfy the lender. An appraisal can be a valuable sales tool!

FHA APPRAISALS

If your home is priced in the moderate range, you should seriously consider getting an FHA (Federal Housing Administration) appraisal or a VA (Veterans Administration) appraisal. (The FHA appraisal is called a conditional

01-19-90

From: John Doe, Appraiser
        000 Main Street
        Somewhere, USA

To: Mr. and Mrs. Smith
        111 Front St.
        Somewhere, USA

Re: Letter of opinion of value of xxx residence

    This partial native stone, 1,350-square-foot, 2-bath,
3-bedroom, 7-year-old home is being appraised for the purposes
of division of equity between co-title owners.

    The subject property is located approximately 4 miles west
and 1 mile north of downtown. The site is located in SouthBrook
III, a modern subdivision around 10 years of age. The neighborhood
is well maintained, clean, and convenient to all modern utilities,
municipal services, and shopping areas.

The subject residence is striking in its cleanliness and maintenance. The square footage appears larger due to the excellent
design. All the home has excellent functionality and all modern
appliances. There is a burglar system. The master bedroom has
an unusually large, attractive bathroom not found in most homes.
the stone fireplace and wood-beamed, vaulted ceilings are attractive.
There was no obvious shifting and cracking of the slab foundation
found in thousands of Tulsa homes. The partial masonry exterior
walls common in this neighborhood, done for economy, is offset
by the excellent maintenance of the neighbors. Value was added
 for the site's location on a cul-de-sac, which attracts most
buyers.

This opinion is subject in accuracy to the acquisition of a
complete appraisal done with comparables and a grid of resolution
of distinguishing factors. No representation is made as to soil
of subsoil conditions effecting movement of the foundation, slabs,
or walls, or surface water run-off or drainage, now or ever. An
engineering survey should be obtained if there is a question of
foundation stability. The property does appear to drain properly
and the neighborhood hasn't flooded.

Due to the excellent appearance, design, and maintenance of the
subject, considered with the appearance, design, and maintenance
of the neighborhood, I determined the value range of this area
between $40 and $48 per square foot. I selected $46 per foot
for the subject property and my estimation of fair market value
as of 1-19-90 is: $62,100.00.

Very truly yours,

John Doe

commitment, and the VA appraisal is called a certificate of reasonable value.) If you sell to a buyer who utilizes FHA or VA financing, the appraisal is good for 6 months. Even if you don't sell to a buyer who gets FHA or VA financing, the written appraisal is a powerful and persuasive selling tool.

ARE APPRAISALS FOR EVERYONE?

Many real estate agents believe that unless you need an appraisal for judicial purposes (for example, you are in probate court or divorce court), an appraisal is not necessary. Agents believe that they can provide you with virtually the same information that an appraisal gives you to help you set your asking price. Real estate brokers in most areas have developed sophisticated data bases that feature all the homes that have been listed, sold, gone unsold, or those with sales pending for the last X months. The characteristics, size, and features of the homes are noted, as are the financing arrangements. Members of the local multiple listing services supply the data.

CMA'S TO THE RESCUE

These data bases allow agents to conduct a computer-aided search for comparable homes that are currently for sale, or have been sold in the past year, or listings that expired without a sale. Data regarding asking (listing) price and actual sales price is supplied, along with the number of days the home was on the market. Utilizing all of this information, an agent can construct a very impressive looking written document on a form custom designed by each agency. Most agencies will title this form "Competitive Market Analysis" or "Comparative Market Analysis." (They are conveniently called CMAs in the profession.) CMAs are very powerful tools that agents use when making a presentation to sellers who are trying to decide if to list or who to list with. CMAs are very helpful to sellers in selecting a good asking price.

You are probably wondering, how do I get my hands on one of these CMAs? Obviously, you can list with a broker and get a CMA from her or him. But suppose you want to try the For-Sale-By-Owner approach first, then what? Do you have any friends or relatives in the real estate business who can get you a CMA? If not, then I recommend a straightforward, honest approach. Call three different agents, and tell them your strategy. You hope to sell your home yourself, and need a CMA. Can they help you? The sharp agents love to help FISBOs, because they realize that at least 50% of FISBOs will turn into listings. The agents will come with their CMAs and will also give you a thorough listing presentation. Agents know they have something much more valuable than comparables—they have experience and access to buyers via multiple listing services that you only dream you had! For an example of a typical CMA, see page 60.

Does the appraiser's data base contain properties that may not have been

Rosetta
REALTORS

9501 South Street • Oxford, MS • (601) 422-0011

PREPARED FOR:

PROPERTY ADDRESS	# UNITS	TYPE UNITS	AGE	CONST	GROSS INC	EXP

FOR SALE NOW:	# UNITS	TYPE UNITS	AGE	CONST	GROSS INC	EXP

RECENTLY SOLD:	# UNITS	TYPE UNITS	AGE	CONST	GROSS INC	EXP

PROPERTY ASSETS:

PROPERTY DRAWBACKS:

AREA MARKET CONDITIONS:

The statements and figures prese

Competitive Market Analysis

T OME	GRM	CAP RATE	FEATURES		

T OME	GRM	CAP RATE	FEATURES	DAYS ON MARKET	CURRENT LIST PRICE

OME	GRM	CAP RATE	FEATURES	LIST PRICE	DATE SOLD	DAYS ON MARKET	SALE PRICE

RECOMMENDED LISTING RANGE

while not guaranteed, are secured from sources we believe authoritative.

sold through multiple listing services? Yes, especially FISBO transactions. In large markets, the size of the data base usually insures representative properties for either source.

Other Factors to Consider

Real estate professionals have to use their judgment to consider other factors besides comparable sales when trying to arrive at a good asking price. You may wonder why a home that sold for $100,000 six months ago will not necessarily sell for $100,000 today. The answer is because nothing is constant in the world of macroeconomics, microeconomics, and local real estate markets. Six months ago it was June and the buyers were out in full force. Now, it is December, and there is a paucity of buyers. Six months ago, perhaps mortgage interest rates were 10%, now they are 11½%. Get the idea—factors and conditions change.

FINANCIAL TERMS

What factors and conditions must be considered? The availability of mortgage financing is very important. Are lenders becoming more conservative in the wake of many failures in the thrift and banking industry? Will larger downpayments be required of buyers? Will larger mortgage insurance premiums be required of buyers? Will interest rates on mortgages rise? Are loan origination fees rising? All these factors touch upon the issue of buyer affordability, and may affect the potential number of prospective buyers interested in buying your home.

What about seller financing? It is prevalent in your market? Are sellers helping out buyers with buy-downs or second mortgages? (See chapter 12 for more on seller financing.) If the seller will help with financing, the price of the home should be higher than a comparable home that does not offer seller financing. The higher price is a risk premium to the seller.

LOCAL MARKET CONDITIONS

Is your local market a buyer's market or a seller's market? In a buyer's market, supply of homes for sale exceeds the demand for these homes. In other words, there are more sellers than there are buyers. This exerts downward pressure on prices. The opposite is true in a seller's market; local real estate professionals know how large the for-sale inventory of homes in your price range is. They can tell you the average number of days a home is on the market before a sale is consummated.

Local conditions, events, and happenings affect price. Are developers planning new construction? Is there a plant closing or opening in town? Is a new school opening? Is there a new highway planned? Is the proposed shopping mall going in close by?

CUSTOMARY MARK-UP

Each local real estate market may practice by custom an unwritten law of mark-ups. Simply stated, how much higher is the asking or listing price from the actual sales price? Are there any observable patterns? Does everyone "know" that the custom in your town is to offer 5% less than the asking price and the offer will probably be accepted? When you study the comparables you may or may not discern a pattern or custom. Also, realize that the mark-up may vary within the same town for various neighborhoods or price ranges that comprise mini-market segments. Review mark-up patterns for your comparables, and incorporate this information into your pricing strategy.

Final Thoughts on Pricing

Are there any "magic numbers" or barriers in pricing strategy? Studies are inconclusive as to whether $99,999 is a better price than $100,000. You may think that an ad that says "under $100,000" may attract a different prospect. Maybe. Again, local custom may provide an answer.

You are now acquainted with the intricacies of setting your asking price, and you have plenty of work to do. Because sellers always ask me, I cannot duck the question: What is a good asking price? The best general answer I can give is this: a good asking price in most cases is a price slightly below the price that your competitive comparables are listed at.

8
A Comprehensive Marketing Plan

Whether you are selling homes or gym shoes or fried chicken, certain principles of marketing apply to all products. Brian Jennings, Field Marketing Manager of Kentucky Fried Chicken's Southwest Division, outlined the basic marketing approach in a recent conversation with me. The California fast food guru began by stressing "you must know your product and its attributes. You should understand and monitor fluctuating market conditions and the actions of competitors." Jennings continues, "Strategic marketing entails three things: 1) recognize that the market is composed of mini-markets or segments; 2) target one or more of these segments; 3) devise a synergistic strategic marketing plan aimed at your targets."

If you are selling your home via an agent, you should get a *written* marketing plan before you sign a listing contract. Stipulate in the listing contract that the marketing plan is part of your listing agreement. If you are selling your home via the FISBO route, you must develop a marketing plan for yourself. With or without an agent, a good marketing plan should include the following components:

1. An overview of current market conditions
   A) Comparative Market Analysis (CMA)
   B) Trends in mortgage financing
2. A profile of most likely buyers (targets)
3. Advertising
   A) Which media?
   B) Message
   C) Frequency of ads
4. Open houses
   A) Preview tours for agents
   B) Open house for buyers
      1. When and how often?
5. Yard signs
6. Listing sheets
7. Fact sheets
8. Brochure box

9. Networking to find buyers
   A) Multiple Listing Service (MLS)
   B) Neighbors, co-workers, friends
10. Handling telephone calls from prospects
11. Showing the home
12. Additional sales tools
    A) Appraisals, inspections, warranties, etc
13. Feedback
    A) Weekly progress report from agent

Let's discuss these components of your marketing plan. We have already looked at the Comparative Market Analysis (CMA) in Chapter 7. The same chapter introduced you to the relationship between selling price and the availability of financing, and Chapter 18 will explore owner financing in greater detail.

Who Are Your Targets?

There are many different market segments in the residential real estate market. For example, there are: first-time buyers, investors, young families, single homeowners, couples without children, empty nesters, retirees, professional/executive buyers, and relocated workers. Markets can be segmented in a variety of ways. Physically, one neighborhood is different than another. A two bedroom home differs from a three bedroom home. Price can also segment one neighborhood from another. Attributes such as being within walking distance of the river or being in a certain school district can segment markets. Segments can overlap and distinctions may be blurred.

Observe your own block or your own neighborhood. Can you sketch a profile of the typical homeowner? Maybe it is easy to do. You live in a new suburban development along with 700 other young couples with small children. Maybe you live in a neighborhood with homeowners from 25 to 90 years old, and homes that have 800 square feet sit next to those with 2,000 square feet. Or, maybe you live in an exclusive neighborhood populated with executives and professionals.

Why worry about the characteristics of homeowners in your area? The odds are very good that the person who buys your home will fit the demographic profile of your current neighbors. This is very useful information! Real estate attorneys, agents, and lenders can also tell you *who* is buying homes like yours. Once you understand *who* is buying, it is easier to ascertain *why* they are buying. (They buy because their needs are met by homes with certain attributes. These attributes should be emphasized in the marketing process.)

Advertising Your Home

Classified advertising is an essential part of any marketing program. Which newspapers or magazines should you advertise in? If a buyer were looking for a home comparable to yours, which source would the buyer read? (That's where you want to advertise!) In most areas, the Sunday newspaper is the one edition that carries the most real estate ads and is read most often by prospective buyers. Which paper do you throw out last? Right—Sunday's paper, because it has more features and you may read it over several days. When I run ads in the Sunday paper, I invariably get calls during the middle of the week that begin with the caller saying "I saw your ad in the paper. . . ."

Some newspapers run a special real estate section on Friday or Saturday. Habits and customs are local in nature. You can watch the number of ads or count newspaper column inches for several weeks to see which day is the big day for real estate in your town. Local or neighborhood newspapers are often found in larger metropolitan areas as well as smaller towns. They can be excellent vehicles to use when targeting a specific segment of buyers. Buyers who are looking for a house on the southside of town will scour the *"Southside News"* for ads.

Some publishers produce a weekly magazine that is devoted only to real estate. Brokers as well as individuals may advertise in such magazines. You may have such a magazine in your town that is normally placed in supermarkets, airports, malls, and other high-traffic locations. The magazine is free to readers, and this boosts circulation. Contact the publisher to determine the feasibility of utilizing this specialized medium.

If you are using an agent to sell your home, she or he will probably write the ad and select the media. Agents advertise your property for two reasons: first, they hope to find a buyer for your home; and second, they hope to find buyers who may not buy your specific home, but will buy a comparable home through the agent. Your home may be used as a "teaser." Real estate agents and firms usually advertise their best merchandise to attract prospects and make the phone ring. Sometimes ads don't even mention the address of the property for sale, because the agent can switch a buyer to a whole MLS listing book supply of comparable homes for sale. Teasers and switching to comparables may work for your benefit, because probably less than 5% of those who are shown a home buy that specific home. Selling is a numbers game, and the more lookers the better for you. Your home may be on an agent's showing list merely as a comparable to back up what the agent thinks is "The" house for the buyer. The buyer may have a different opinion and fall in love with your house. The essential point regarding ads run by brokers is this: get some ideas from them, but do not copy them because brokers have several motives for running an ad. You can compare your ads to those your competition is running for comparable homes. If you were a buyer, which of those competing ads would you call, and why?

Classified Advertising Tips for FISBOs

If you are selling by owner, the decisions about layout, headline, and body are yours to make. Regarding layout, there is no doubt that larger ads with a border of white space attract more attention that the usual 3 or 4 line ads. Pick up the real estate ad section yourself, and see what you look at first. Is it worth the extra money to have an ad that stands out? Maybe. (Nice bit of waffling, huh?!) Big ads are noticed first, and may be called first. However, some experts present this view of prospective buyers: serious buyers will read *all* of the classified ads with big and small layouts, because they don't want to miss anything.

In most cases, the words "By Owner" should be used above the headline. This immediately signals the prospective buyer that the potential for savings exists, and a bargain may be possible. The purpose of the headline is to get the buyer's attention and induce him or her to read further. The headline should identify the most important feature of your property and house, compared to all the other ads for comparable homes. That feature may be a variety of things, from price to location to privacy. If you can work several features into the headline, that is advised. A headline "Below Appraisal in Lorenz Heights" tells the reader both the location and the potential for a bargain. One or two features in the headline is enough. Keep the headlines short and direct.

The body (or copy) of the ad should be composed of facts that support or prove the headline. If the headline says "Below Appraisal," the body should tell the reader who did the appraisal (FHA?) and how much the selling price is below the appraised value. If the headline mentions the word "convenient," the body should spell out the details such as close to the highway, public transportation, schools, shopping centers, whatever. If the headline says "Carefree" the copy should stress things such as new or superior electrical, mechanical, and plumbing components, and low maintenance features such as brick exterior and minimal yardwork. Should the phrase "energy-smart" appear in a headline, it should be followed in the body of the ad with talk about storm windows, insulation, and low utility bills.

What else should appear in the body of the ad? The price is the most important information that buyers seek, followed closely by location or neighborhood, and the number of bedrooms and bathrooms. Extras and amenities, school districts and financing and terms may also be important information to certain target markets.

Avoid the use of abbreviations, if possible. "Words" like FP, 2G, EIK may be familiar shorthand that agents recognize as fireplace, two-car garage, and eating space in kitchen; but to most buyers this is real estatese and gibberish that distracts from mental images the adwriters try to paint. You can attract attention in the first week or two by using words such as "New

Listing" or "New On The Market" or "Just Advertised." This will alert buyers who have diligently been searching the ads week in and week out that your product is new.

Some FISBO sellers put "principals only" in their ads to discourage agents and to also encourage buyers to bargain directly with the owner. Many ads close with some action-oriented positive words such as "Won't last—call now" or "See Sunday 1–4 P.M. before it's gone." A phone number should be included in the ad, together with any comments such as "call after 6 P.M."

Sellers should check on the accuracy of the ad they are running. A misprinted price or phone number can cost time and money. Sellers may run ads in several different publications and may even run different copy aimed at different target markets. Such a strategy increases your chances of finding a "crossover" buyer who is outside your primary target market.

FISBO sellers often ask how much money they can expect to spend on advertising. The answer depends to a great degree upon market conditions, especially the average number of days on the market before sale. Spending ½ of 1% to 1% of the sales price on advertising is fairly common.

Previews for the Pros

If you have listed your home for sale with a brokerage firm, your agent will arrange a private open house for agents. These agents' open houses may take several forms. If you have listed with a large firm, the firm will arrange a "caravan" tour of your home and others that have been recently listed with the firm. These caravans are usually scheduled on a Monday or Tuesday as the wrap-up to a meeting for the entire sales staff. All the agents from the listing firm inspect your home and fill out questionnaires that ask a few questions; what price should this home sell at or what do you suggest to make this property sell faster? These comments will be collected by your agent, and the highlights reviewed with you. The preview caravan is helpful to you the seller in another big way—the agents have been exposed to your home and now put it in their mental inventory. The home comes alive and is not just something described on a sheet of paper. Agents tend to show homes they have seen before more frequently and with more enthusiasm.

If your home is offered through a multiple listing service (MLS), your agent may hold a separate open house just for member agents of the MLS system. Agents may visit together in groups from the same firm or they may come alone to inspect your home. Your agent again seeks the opinions of her/his peers and passes on the comments to you. The increased exposure helps your chances of finding a buyer.

An Open House for Buyers

A well designed marketing plan will include plans to hold an "open house" so that the public can come by to view your home without having made an appointment. If you are using an agent to sell your home, ask the agent to stipulate in writing how often and when the house will be held open. Honest agents will tell you that rarely does an open house produce a buyer for the house being held open that is listed with a broker. (FISBO open houses and model home houses for new developments are more successful in producing sales.) Agents like to hold open houses for three reasons: the effort and activity impress the owners because they can "see" the agent earning the commission; agents will meet prospective buyers who will not buy your particular house for sale, but the agent can show and sell them other homes; and the agent will meet some people who are thinking about selling their homes, and may be potential listing prospect.

WHEN TO HAVE IT

If you are a FISBO, I suggest that you hold an open house several times a week. The best time slot is usually 1 P.M. to 5 P.M. on Sunday. Saturday from 1 P.M. to 5 P.M. can also be a good time. I also believe you should try a week night to catch people on the way home from work, as well as those who work or do something on the weekends. Try Wednesday or Thursday night from 4 P.M. to 8 P.M. Monday and Tuesday are usually bad nights for customer traffic in any business. (Ask any merchant or restaurateur). Experiment a bit with Wednesday or Thursday. Some local or seasonal events may influence your choice of days and times. (Is Wednesday church night? Does the high school team play on Thursday nights? Are the times picked conducive to capturing the traffic flow?)

Some preliminary details must be attended to several days before the open house. You and your broker should be sure that your classified ad that runs the day before and the day of the open house mentions the time and address of the open house. Four or five days before the open house, a sign should go up on your lawn that says "Open House This Sunday 1–5 P.M.," or whatever is appropriate. This allows the auto and foot traffic to take note. Some of this traffic will not be driving by on Sunday, since some people only go down your street Monday through Friday during the day when going to work or taking the kids to school. So get that sign out early! Neighbors will also see the sign and start to buzz a bit. They wonder "Why are the Mosebys selling? Is Jane expecting another baby? Did Brian get transferred? I wonder who will move in—not some geeks, I hope. Hey, wait a minute. My cousin is looking for a house in this area. I'd better call her. I wonder what the home is selling for? It looks about the same size as mine. I wonder what the inside looks like?"

Attention, All Magpies

They wonder, they phone their cousin, they drop a tidbit into their next conversation over the backyard fence, and the networking and word-of-mouth advertising begins. Two or three days before the open house, every neighbor on the block should receive a personal invitation to attend the open house. If you hire an agent, the agent should invite the neighbors and tell them that the owners will be gone. Neighbors like to hear that, because they can inspect the house without feeling like they are invading your privacy. Neighbors will want to compare their house to yours and get some idea of what their house is worth. Obviously, a FISBO cannot tell the neighbors that the owners will not be there. The FISBO seller must use another approach such as "Come on over and look the house over. A lot of of the homes on the block are similar in design, but sometimes we can all pick up a decorating idea or two from each other."

Either the agent or FISBO seller must also plant another idea in the neighbors mind. That idea is that maybe the neighbor knows a friend, relative, or co-worker that wants to buy in this area. A FISBO seller might say "We sure hate to leave this neighborhood, we love it here. But we're expecting another baby soon and need more room. I hope your new neighbors enjoy living here as much as we do. You might think of a relative or friend that would like to move into this area, so feel free to bring them by the open house."

What about neighbors who live one block down, over, or behind you? I advise you to photocopy a "cover letter," an open house announcement (create one yourself!) and staple it to your fact sheet or the broker's listing sheet. You (or those expensive kids of yours) can then distribute them in the neighborhood. I've seen some very creative cover letters that grab attention. One letter had a headline "Guess who your new neighbor is going to be?!!" The letter then had several pictures that were cut out of magazines. One picture was a grizzled, unshaven old man with a bottle of muscatel peeking out from his pocket. Another picture was of a gruff-looking male and female couple in matching quasi-motorcycle outfits. The getup and the couple both looked like forty miles of bad road. Picture number three was of a young couple with two cute little kids that look like they were dressed to visit Grandma. The cover letter then said, "The selection process begins this Sunday!" Then the letter noted the time and place for the open house, and gave a phone number. The cover letter served to remind nearby residents that they have a small stake in the seller's actions because their quality of life may be affected. Self-interest serves as an incentive.

Two or three days before the open house is also the right time to scout out the best places to put your directional signs and arrows. You've seen these types of signs before. Their purpose is to lead strangers from recognized arterial streets and cross streets to the site of your open house. Be sure you understand local ordinances regarding signs, and also be careful not to put your sign on somebody's private property without their permission. Don't wait until 30 minutes before the open house begins to worry about placement, because you may need to put a sign on private property, but the owners are not home. Plan ahead and get permission. (And while you are there, drop off a listing sheet or fact sheet.)

On the day of your open house, attention to detail is important. Your signs and arrows should be in place one hour before the scheduled time. You may get an early-bird or cruiser who notices the signs and comes in early. Your home should be clean, well lit, and dressed to kill. (See the section on showing your home in this chapter.) All valuables, keepsakes, and breakables should be stored, hidden, and locked up. Remove temptation. The old adage "out of sight—out of mind" is good advice. Children of visitors can quickly pull an expensive vase off a coffee table.

Coffee, soft drinks, fruit, snacks, or cookies are usually welcomed by visitors. When placed in the family room or kitchen, they help to slow the visitors down so that you or the agent can talk and listen to them. If you make a great snack or cookie or dessert, have some on hand and in view. It may be the icebreaker you need to start talking in a relaxed way. A perfect cookie can lead to talk about your oven's temperature, ease of cleaning, and the functional efficiency of the kitchen. A cookie given to a child can lead to talk such as "He's a good-sized boy. What grade is he in? What school district are your folks in? Do you like it? We're in the Einstein District, and think the schools are great. The kids from Einstein consistently outscore kids from Moe Howard Junior High School on standardized tests. We can get you some more information on the local schools and mail it to you or drop it off."

You should have plenty of fact sheets on hand, as well as financing worksheets that would show a prospective buyer what monthly payments would be with an average downpayment. You should also have a sign-in sheet or guest book ready for use. You can reproduce the form on the next page and attach it to a clipboard.

A Variety of Visitors

When the visitors arrive, you want to greet them in a relaxed, non-threatening manner. Body language and space communicate with others. If you open the door to let them in, step back a comfortable distance—don't crowd them. After introductions, hand them the visitor sign-in sheet or guest book. The sign-in list may already contain a few dummy names of your relatives or friends. Few people like to be first to sign anything. If the visitors balk, tell them your insurance man, your attorney, and the local police recommend getting a record of all visitors in case a dispute arises later. If in doubt, a driver's license and verification of car license plates may be in order. It is your home, and they expect to follow the rules of the house. You may ask the visitors how they learned about your open house. This feedback helps you decide which methods of advertising have the most punch.

All types of visitors may show up to view your house, and not all are serious buyers. Other sellers may drop by to view the competition. Nosey neighbors may be curious to see your home to compare interior decorating schemes with theirs or to see what their own property is worth compared to

OPEN HOUSE GUESTS
Visitor Sign-In Sheet

Name	Address	Town	Phone	Ad	Sign	Other

LEARNED OF OPEN HOUSE BY

yours. Walk-by gapers, out for a leisurely stroll, may pop in to pass some time. Drive-by cruisers may come in because they are interested in real estate, but think they aren't quite ready to take the plunge. Agents may also visit, especially if you are a FISBO. Don't let appearances or attire fool you. The lady in gym sweats may be a lawyer, and the man in the flannel shirt could be an executive. You should treat everyone warmly, and realize that each one of them will talk about your home to others. The walk-by gaper may visit your home and later phone her nephew about your place.

There are different approaches and theories to showing a home. Many people who visit an open house do not like the rigidity of a formal appointment with you or an agent. They prefer a more relaxed environment. I believe that you should tell the visitors to "explore this fine home by yourselves. I'll be here in the den, and if you have any questions about the neighborhood, or schools, or any part of the house, I'll be happy to help."

This approach lets the buyers discover your home, and they can linger and talk about certain rooms or features at their pace. It lets them get the feel of your house, and gives them time to imagine themselves living in your house. Those real estate professionals who disagree with me say that buyers will not be made aware of some unique features without a tour guide. Maybe so. If that is your worry, try placing small index cards with information at appropriate spots in your home. Tape them or tie them to an item. For example, your hot water heater may have a card saying "40-gallon capacity, gas fueled, one year old, under five-year warranty." Your kitchen cabinets may have a tag or card saying "all oak cabinets, custom built by master craftsman Wallace Reed." The serious lookers are usually the ones who ask questions or want to return with a relative or friend. Set an appointment for those who want to return. If they are not sure of a good time because they don't know Uncle Chuck's schedule, tell them you will call them at 9 P.M. tonight. If they are hot prospects, stay in touch. A second private showing will allow you to concentrate on the benefits and features of your home and neighborhood. It will allow buyers to voice objections. It is good to remember that over half of all homes sold are bought by buyers who visit the home two or more times. It is good to have at least two hosts if you are holding a FISBO open house. One can be available for serious questions and discussions while the other greets visitors and signs them in.

Yard Signs: More Bang per Dollar

The most cost-effective form of advertising is the For Sale sign you put in your front yard. The yard sign is a great promotional tool, yet some sellers shy away from using them. Why? Some sellers worry about what the neighbors will think and hope to keep their listing a secret. This seems counterproductive, not to mention silly. Neighbors can be an important part of your word-of-mouth sales network. Neighbors also know you're selling when they see a car with a logo on the door pull up, and an agent dressed in a colored blazer that is identified with a national franchisor leaps out to open the door for a couple. Later, the neighbors see the blazer-clad agent with two strangers out in your yard looking around. The neighbors find out despite your reticence, so why hide the fact that your house is for sale?

Some sellers tell brokers that they don't want a For Sale sign in their yard because it attracts lookers that are not financially qualified and lookers who ignore the sign's words "by appointment only." The obvious response to this concern is that the sellers should not answer the door! Some sellers put a sign next to the doorbell that says "day sleeper—do not disturb" or "please do not ring bell—baby is asleep," followed by "Call broker for appointment at 777-1000." A FISBO seller might leave a note saying "Come to our next open house this Sunday, 1–4 P.M., or "call us tonight after dinner to schedule an appointment."

Signs not only signal the neighbors that your house is for sale, but they also broadcast the news to the mailman, people who drive by, and especially to the buyers who cruise particular neighborhoods they are interested in.

SIGNS FOR FISBOS

If you are selling through an agent, the agent will provide a sign for you. If you are a FISBO, you'll have to procure your own sign. Your sign should be of good quality and look sharp. Hardware stores carry FISBO signs, and sign companies will custom make one for you. (Check your local yellow pages for help.) If you purchase the sign, you might also buy an open house sign and directional arrows while you are at it.)

Homemade signs are OK, providing they look good and don't warp, wilt, or peel in rain, sleet, snow, or blistering sun. I've seen sharp looking signs made of plywood and large peel-off and press-on vinyl letters and numbers. The sign is then sealed with a clear polymer to protect it from the elements. The best heading is "For Sale By Owner," and the words "For Sale" should be big, as should your phone number. You want traffic to be able to read your sign, so put it close to the street in a good vision lane not obstructed by a tree trunk, shrubbery, or parked cars. A white background on the sign with dark letters (red is best) will show up well at dusk or night. Your sign should be well-anchored and standing up straight. Be sure you are not violating any restrictive covenants, zoning codes, or local ordinances with the size or placement of your sign.

Listing Sheets

Real estate agencies put out a listing sheet that describes your home and property and usually has a photo of your home. The listing sheet is primarily distributed in-house to other agents and buyers who are working with the agency. Each brokerage office may have a standard design and format they employ. Some feature just your home on one sheet, front and back. Others feature several homes on one sheet if the homes have something in common, such as price range or neighborhood. If your listing broker uses listing sheets, review them for accuracy and make suggestions about content.

Your Own Fact Sheets

If you are a FISBO, you must develop your own promotional handout, called an information or "fact" sheet. The aim of the fact sheet is to provide prospective buyers with the facts, figures, and features of your home and the neighborhood you live in. It is an indispensable tool for the FISBO, and even sellers who utilize the services of agents that issue listing sheets should consider making up their own fact sheets.

Be creative and customize your fact sheets to emphasize the features you believe your target markets seek most in a home. Before putting together the fact sheet, you should gather all the information you can about your home. The survey will help, and so will utility bills or old floor-plan brochures. Measure your rooms carefully. Check the accuracy of all your facts. Take several photographs of your home from various angles in various conditions from sunny to cloudy. Select the best three or four photos and run them on a photocopier. Then, pick the best one of the photographs, based not only on the picture itself, but also on the quality of the reproduction. When you lay out your copy to design the fact sheet, almost anything goes. I make just a few recommendations. The top one-third of the front page may be the most important section. In this section you should include your photograph, the property address, the neighborhood, and the pertinent numbers (price and the number of bedrooms and bathrooms). After this basic information is given, emphasize anything in any order. Listed below, in no particular order, are some items you may want to include in your promotional fact sheet.

Owner's name and phone number(s)	Basement
Neighborhood or addition	Foundation
Directions to the home	Attic
Map showing the home with directions	Inside storage space
	Closets
Open house schedule	Average monthly and annual utility bills
Price and terms	
Financing and mortgage information	Insulation
Drawing/floor plan of home	Storm doors and windows
Total square feet of living space	Type of heat
Room dimensions and sizes	Type of air conditioning
Size of lot	Capacity and type of water heater
Age of house	Annual assessments
Style type of house (ranch, bungalow, tudor, etc.)	Fireplace
	Electrical wiring
Exterior construction (brick? siding? etc.?)	Fenced yard
	City water
Neighborhood schools	Water softener
Neighborhood shops	Sewer system
Neighborhood churches	Kitchen layout
Public transportation in neighborhood	Brand name and description of major appliances (stove, range, oven, dishwasher, microwave, disposal, refrigerator, freezer, etc.)
Access to highways	
Type and age of roof	
Garage	Eating space in kitchen
Patio or deck	Breakfast nook
Storage or tool shed	Dining Room
Porch	Family room/den
Bathrooms and their fixtures	Additional bedrooms and details
Living room	Personal property that goes with house
Carpets, flooring, drapes	
Master bedroom size and features	

Again, I stress creativity and emphasizing your home's best features. Avoid abbreviations and shorthand. Be honest. You can run off hundreds of copies on a photocopier. The only sellers who should consider having a professionally designed and printed brochure are those sellers who are marketing a very exclusive and high-priced executive home.

Fact sheets are an absolute must for FISBOS. Create your own. For an example of a FISBO fact sheet, see page 78.

Shown by Appointment Only

If you have listed your home with a broker, you should stipulate that the property be shown on a "by appointment only" basis. This helps save you time and worries. "By appointment only" showings are very effective at separating the financially qualified prospects from the day dreamers, lookers, and no-money-down bargain hunters. They also help screen out undesirables who prey upon homesellers physically, or burglarize the house. "By appointment only" showings also do less to disrupt your family's living pattern and habits.

Agents are generally courteous, well-prepared, and cognizant of the seller's concerns. Nonetheless, your agent and all the MLS agents trying to sell your home will miss showing appointments, be very late for showings, fail to show up for showing appointments and never call to cancel and on occasion knock on your door hoping to show a prospect your home immediately. Understand this, and prepare for it! To understand why and how this happens, let's take a glimpse at buyer behavior and the best laid plans of agents and brokers.

Suppose you get a phone call from an MLS agent. "Hello Mrs. Rumley, this is Susan Duncan. I'm a real estate agent with the McDonald Real Estate firm. I have a nice couple that would like to see your home! Is tomorrow around 1 P.M. a good time? Fine, thank you." The agent, Susan Duncan, then proceeds to call three or four other owners to make showing appointments for comparable homes the buyers may also be interested in. Suppose there are five homes on the agent's showing schedule. Are you the first home to be shown, the last one to be shown, or somewhere in between?

Some agents will schedule the visits so that the "best" home (by the agents' prognosis) is the last home on the showing tour. This psychological approach is similar to a chef's—whet their appetites with light courses before serving the main course. Suspense and excitement builds, and the comparables serve as reference points.

Other agents go right for the kill and visit the "best" home first! From a behavioral standpoint, perhaps the buyers have been looking at comparables for days, and don't need any more appetizers or reference points. Still other agents arrange the homes in random order for two reasons: trying to guess which home the buyers will like best is fruitless; and certain owners would/would not allow a showing at a certain time.

No Shows and No Appointments

Suppose agent Susan Duncan thinks your home is the "best," and you are the last stop on the buyer's magical mystery tour. What might happen when the buyers see the first four homes? Anything can happen! The buyers may spend only five minutes looking at one home, but one hour or more looking at another. This may cause them to be very late for your 1 P.M. appointment. The buyers may like one of the previous homes so much that they decide to make an offer. They will not be visiting your home, they are "no-shows." Perhaps the agent will call you around 1 P.M. to cancel, perhaps not. The agent may be involved in negotiations or paperwork, or maybe you just are forgotten in the excitement and activity.

Agents may also surprise you, and without making an appointment ring your doorbell. "Hello Mrs. Fixico, I'm Elizabeth Ahow with Jefferson City Home Finders. I have two buyers in my car. We have just finished looking at a home two blocks over, and noticed your home while heading back to the highway. We've been parked out front for five minutes, looking at your house in the MLS book. The buyers love the outside of your home, and would like to see the inside. May we come in?" Is Mrs. Fixico surprised? Darn right she is! The twins, Alicia and Kametra, just threw their food all over the kitchen floor, and little Howie has dirty pants. Darby the dog is growling through the front screen door, and the soup is boiling over. What should she do?

Surprised sellers should try very hard to accommodate the unexpected prospects, but *only* if they are with agents. Agents are well aware of the hassle caused by a surprise visit. A good agent would not disturb you unless the buyers were financially qualified and really hot to see your home *immediately*. Mrs. Fixico could tell agent Elizabeth to give her five minutes. In five minutes the kids and mom can go to the backyard, and Darby the dog can be tied to the back corner fence. If the weather is bad, a phone call and visit to a sympathetic neighbor is plan number two. Plan three is the basement or a big family room. (*Never* crowd the kitchen!) A good agent can kill five minutes in a variety of ways: activities such as a slow drive around the immediate neighborhood, a return to the car to review the buyer's objections to the homes previously visited, or a tour of the exterior. All will buy some time for the seller to tidy things up a bit.

The Brochure Box

Some brokers and FISBOs use a "sales box" or "brochure box" as a promotional tool. The mailbox-like container is placed as close to the street as possible to attract drive-bys and walkers. The box is filled with your fact sheets or listing sheets or sales brochures. Both sides of the box should say "Free Info" or "Free—Take One!" If you cannot find a sales box in your area, make one. All you need is a five-foot-long, 2″ x 4″ piece of lumber, an inexpensive aluminum or metal mailbox, and a few screws to mount the box to the post. Most boxes are red, so you may want to invest 99¢ in a can of spray paint for use on the wooden stake and box. If being the same as most sellers goes against your grain, try a bright neon color, such as orange, that

BEVERLY/MORGAN PARK CONDO

Beautiful, modern 2-bedroom, 3-story condominium in historic
Beverly Hills/Morgan Park area of Chicago

--1½ blocks from Rock Island train; 36 minutes to Loop

--Townhome layout (see reverse) includes 3 stories, 2 large
  bedrooms, large family room, all with central air conditioning.
  Hardwood floors upstairs, carpeted living room w/ hardwood floors
  underneath; ceiling fans in kitchen and upstairs; all window
  treatments and miniblinds; storms and screens; programmable
  thermostat.

--Gas budget: $47 per month; Electric budget: $50 per month.

--Large condo association (48 units

--Assessments cover water and garbage fees (garbage pickup twice
  weekly), snow removal, all lawn care and landscaping, repairs
  to common areas, all exterior maintenance.

--Newly paved parking lot (1990) and new bright lights in lot (1990),
  new cedar fences throughout complex (house backyard has fences on
  three sides), new roof (1985), newly painted exterior (1989).

  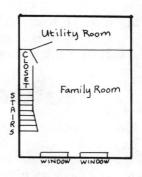

First Floor	Second Floor	Lower Level
Living room: 14' x 16'	Master Bedroom: 14' x 14'	Family room: 14' x 20'
Kitchen: 16½' x 8½'	Guest Bedroom: 11' x 15'	Utility room: 18' x 17
Bath: ½ bath	Bath: Full	Closet under stairs
Closets: Linen/Pantry	Closets: Large closet in	
Front hall	each bedroom	
	Hall linen closet	

Schools:
    St. Cajetan Grammar School and Church
    Clissold Public Grammar School
    Marist High School
    Mother McAuley High School
    Morgan Park Public High School

Library:
    Walker Brank Library

Grocery Stores:
    Fairplay
    Countyfair
    Dominicks
    Jewel

Post Offices
    111th Street station
    Mount Greenwood station

Churches:
    St. Cajetan Catholic Church
    Morgan Park Baptist Church
    Church of the Mediator (Episcopal)
    Morgan Park Presbyterian Church

        ASSUMABLE 8.5% MORTGAGE; CALL OWNER FOR DETAILS!

will show up well at night. Some sellers stake the box at car door-level height, so motorists can grab one and go. Check your ordinances and covenants for any local prohibitions.

Networking for Buyers

The most powerful network of buyers and sellers is the Multiple Listing Service (MLS) that is controlled mainly by the local member brokers of the National Association of Realtors. How powerful is it? Eight in ten homes sold in America are offered through an MLS system! Eight in ten—that's 80%! How does this powerful network function? MLS is essentially an information service that publishes photos and descriptions of all the homes that are currently offered for sale by MLS subscribers or members. (MLS also keeps data on properties that have sold or have been listed but did not sell.) To be a member, you must pay an annual fee and meet any membership requirements set by the local MLS system. In the overwhelming majority of states, you must be a realtor to join the MLS system.

MLS information is usually published weekly in booklet form for use by subscribers/members. Subscribers may also access the data via computer terminals that are located in member brokerage offices. This service is very useful for rapid sorting through thousands of homes to find all the homes currently for sale (via members) within a one-square-mile area that have X bedrooms, Y baths, and certain features the user specifies. This service is the data source for the Comparative Market Analysis (CMA) discussed in Chapter 7.

Participating MLS members share information about their listings and invite other members to bring buyers for the listings in return for a co-brokered or shared commission. By listing with a broker who participates in the MLS system, your home is exposed to virtually all of the brokers and agents in your town or neighborhood area. Via the MLS system, you theoretically have almost every agent in town trying to sell your home. Those agents work with many, many buyers, one of whom may be very interested in your home.

WORD-OF-MOUTH NETWORKS

How many people do you and your family talk to or see in a given week? That's a tough question—you probably have to stop and think a minute. The neighbors . . . our relatives . . . people at work . . . the school crossing guard . . . teachers and coaches . . . fellow church goers . . . club members . . . supermarket clerks . . . beauty shop operators and patrons . . . schoolmates of kids . . . the mail carrier . . . the pharmacist . . . doctors, lawyers, CPAs . . . pizza delivery people. . . . Whew! That's a lot of people, and we've probably missed a few.

How many of these people have you or will you tell about your home for sale? Probably just a handful. Why? Because you are a bit self-conscious and think that you'd be boring people or imposing upon them. That assumption could be dead wrong. For all you know, a lady just told the hairdresser yesterday that they were tired of renting and wanted to buy in the neighborhood. For all you know, the guy down the block has a brother who is looking for a home close by. For all you know, a friend of your teenagers knows a cousin who is getting married soon and wants to buy in the area.

REAL ESTATE! A NATURAL TOPIC

It does not surprise me that most adults are interested in real estate. Consider these signs: does a For Sale sign across the street get your attention? Sure it does, because your life is going to change. Your neighbors had children that played with yours. Will the new family? What if some jerks move in?! People who don't keep up their property values.

Because two of three households own their home, and because the home is most people's largest single investment, people are always curious about selling prices and market values. Watch those real estate magazines disappear from the racks by the supermarket doors every week!

Have you ever walked by a house and wondered—"Gee, what does the inside look like?!" Have you thumbed through magazines (and looked at other people's houses) to get some decorating ideas?

Still not convinced? Try this out at your next bridge club game or bowling night: "You know what I heard from some real estate agent the other day? She said that prices in this area have cooled off. I'm no expert, but I found that hard to believe. What do you guys/gals think?" A typical response may be "That sounds like a bunch of bull to me, Bob. My neighbor sold last month and made a bundle. His home appreciated 25% in two years." Or you may hear "that sounds true to me, Mary. My sister and her husband had a terrible time finding a buyer, and had to take a loss on their place." Believe me, when you mention local real estate trends, people tune in fast! Why not tune them in to your real estate, and let them broadcast the message for you? Tell everyone about your house for sale, and give them a fact sheet. Neighbors are treated in a special way, and the section dealing with the open house explains how to build a neighbor referral network.

OPPORTUNITIES FOR FREE ADVERTISING

There are many businesses and community organizations that have bulletin boards that are available for public use. Supermarkets are prime examples of such opportunities. Parks, libraries, small retail and service businesses, barber and beauty shops, and schools may have bulletin boards for public use. You may put up your fact sheet, or you may be limited to using only an index card supplied by the owner of the premises. Stuff you put on bulletin boards has a way of disappearing or getting covered up by other notices. You must check every 10 to 14 days to be sure your ad is still surviving and in good shape. It is a good idea to keep a list of all the locations where you have put up your material. Hit all the free spots you can, and shoot for coverage within a reasonable radius from your home's location.

You should also check for local newsletters that run free ads. Company newsletters, bulletins of information at houses of worship, community service publications, and school information handouts are fertile sources to investigate. Large employers (a college, a military base, a large corporation) usually have personnel officers that work with new employees to find housing. Call them, stop by, and leave them with a supply of your fact sheets.

Feedback

A marketing plan must be monitored so that you can assess how well its various components contribute toward the achievement of your objective. Feedback helps you adjust your selling program if and when it becomes necessary to do so. Seeking feedback from others is a continuous process, and emphasis should be placed upon reaction to advertisements, showings, and buyer objections.

How do you know which ads and which advertising media are the most useful? Your agent will keep records of where each caller or looker learned about your house for sale. Agents on "floor duty" at the broker's office maintain a log that documents this information so that advertising dollars can be allocated to the most efficient and effective media. If you are a FISBO, you need to find out how and where people are learning about your home. Did they see an ad? Which one and where was it? Did they see your fact sheet? Did your word-of-mouth network help out? Ask your telephone callers and open house visitors for this information.

Showings provide a great opportunity to assess buyer reaction. Agent preview caravan tours often feature a contest for the agents to guess the selling price and also give the listing agent a chance to seek recommendations from her/his fellow professionals. Agents can solicit reactions from buyers and can also check with multilist agents who show their buyers your home. These other agents leave their cards so that your agent or you can call later to get the buyer's reaction to your home.

Agents can also alert you to buyer objections (The price is $4,000 too high; the condition of the exterior is poor; etc.). If you are a FISBO seller, it is tougher to get this type of information because you are not as likely to receive truthful feedback and it is harder for you, as opposed to an intermediary or third party, to follow up with buyers.

More marketing information regarding telephone calls, additional sales tools, and showing the home is provided in later chapters that are aimed primarily at FISBO sellers.

9
It's Almost Showtime!

Once the "For Sale" sign goes up, you must be ready for visitors, expected or otherwise. You may be asked to show the home with only five minutes of notice. In the earlier Chapter 3, you learned how to spruce up your home for sale. Now, we talk about fine-tuning your home to make it appeal to the buyer's needs and senses.

You better face it—your normal lifestyle is going to be disrupted! You will probably keep your house cleaner than you ever have; you will drive your family nuts following them around with sponges and brooms; your spouse may grumble about turning off the TV set right in the middle of a titillating scene of a soap opera, or during a two-minute drive in the big football game; your children will think you've hit new lows on the mean, bossy, and crabby scale; your neighbors and relatives may grow weary of your unexpected visits; and even your pets may snub you.

Keeping Your House Ready to Show

You must accept one of real estate's rules: houses in good condition show better and sell faster. By now, you have your house in good condition, so it really becomes a matter of *keeping* the house clean, presentable, and attractive. Outside your home, a regular schedule of chores will help insure that your lawn and shrubbery are trimmed and maintained, the rubbish is disposed of properly, and the front steps and porch are swept clean and free of debris. Inside the home, pay particular attention to the tidiness of your kitchen, your bathrooms, and your bedrooms. In the kitchen, keep your sink clean and do not leave dirty dishes there or on the counter tops. Keep the counter tops clean and free of clutter. Your oven and range/stove should be spotless. (If your oven is a built-in unit, any serious prospect will open it up!) Wipe those smudges off the refrigerator and the windows, and look for grease stains around the stove/range. Bathrooms should also be spotless. Put out those new towels, eliminate any odors, and put the toilet seat down. In the bedrooms, be sure the closets are spacious and well organized. Eliminate unneeded clothes, toys, shoes, etc. and store them elsewhere. Pick up clothes, toys, and other items. Make all beds, and put your best bedspread on.

Prelude to Showtime

Before any prospective buyers arrive to your open house or for their scheduled appointment, go through your entire house and turn on every light (even in the daytime!). If the areas are too dim, put in brighter bulbs, or use a table lamp. Make your home as bright as possible. Pull back your drapes, open all the window shades and let as much natural light inside as you can. If one of your windows has a bad view, you may decide to keep the drapes or blinds closed. Your windows should all be clean, and free of paw prints and smudges. You should observe a regular inspection and cleaning schedule. You are probably wondering why light is so important. That's a good question, and here are a few good answers.

1. A bright, well-lit house appears larger, and space is one of the major attributes buyers seek.

2. Psychologically, light creates an impression of warmth and cheer.

3. Worn carpets and old furniture appear brighter and more attractive in the right lighting.

4. Your prospects will not know where all the light switches and fixtures are, so make it easy for them—turn them all on. You also make it safer for them to navigate the basement and attic stairs.

If you are showing your home after dusk, do not forget to turn on all your outside lighting. Put a really bright bulb in the front porch light, as well as the back. Don't forget to check the lighting in the garage and the yard.

It can be argued that buyers make a decision for emotional reasons, and then they try to justify a decision that they have already reached based upon factual information. To some readers, that process sounds a little bit like falling in love with a person, or buying a car. Can one really "fall in love" with a house? Yes, and words of buyers confirm it. How often have you heard a buyer say "As soon as we walked in, we knew right away this was the house for us," or "We saw dozens of great homes, but we really loved the one on Winston Street."? Buyer behavior can vary, and the emphasis upon emotional versus rational factors may differ from one buyer to another. Nonetheless, your home should appeal to the senses as well as the mind. The sense of sight dominates in the house-hunting process, and that is why we have emphasized reducing clutter and creating the impression of spaciousness. Do you realize that humans can also clutter up a house? An agent, two buyers, a homeowner and her two children having lunch in the kitchen can "crowd" a kitchen and detract from the feeling of spaciousness the seller hopes to create. Homeowners, as well as their children, relatives, and pets can be distractions to potential buyers and can cause the buyer's mind to wander from the central issue, "Can I picture myself living here in this house?" A buyer wants to mentally try the home on for size and test-drive it. A serious prospect wonders if "our furniture will look good in the living room . . . is our bedroom suite too large for the master bedroom . . . and will all the relatives fit in the living room at our Christmas party?" Buyers have a hard time imagining your home as theirs when you and your family are present. For these reasons, you should leave your home when a broker or agent is showing it. Take the kids with you. If you are a FISBO, try to send the kids to a neighbor's or a relative's house. If that is impossible, put them in the yard or basement.

What to Do about Pets

Pets can create problems when your home is being shown. Some buyers will not walk around in a yard if your dog is out there. Dogs can get all worked up just watching your buyers get out of their car. I had two good-sized dogs named Colorado and Bosco that barked wildly when anyone merely walked on the sidewalk in front of my property. Anyone walking up the front steps sent the dogs into really high gear! To most dogs, a stranger on your turf is a deadly emergency.

What can you do about your dog? The best approach is to get the dog off the premises. Have the kids take him for a walk to the park or to a neighbor's house. The next best approach is to securely tie the dog to the fence or a stake in the farthest corner of your backyard. You can also rig a small dog pen in the farthest corner of your lot with a small section of wire fencing and a few stakes. Some homeowners use travel boxes or doggie crates to lock up their pet, and put the box in the basement or yard or garage. Some owners lock the dog in the garage. No matter where you lock up a dog on your premises, his barking may be a distraction.

Cats are not as troublesome, especially if your cat is allowed outdoors. House cats who live indoors can be a problem if the buyers have small children who grab at the cat or surprise the cat while he is napping. A house cat should be put in a travel box for safety reasons. If you don't have a travel box, put the cat in the basement or garage with the doors closed. You should also leave a note on the doors to let the agents know that the cat should not be allowed to sneak out.

Pets can be offensive to the buyer's sense of smell. A cat's litter box can cut through blocked sinuses faster than ammonia! Hamster cages and bird cages can smell bad, too. Pets can get loose, so make sure those cages are closed and locked securely. If your home is listed on an MLS system, you should note what kind of pet you have, and where the pet is when you are not home. Remember, many people do not like pets, period. Some are allergic to pets. Some are afraid of pets, even your miniature poodle. You don't want to lose a potential sale, so avoid the problems pets cause.

The Art of Noise

Noise can be distracting and divert a prospect's attention from your home's features. We have already talked about children and pets. Have you considered other sources of noise in your home? Appliances such as washers, dryers, and dishwashers should be turned off or not used during a showing. Never have a television set on during a buyer's visit. You may wish to turn on your radio or stereo. The *only* type of music to play is the "elevator music" played on your local easy-listening channel. Those are the channels that have groups like "1,001 Violins" playing a Roy Orbison tune. Classical music is good background music if you don't have a soft music station. Music helps create a pleasant mood, and also masks some outside street noises. Street noise can be a special problem if your home is located near a busy street, a highway, train tracks, a factory, an airport, or a school yard. If you have this problem, you should try to schedule your showings during the time periods when the noise is at a lower level.

Olfactory Signals

Smell is a sense that sells many products from perfume to foods to automobiles. The sense of smell can influence a homebuyer's decision. The smell of cigar or cigarette smoke can make a buyer think they stepped into a tavern. Owners need to air out the home, or freshen the air with a neutral spray.

Some real estate pros recommend an old technique: let the buyers smell warmth, love, and "home." Baking a cake, a pie, some bread, muffins, or cookies can subtly say "welcome home" to a buyer. Fresh coffee delights others, as does a slow, simmering stew or post roast. Some agents will recommend boiling a small pot of water laced with vanilla or a spice.

Special Effects

A crackling fire can appeal to the buyer's sense of sight, sound, and smell. You can buy products and additives to make your flame various colors and hues or to add more snap, crackle, and pop to the fire. Another effective visual ploy is to set your dining room table in a beautiful and lavish manner.

Use your best tablecloth, china, glassware, and settings. Some fresh flowers are a nice touch. You are selling emotions and benefits, and the buyer needs to vividly see what possibilities your home offers for entertaining others. Remember, the home is your castle—no matter how humble it may be. Not every home is a candidate for one of those "opulent lifestyles" television programs, but almost every homeowner wants to experience a bit of those emotions and pride of ownership. Dress up your home to interact with their dreams and imaginations. An imaginative seller can stage a scene or mental image.

One builder told me that he uses standard props in his hot tub area of the home. Wine glasses, wine bottles, and fruit juices are arranged on a tray on the deck. Health, fashion, and sports magazines are arrayed nearby. Towels and a swimsuit for him, and one for her, rest on nearby hooks. A cordless phone and television are close by. Sometimes the builder experiments a bit, and adds an exercise bicycle to the scene. What kind of images does this builder's scene connote in your mind? Did your mind interact with his inanimate objects? Did you picture yourself in that scene? If so, the builder showed that room well.

Valuables: Out of Sight— Out of Mind

Before you allow strangers to visit your home, you should pack away in a safe place all your valuables. You may rent storage space or a safe deposit box. Objets d'art, jewelry, guns, collectibles and even doorknobs are temptations to those with larceny in their hearts. Even toddlers, with no malice aforethought, can knock over that vase that grandmother gave you years ago. If it has value to you, store it or hide it. A For Sale sign sends a message to burglars. It says "C'mon in! Browse around and see if we have something you like. While you are here, check out our floor plan and look for any security devices and ease of entry."

Keep Your Home Ready to Show

Keeping your home clean and in tip-top shape between showings is a constant struggle. Scheduled appointments make the task somewhat easier, but you must remember that unscheduled appointments are possible. Remember, too, that if your home has a keybox, that buyers and agents are apt to visit anytime. Keep that in mind every morning before you rush off to work with the bathroom and kitchen a mess, and your bed isn't made and clothes are thrown all over the place, and who knows what kind of a mess your children have left!

To win the war against dirt and disorder you need the cooperation of all household members, and you also need a regularly scheduled cleanup routine. Children and teenagers should be made aware of the importance of keeping the house clean. Don't just tell them to do this or don't do that, explain to them *why* it is important. Children who are old enough should be told about concepts such as buyer behavior, creating spaciousness, and selling benefits and attributes. If their mental faculties can handle it, tell them about it. Involve them in an important family undertaking.

Once a week you should have an all-out, hard core cleaning session of the entire house. Set aside a few hours to do this, and divide up the chores. It may be best to schedule the "Big Cleanup" on Thursday or Friday, since weekends tend to be the days of heaviest buyer traffic through most homes. Between your weekly big cleanups, you can institute some special rules to reduce your headaches. Some sellers employ rules such as: do not use the dining room—stay out of there; use only bathroom number one; don't play near the new grass or sod in the yard; $2.00 will be deducted from your allowance if your room is messy; etc., etc. You may decide to make everyone use the back entrance only to reduce the dirt and smudges on the front door and entrance hall. Throw rugs may be helpful in high traffic areas, especially in the kitchen. The ever popular battlecries of moms may ring out more often: "Wipe your feet" and "Take your shoes off before you come in here."

Establish daily habits for everyone. Before going to bed, is the family room picked up? Is everyone's bedroom orderly? In the morning, encourage all family members to be responsible for the neatness of their rooms and articles of clothing. Put special emphasis on the kitchen and bathroom clean-ups.

When you have a scheduled showing appointment for a certain day, you can take your preparations a step further and pay special attention to details. The "It's almost showtime" checklist that follows should be used as a helpful reminder of the ideas we have discussed.

"It's Almost Showtime" Checklist

- Kitchen sink clean and empty
- Kitchen table and counter tops clear and clean
- Kitchen floor clean
- Bathroom fixtures scrubbed
- Bathroom odors eliminated
- Bathroom guest towels out
- Bedroom floors clear of toys, clothes, shoes
- Bedspreads on
- Floors clean, carpet vacuumed throughout house
- Garbage taken out
- Garage doors shut
- Yard picked up, trash removed
- Curtains, drapes pulled open (daylight hours)
- Window shades up (daylight hours)
- All lights turned on
- All light bulbs working
- Noise reduced (TV, washer, dryer, dishwasher)
- Soft, easy-listening music on
- Special effects staged (fireplace, table set, kitchen smells)
- Pets in proper place
- Children out of home

Let Your Agent Do the Showing

If you have hired an agent to sell your home, let her or him make all the appointments with the prospects. You should also let the agent do all the showing, preferably with you out of the house. You may think this is a little odd. After all, you know your home and its features better than anybody, including the agent. That is true! But what really counts is do you know the wants and needs of these particular buyers? No! (But your agent does.) Your agent knows the buyers want a hardwood kitchen floor. (Underneath that old linoleum, your house has hardwood floors that you hate. You would have offered the buyer a $700 discount for new tile!)

Agents are adept at handling serious buyer objections in a non-defensive manner, and know when to listen and when to speak. Agents are schooled to recognize body language and non-verbal cues. Agents know the buyer's thoughts on the comparable homes for sale that they have already visited. Agents get a more direct reaction to your home because they are third parties.

If circumstances force you to be at home when an agent and buyer tour your home, you should do two things: shut up and get out of the way. Be polite when introduced, then immediately excuse yourself and take any children with you to the biggest area of your home. The backyard or basement is your best bet, followed by the family room or living room. Stay out of smaller areas, because too many bodies creates a cramped feeling and make the room seem small, not spacious. Do not congregate in the kitchen or master bedroom. Do not speak, unless the agent invites you to converse with the buyers.

FISBO Sellers

Chapter 18 is titled "A GUIDE TO FISBO SHOWINGS." For-Sale-By-Owner (FISBO) sellers will find chapter 18 to be most helpful.

10
Negotiating Price

When was the last time you negotiated the price for an item you wanted? Maybe it was at a garage sale or a flea market. In reality, virtually all of your purchases in the past year have been of items that had fixed, set, predetermined prices. (Think of your purchases at the grocery store, the shopping mall, etc.) There are two major items that buyers and sellers are accustomed to haggling over the price of: automobiles and houses.

You must remember that important point: people expect to bargain, bicker, and negotiate over the sale of a house! People expect to give up a little, and to get a little. Since most Americans do not have many opportunities to practice and refine their negotiating skills, they feel uncomfortable and ill-prepared to negotiate price. Negotiating can be an emotional endeavor charged with tension and stress. This tension is the natural result of trying to forge an agreement between parties with different objectives. The seller wants to sell his home for as much money as he can possibly get; the buyer wants to pay as little as possible. Add to that the fact that for most buyers and sellers this will be far and away the biggest and most complicated financial transaction of their life. To further get things boiling, realize that the hopes and dreams of both parties are tied to a home. Lifestyle and security stir powerful emotions.

Because of these high emotional and financial stakes, many sellers seek help from professionals who are experienced negotiators. Agents, brokers, and attorneys often handle most of the negotiations for buyers and sellers, but they get their direction and authority from the party that they represent. They can buffer you from face-to-face negotiation and confrontation, they can follow up on details, but they generally do not make big decisions for you.

How Strong Is Your Position?

Nothing is constant in the world of real estate, and this makes each transaction unique. What worked for Uncle Larry when he sold his executive home in the Wewers Hills subdivision last spring will not necessarily work for you. The big variables in determining the relative "strength" of each party's negotiating position are these:

1. **Local Market Conditions**
   Is it a buyers' market where the number of homes for sale (supply) exceeds the number of buyers (demand)? Or is it a seller's market

where demand for homes exceeds supply? Or is the market in equilibrium, with demand and supply roughly equivalent?

2. **Financial Conditions**
   Are home loans affordable and plentiful, or is mortgage money tight? Are interest rates at moderate levels so that buyers can qualify for and afford the monthly payments to buy your home? Do sellers have to help buyers with the financing?

3. **The Buyer's Motives**
   How badly does the buyer went your home? Is he pressed for time to vacate his current residence?

4. **The Seller's Motives**
   How badly do you need to sell? Are you pressed for time? Are you closing on another home you bought? Have you been transferred? Do you need all cash at closing?

There are other variables and factors unique to each individual transaction and the parties. The weight that each party assigns to different variables is something to determine through good communication. Questions such as "What is most important to you?" or "What would make this a perfect deal for you?" help smoke out priorities.

Because each transaction is unique, intuitive judgments must be made. Successful negotiators offer some general tips that you may find helpful.

1. Let buyers know you understand the game. Unless your price is firm, always use the phrase "asking price" on your fact sheets and in your telephone and personal conversations to tell prospects "we are serious about selling, and we invite all serious offers."

2. Always keep communication channels open. Never shut the door on talk forever. Always respond, and use counteroffers when necessary. Asking for a day to "consider things" or to "sleep on it" or "discuss matters with my lawyer" will buy you time.

3. Do not negotiate on the phone. Real estate transactions are complicated, and writing is required to make a sales contract binding.

4. Avoid face-to-face negotiations if you have hired a pro. Let your hired gunslingers utilize their talents. The only time you should enter the scene is with their advice. (Usually when an impasse cannot be resolved, and the deal will fall apart.) If you are a FISBO, decide what role, if any, your attorney will play in negotiations.

Getting That First Offer

Your heart will pound a little faster when you receive your first written offer. Let me prepare you for the big event by asking you a very important question: How many sellers actually sell at their asking price? What is your guess? Nationwide, it is estimated that less than 5% of sellers get their asking price. And some of those 5% have to help the buyer with financing. Right now, in your town and in your price range, what percent of sellers get full asking price? (If you have a great agent or appraiser, you already know that answer.) It is a general rule in real estate sales that the first offer should be taken very seriously, and is often the best offer! You are probably wondering what the rationale is behind that general rule. The first offers you receive tend to be made by very serious, qualified and motivated buyers who have been in the market for awhile. They study the market and even patrol the neighborhood they want to buy in, and watch it like a hawk for new listings. If they work with brokers, they hound them to stay up on new MLS listings. These students of the market have shopped comparables, and have a good feel for property values.

With that background information in mind, what do you do? If comparable home sales in the past year show that it is customary in your area that homes sell at 95% of their listing price, and the first offer you receive is 95% or more of your listing price, it sounds like a darn good offer to me. If the first offer is 90% to 94% of your listing price, you should probably consider making a counteroffer. At this point, you should be confident that you have priced your home right, because you used an appraiser or agent or had relevant current data from other sources.

If the Buyers Do the Limbo

Suppose that the buyer makes you a written offer that seems ridiculously low to you. How do you respond? Try to remain cordial if the buyer is present, and tell him you will consider it later that evening with your spouse and agent or attorney. Later, you can vent your anger and use some colorful expletives to describe the offer and its maker. Realize that low offers are part of the game. They may be made by professional bargain hunters who hope you're foolish enough or desperate enough to sell at 80% of listing price. Or this offer may be from a tentative buyer who had to work up the courage to sign a complicated, written offer; or this low offer may be just a feeler by someone who wants to play the negotiation game with you. It has been said that "a low offer is better than no offer," because it is at least a starting point.

What do you do about low offers? You try to flush out the bargain hunters from the motivated buyers. If you have an agent, it's time to learn a little about how agents present offers to sellers. Listing agents will present offers made through them or the MLS system in person to you. If the offer is made through another agency, the co-brokering agent may also come along to make the presentation. When your agent calls you to set up a presentation, you naturally will ask "What's the price they are offering?" Agents usually sidestep the question and mumble something about considering all the terms and conditions in person, or they are *required* to submit all offers in person. In her presentation, your agent will go over the details and conditions, and summarize the pros and cons from your perspective. The agent may also show you what you would net at closing if you accepted this offer, utilizing a form titled something like "'Estimate Of Seller's Proceeds."

Involve the Agents

You should be able to learn something about the buyer and his, her, or their financial status and motivation to buy. The agent or co-op agent should know if the buyers are serious or not, and if they are trying to sell their own home or not, and if they are facing a time limit to buy. If the agent working with the buyer is reticent about disclosing the buyer's status, you or your agent or lawyer should remind the buyer's agent that they are legally a sub-agent of the seller's agent, and they work for you. You pay their co-brokered commission and they owe you the fiduciary duty of disclosing all material information. All listing agents and sub-agents also owe a duty of loyalty to you, and must act in your best interest. That means that an agent cannot say "it's listed at $90,000, but the seller said he'll take $86,000" to another agent or a buyer, unless you have instructed your agent to do so. Nonetheless, agents do not always observe this fiduciary duty. For that reason, many real estate advisors warn against disclosing what your bottom taking price is to your own agent.

FISBO Price Negotiations

If you are a FISBO selling on your own, you probably will have to negotiate price on your own. You may find some real estate attorneys who will assist you, while others do not advise on price, but on the terms and conditions. When negotiating on your own, avoid becoming argumentative and too emotional. You must find out something about the buyer's motivation and financial status. After all, if you accept his offer, your home could be off the market for weeks while he tries (unsuccessfully, perhaps) to get financing. You can ask a buyer to provide a credit report and a personal net worth financial statement. You can negotiate price, and your attorney will take care of the other conditions in the sales contract. Your attorney should give you a form (binder or earnest-money deposit or good-faith deposit) that varies with locale.

A FISBO seller who is negotiating price on his own can argue his position strongly if he has an appraisal that documents value. (Seller's agents will show the buyer information about comparables sold and comparables in current listings.) A FISBO seller also can use the saved commission argument: "look Mr. & Mrs. Buyer, we can both save some money because no agents are involved and we save a 6 or 7% commission." The buyer will say great—knock 7% off your price. The FISBOs should reply, "We can't give you the whole 7%. We've already spent about half that on advertising an legal fees, not to mention the time we've spent showing the home. If we wanted to give away the whole 7% commission, we could have hired an agent and saved my time showing and money on lawyers and advertisements. If we don't get greedy Mr. & Mrs. Buyer, we can split the 7% and all come out winners." The buyers may wonder if you just marked up your asking price 7%. Your appraisal will document that your price is right.

Counteroffers May Help

Some buyers don't like to make more than one or two offers, and will not get involved in a time consuming series of counteroffers with you. Experienced real estate pros claim that most buyers will not make more than three offers. If you have hit an impasse on price, perhaps you can throw a few non-price sweeteners into the deal to make it go. You could give the buyers some personal property such as appliances, or you might move the closing date to help them save more cash, or you may carry a small note for the disputed price differential. You may have to give a little to get a little. In certain instances, participating brokers may reduce their commission to make up the amount in dispute. (Don't be afraid to ask! Your agent will have to confer with his or her broker.) In a buyer's market or a depressed market, you may have to assist the buyer with financing or try some creative financing techniques. If you help with financing, you should negotiate for your full asking price as compensation for your risk. We'll talk about owner financing in great detail in Chapter 12 and about negotiating the non-price items next.

11
Negotiating Non-Price Matters: A Layman's Guide to Written Offers and Real Estate Contracts

After the parties have negotiated and agreed upon a price and perhaps a few other basic points, such as what type of financing the buyer will seek and when closing/settlement shall be, the parties must memorialize their mutual assent. Contracts for the sale of real property must be in writing to be enforceable. All states have this law to prevent fraud. Oral contracts are not enforceable for the sale of a home.

How do the buyer and seller get their hands on a written contract? Customs vary in the different states. In many states a "Binder" is used. A binder may also be called a "memorandum of sale" or an "offer to buy" form in some areas. The binder will state the basic terms of the sale (such as price, financing, and earnest money deposit) and also says that the parties agree to seek approval and legal help from their attorneys to draw up the final formal documents. Your lawyer or broker can provide you with a binder form. Lenders and stationery stores may also have them. The purpose of these short form contracts is to bind or hold the parties to their agreement until the attorneys take over.

In many other states, it is customary for buyers and sellers to sign a detailed contract right from the beginning of their meeting of the minds. This contract may be called a "real estate contract," "contract of sale," "contract for the sale of real estate," or other similar phrases. These contract forms have evolved through custom and usage, and may be referred to as a standard form contract. The drafters may be the state or local bar association, a group of real estate brokers, a title company, local lending institutions, or even a stationery/office supply store. In most areas it is the seller's responsibility to have the contract prepared, usually by the seller's attorney or agent. Realize that these standard forms may have been drafted to favor one party over the other. It is up to each party to fend for himself, and you are free to negotiate anything and everything in these preprinted standard contracts. The word "standard" connotes some feeling of legal origin, but in fact the legislative branch of your state government did not pass a law making it mandatory to use a specific form. Once again, you must understand that it is up to you to protect your own interests. You can modify a so-called standard form, add additional clauses, delete anything, and generally make any change the parties all agree to. You do not even have to use standard forms, although it is generally advantageous to do so because of the economy of scale cost benefits (you do not have to draft a contract from scratch), and the local lenders, brokers, attorneys, title insurance companies, and others in real estate are familiar with these forms.

Unless you are an expert in real estate practices, customs, and law, you are foolish if you do not have an experienced professional represent you. In almost all cases, get yourself a good real estate lawyer.

Earnest-Money Deposits

An earnest money deposit is a sum of money that the buyer deposits with a third party to hold for later application to the purchase price or for later return to the buyer if the deal fails through no fault of the buyer. The purpose of an earnest money deposit is for the buyer to show the seller that the buyer is serious, and if the buyer frivolously decides to withdraw from the contract, the seller will have access to some funds to compensate for legal damages due to having his home off the market.

Again local customs vary, and in some areas 6%–10% of the purchase price is customary, although not required. There are circumstances when little or no earnest money may be appropriate. Perhaps the buyer has all his equity tied up in a home that has not sold or closed/settled yet. Brokers like big earnest-money deposits, and they like to be the party holding the deposit in trust. Why? Because if the buyer backs out of the deal wrongfully, the broker is still entitled to his or her commission for producing a ready, willing and able buyer—whether your home actually sells or not. If the broker is holding 6 or 7% in trust, the broker is in good shape. I believe it is best to let your attorney hold the funds in trust. Escrow agents, closing agents, and title companies that offer settlement services are also fiduciaries that sometimes hold the earnest-money deposit.

Contracts for the Sale of Real Estate

As mentioned earlier, there are many different forms in use. However, these standard forms all have the same basic elements, plus or minus a few frills. Here is a survey of what you can expect these forms to contain:

1. SALE AND IDENTIFICATION INFORMATION
   This is usually the first thing contracts cover. The buyers and sellers are named, and their intention to transfer real property is stated.

2. LAND AND ALL PROPERTY BEING SOLD
   The land is named by its legal description. The house and other structures (garage, tool shed, etc.) are referred to as "all improvements" on the land. The personal property involved in the sale is specifically defined (Example: refrigerator, washer and dryer). Certain property may be specifically excluded from the sale, such as a crystal chandelier that Grandma gave the sellers for their wedding.

3. TYPE OF DEED
   There are five common types of deeds and numerous special-purpose deeds. These five types are: 1) the general warranty deed; 2) the special warranty deed; 3) the bargain and sale deed; 4) the deed of trust; and 5) the quitclaim deed. While each one affords the buyer different guarantees or warranties, they may be used in conjunction with title insurance. Customs vary, and this is work for your attorney.

4. PURCHASE PRICE
   The total purchase price is stated. The earnest deposit is stated and noted to be partial payment, with the remainder to be paid upon delivery of deed at a closing, unless otherwise provided.

5. FINANCING CONDITIONS
   States which type of financing buyer wants to use. If a loan is needed, the type is specified and so is the interest rate, loan length, loan fees, points, etc. Should the buyer fail to be granted a loan of the exact type specified, the contract is null and void. The buyer is given a certain amount of time to get the loan approved, usually three to six weeks in most areas. Also spelled out is which party is responsible for which escrows and closing costs.

6. TITLE
   In some states, after loan approval, seller has a certain number of days to furnish the buyer with a certified abstract of title and a current UCC search certificate. The buyer has a certain time to examine the title and state any objections. A certain time is allowed to clear any objections to title.
   Another period of time is allowed to clear any objections to title. In other states, title insurance companies will search title records and issue title insurance to the lender (and sometimes buyer) if no liens or encumbrances present problems.

Negotiating Non-Price Matters   **97**

7. TAXES

This provision generally calls for seller to pay all special assessments, and the current ad valorem taxes are prorated between the buyer and seller.

8. LIENS ON THE PROPERTY

Seller must pay in full any existing liens on the property before closing. (Example: labor or material liens.)

9. TERMITE CLAUSE

Either party may pay for the termite inspection. There are two basic types of certificates that termite companies give: a) states that property is free of visible termite infestation; b) free of infestation plus visible terminate damage. Ask for the second. If termite infestation or damage is found, the contract may give the seller the option to remove the pests and fix the damage, or if the cost exceeds a certain amount the seller can rescind the contract.

10. CONDITION OF THE PROPERTY

One of the buyer's biggest worries is that one of the major components of the house is broken or does not function properly, and the buyer does not want to get stuck with hidden repair costs. The seller's main concern is that after closing/settlement he is free of all worries about the furnace breaking down and other maintenance problems with his old house. Buyers in various cities handle this problem differently. In some areas, the buyer has the right to inspect the house within 7 days after signing a binder, but before a formal contract of sale is drafted. In other areas, buyers sign formal contracts and are given 7–10 days after signing to inspect the house. In still other areas, it is customary to give the buyer the right to inspect the house 7 days prior to closing/settlement. Wise buyers will hire an engineer or other professionals to inspect the electrical, mechanical, and plumbing components of the home, as well as the structural fitness. A common clause in a contract will give the buyer a certain time limit to inspect the house, and provide the seller with a written report of defects. If genuine problems exist the buyer can usually elect to rescind (cancel) the contract and receive his earnest-money deposit back; require the seller to repair and correct the problem(s), at the seller expense, but in no event shall that expense exceed $XYZ; renegotiate the price and terms of the contract.

Another common clause in the contract will state that the seller represents, but does not warrant, that all fixtures, equipment, and systems shall be in normal working order at time of closing/settlement.

11. CLOSING/SETTLEMENT TIME AND PLACE

Closing/Settlement is specified as occurring "on or about" a certain date. Your contract may state "on or before" a certain date. Many contracts contain the words "time is of the essence," which has been interpreted by some courts to mean that a specific date is important to the parties, and if closing/settlement does not occur on that date, a breach of contract occurs. Other jurisdictions hold the mere recital of the phrase "time is of the essence" does not by itself make time critical.

The place of the closing/settlement is noted, and some contracts detail the closing costs that will be the responsibility of each party. Buyers sometimes want a clause that makes the seller pay rent to the buyer if the seller does not vacate when time of possession is specified; and also makes the late vacating seller responsible for the buyer's alternate lodging expenses and any storage costs of the buyer. Buyers normally are contractually entitled to take possession at closing, but, like everything, this is negotiable.

12. BREACH OF CONTRACT

This clause defines the consequences to a party that fails to live up to the terms of the contract.

13. SPECIAL CONDITIONS

On most form contracts there are a couple of inches of blank, white space with a heading above it titled "special conditions" or "other conditions" or "additional covenants." This space is reserved for adding any conditions or promises the parties want included in the contract. If there is not enough space here to type in additional matters, your attorney may note "see attached amendments," thus incorporating by reference another document. An amendment may also be called a "rider" or an "addendum" or a "supplement," or something else.

There can be literally thousands of clauses that may appear here in this "catch-all" section. Hard to believe? Here are just a few examples.

—SALE OF BUYER'S HOUSE

Buyer #1 may make the purchase of the seller's house contingent upon the prior sale of the buyer's house. A seller might agree to that contingency, with the stipulation that the seller can continue to look for another buyer. Should the seller receive an offer from buyer #2, buyer #1 has the option of matching #2's offer and closing within X days, or to step aside and withdraw. Sellers want to keep the time limit to no more than 60 days, and often ask buyer #1 to forfeit his earnest-money deposit if he fails to close.

—RISK OF LOSS CLAUSE

Suppose the house is damaged or destroyed after contract, but before closing/settlement? Fires, floods, earthquakes, vandals,

REALTOR®

REAL ESTATE CONTRACT

FORM APPROVED BY THE SOUTHWEST BAR ASSOCIATION AND
FORM APPROVED BY THE SOUTHWEST SUBURBAN ASSOCIATION OF REALTORS

EQUAL HOUSING
OPPORTUNITY

☐ Single Family
☐ Multi-Family
☐ Townhouse
☐ Condominium
☐ Vacant Lot

(check one)

SELLER: _____

ADDRESS: _____
　　　　　(City)　　　(State)　　　(Zip)

BUYER: _____

ADDRESS: _____
　　　　　(City)　　　(State)　　　(Zip)

Buyer hereby agrees to purchase and Seller agrees to sell the following described real estate, on the terms and conditions herein set forth.

DESCRIPTION OF PROPERTY: LEGAL DESCRIPTION: (Permission to enter at any time hereafter)

STREET ADDRESS _____
(Include "Unit Number" if condominium or townhouse)
　　　　　　　　　　　　　　　　(City)　　　　　(State)

LOT SIZE: APPROXIMATELY _____ X _____ X _____ X _____ feet.

IMPROVED WITH _____

together with all appurtenances attached to and forming a part of premises, for which owner shall deliver a Bill of Sale at time of delivery of Deed; existing heating, plumbing, electrical lighting fixtures; storm windows, storm doors and screens, if any; drapery rods, curtain rods, if any; fencing, if any; attached air conditioners, if any; attached outside TV antenna, if any; and specifically including the following items of personal property now on premises:

_____

_____

PRICE AND TERMS:

PURCHASE PRICE .... $ _____

EARNEST MONEY DEPOSIT
In form of (cash) (personal check) (cashier's check) or (judgement note due _____) .... $ _____

.... $ _____

BALANCE DUE AT CLOSING .... $ _____

FINANCING:

This contract is subject to the Buyer obtaining within _____ days, a mortgage commitment, in the amount of $ _____ or such lesser sum as Buyer accepts amortized by monthly payments over a period of not less than _____ years at an interest rate not to exceed _____ per annum, for which Buyer shall make application within 10 days from date hereof, and the proceeds of which are to be used as part payment of the purchase price herein and the expenses of which purchaser agrees to pay. If, after making every reasonable effort, Buyer is unable to procure such commitment within the time specified herein and SO NOTIFIES SELLER THEREOF IN WRITING within that time, this contract shall become null and void and all the earnest money shall be returned to Buyer. IN THE EVENT THE BUYER DOES NOT SERVE NOTICE of failure to procure said commitment upon Seller as herein provided then this contract shall continue in full force and effect without any loan contingencies. Buyer shall be allowed to have a Mortgage or Trust Deed placed on record prior to closing, but any delays caused thereby shall not constitute default by the Seller. Seller must allow reasonable inspection of the premises by Buyer's financing agent.

CLOSING:

The closing shall be on or before _____ at the office of Buyer's lender, or _____

POSSESSION:

Seller shall deliver possession to Buyer (within _____ days from date of)(at) closing. In the event possession is not delivered at closing, Seller agrees to pay Buyer for the use and occupancy the sum of $ _____ per day for each day after closing that Seller retains possession. Seller shall be responsible for heat, utilities and maintenance expenses during said period. Should Seller fail to deliver possession to Buyer as agreed, Seller shall pay to Buyer beginning on the _____ day after closing, the sum of $ _____ per day until possession is delivered to the Buyer.

Seller shall deposit the sum of $ _____ in escrow with _____, as Escrowee, at the time of closing and any monies due the Buyer for Seller's use and occupancy hereunder shall be paid to the Buyer from this deposit and the balance, if any, refunded to the Seller. Possession shall be deemed delivered to the Buyer when Seller has vacated the premises and delivered the keys to the buyer or the Escrowee. Escrow money to be limited to delivery of possession. Funds held pursuant to this paragraph shall be used only to satisfy claims made under this section exclusively.

Revised 3/90

TITLE EVIDENCE:

Seller, at his expense, shall furnish not less than five days prior to closing:

A Title Commitment for an Owners Title Insurance Policy issued by an Illinois Licensed Title Company in the amount of the purchase price to cover date hereof showing title in the intended grantor subject only to (a) the general exceptions contained in the title policy where the subject property qualifies thereunder as a residential parcel; (b) the title exceptions set forth below; and (c) title exceptions pertaining to liens or encumbrances which have been assumed by the Buyer under the terms hereof or which the Seller has agreed to remove at closing from the proceeds hereunder and additionally, if applicable, a Torrens Certificate of Title and Torrens Tax Search. Any delay in delivery of title commitment which is caused by the Buyer, his agent or his lending agency, shall extend the time for delivery thereof by the Seller by such period of delay.

If the Torrens Certificate, Tax Search or the title commitment discloses exceptions not provided for herein, Seller shall have until closing to remove said exceptions or to acquire title insurance covering said unpermitted exceptions. If Seller fails to remove said exceptions or obtain additional insurance within the time stated herein, Buyer may elect to terminate this Contract and all monies paid by the Buyer shall be refunded.

CONVEYANCE, LIENS, ENCUMBRANCES:

Seller shall convey, or cause to be conveyed, title to the Buyer by warranty deed with release of homestead rights (or by other appropriate deed if title is in trust or an estate) subject to (a) general taxes for 19_____ and subsequent years; (b) building lines and building laws and ordinances; (c) zoning laws and ordinances, but only if the present use of the property is in compliance therewith or is a legal non-conforming use; (d) visible public and private roads and highways, (e) easements for public utilities which do not underlie the improvements on the property; (f) other covenants and restrictions of record which are not violated by the existing improvements upon the property; (g) party wall rights and agreements; (h) existing leases or tenancies, if any.

PRORATIONS:

The following items, if applicable, shall be prorated as of the date of closing; (a) insurance premiums; (b) general taxes; (c) rents and security deposits; (d) interest on mortgage indebtedness assumed; (e) water taxes; (f) fuel; (g) prepaid service contracts. Proration of general taxes shall be on the basis of the last ascertainable bill plus homestead exemption, if any. If said bill is based on partial assessment or on an unimproved basis for improved property, a written agreement for final proration when the complete assessment information is available from the County Assessor shall be signed at closing by the parties hereto.

DAMAGE BY CASUALTY BEFORE CLOSING:

If the improvements on the property shall be destroyed or materially damaged by fire or other casualty prior to closing, the provisions of the Uniform Vendor and Purchaser Risk Act of Illinois shall apply.

SURVEY:

Seller, at his expense, shall furnish to Buyer a current spotted survey (not more than 6 months old) under certification by an Illinois Licensed Land Surveyer certified in the name of the Buyer, showing the location of the building and improvements on subject property to be within the lot lines and not encroaching over any setback line or easement, and showing no encroachments of buildings or other improvements from adjoining properties.

BROKER:

ATTORNEYS: Seller's Attorney _____ Buyer's Attorney _____

PERFORMANCE:

The earnest money and this contract shall be held by _____ for the benefit of the parties hereto, and applied to the purchase price at closing. If the Buyer defaults hereunder, the deposit is to be first applied to the expenses of the Seller; such as title expenses and survey costs, then to the broker's fees, and the remainder to the Seller. If this contract is terminated without Buyer's fault, the earnest money shall be returned to the Buyer.

GENERAL CONDITIONS AND STIPULATIONS:

(a) Both Seller and Buyer agree to execute all documents and provide all information necessary to enable any lender to issue a commitment for mortgage or trust deed and to close this sale.

(b) Seller warrants that as of the date hereof neither he nor his agent has received any notice issued by any city, village or other government authority of a building code violation concerning the subject property which will not be cured by date of closing.

(c) All notices herein required shall be in writing and served upon the parties at the addresses shown on this contract or upon the attorney for such party. In the event the name and address of the Seller or the attorney for the Seller is unknown, written notice may be served upon the listing broker as agent for such Seller. Facsimile transmission of any offer, acceptance, notice or rider herein provided to the parties, their broker or attorney, shall constitute sufficient notice or acceptance. Original documents shall be forwarded in all instances within three business days of such notice.

(d) Seller agrees to arrange to leave the subject property in broom clean condition. All refuse and personal property not to be conveyed to Buyer shall be removed from the property at Seller's expense before the date of Buyer's occupancy.

(e) Prior to closing; Buyer shall have the right to enter into and inspect the premises.

(f) Buyer agrees to purchase Flood Insurance, if required by Lender.

This contract and riders numbered _____, _____, attached hereto and incorporated herein, shall be executed and one copy thereof delivered to Seller and one copy to Buyer.

THIS IS A LEGALLY BINDING CONTRACT WHEN SIGNED. IF NOT UNDERSTOOD, SEEK LEGAL ADVICE BEFORE SIGNING.

BUYER: _____   SELLER: _____

DATED: _____   DATE ACCEPTED: _____

civil disorders, and other occurrences happen. Your contract should state which party bears the risk of loss until possession & title is transferred at closing. If the property is damaged, can the buyer avoid the contract and receive his earnest money back? What about other fees the buyer has paid to attorneys, lenders, and others? Does the seller have the option to repair the damage within X days and hold the buyer to the contract?

—CODE VIOLATIONS

It is common for contracts to contain a clause or representation by the seller that he is not aware of, nor has he received any official notice of any building, fire, health, safety, pollution, or other code violations at time of closing/settlement.

—DURATION OF OFFER

Remember, before this form contract is agreed to by both parties it is merely an offer that is not yet accepted. Generally, an offer can be withdrawn anytime before acceptance. An offer is open for a reasonable time, unless the offeror specifies a time period. If you make an offer or counteroffer, you should limit its validity to several days at most.

—CONDITION OF PROPERTY UPON TRANSFER OF POSSESSION

The seller may agree to cut the lawn, remove the trash, and keep the exterior of the home in good condition. The most common clause referring to inside the home calls for "broom-clean" condition, which means the inside is swept out and all non-contracted-for items are removed.

—BROKER'S COMMISSION

The seller normally pays the broker, and in the amount specified in the listing contract. If the commission is changed, this clause serves as evidence of this later modification of the existing listing contract.

—INTEREST ON EARNEST MONEY DEPOSIT

If some state's laws are silent on this issue, the buyer may wish to claim any interest earned on his earnest money.

—CONTRACT SUBJECT TO THIRD PARTY'S APPROVAL

Either party may want a clause added that makes their performance contingent upon a third party approving the contract and its terms. These are sometimes called "escape clauses" or "weasel clauses." Courts have held that this third party (attorney, relative, knowledgeable friend) must have a reasonable objection, and cannot capriciously object to the transaction.

12
Seller Financing May Be Helpful

There may be situations where you as a seller have little hope of selling your home and receiving all cash for your equity at closing. In soft or depressed markets, you may have to help the buyer with financing just to make the sale.

In times of soaring interest rates, such as 1981–1983, as many as half of all home sales utilized some sort of seller financing. This chapter explains the basics of owner financing, with legal and financial advice.

Why would a seller want to play the role of a lender? There are several good reasons:

1. The seller has not received any other offers for his home that are close to his desired price.

2. The home is too old, in need of many repairs, or in a neighborhood that the lending institutions consider to be too risky.

3. The owner does not need to receive a large bundle of cash at closing. He can afford to have the payments deferred.

4. The owner views his decision to carry the mortgage as one that will provide him with steady monthly income. The loan is secured by the home itself, and the owner receives a very good rate of return that tops any other investment he could make. (Usually the interest rate is the same as the going conventional rate, or slightly higher. But, it is always up to the parties to negotiate!)

The Contract for Deed

The contract for deed is one method an owner can utilize to finance the sale of his own home. In some states this is also called a "land contract," because it is often utilized in financing vacant land that institutional lenders usually avoid lending money on. It is also a common financing method for rural property, particularly midwestern farms.

Let us see how the contract for deed works in practice. You have been trying to sell your home in a buyer's market for 8 months. You want $70,000, and have an interested buyer, but the buyer lacks the income to qualify for a new loan, and he does not have enough cash to make a 10% down payment. The buyer offers you $3,000 down, and wants a 20-year loan at 10% interest on the balance of the purchase price. You accept the offer.

When the contract is signed, the contract and deed are usually delivered to a third party. The third party holds them, acting as an escrow agent or trustee. This third party is instructed to deliver the deed to the buyer after all, or a specified portion, of the loan balance is paid by the buyer to the seller. This practice of letting a third party hold the deed is to guarantee delivery to the buyer at the proper time. Should the seller die while holding the deed himself, the buyer could get involved in a real mess with the estate. Another potential nightmare would be chasing after one of the sellers, for his or her signature after a divorce and subsequent move to another city under a different name.

CONTINGENCIES AND VARIATIONS

Often, a seller will finance the purchase for five years, with the stipulation that the buyer refinance the loan with a regular loan from an institution.

Most contracts for a deed contain language that purports to define what happens should the buyer miss a payment. The typical language states that "time is of the essence"; and should the buyer miss a payment, the seller may declare a forfeiture and all rights of the purchaser are terminated. The buyer's payments will be treated as rents and liquidated damages, should the buyer default. The seller is often given the right of re-entry. Another form the language might employ would be to give the seller the option to declare the total balance to be due upon default or late payments, or to foreclose at the seller's option.

What are the rights of both parties upon default or late payment? To be quite frank, different jurisdictions treat these problems in different ways. Most courts will treat contracts for deeds or land contracts as equitable mortgages, and give the buyer a specified period of time to redeem the property. Other courts may require a public sale with the buyer and seller sharing the proceeds in an equitable way, and a few might even construe the contract strictly.

If you are going to use a contract for deed (land contract) as the financing vehicle, see a lawyer before you sign the contract. Your attorney can explain your state's laws regarding land contracts and advise you of all the legal ramifications.

In summary, you can see that the contract for deed (land contract) has several advantages for the purchaser, namely: 1) lower downpayments; 2) no loan origination fees, closing costs, private mortgage insurance premiums, or escrows; 3) no rigid loan qualification standards; 4) any interest rates and loan terms can be negotiated.

The disadvantages of contracts for deed are the uncertain legal rights that accompany such arrangements.

Sellers view the buyer with little down a higher risk, and are justified in seeking a risk premium, such as a higher than market rate of interest. Ultimately, the seller is relying on the credit-worthiness of the buyer.

The Purchase-Money Mortgage

A second method of owner-financing is the purchase-money mortgage. It operates in essentially the same manner as the contract for deed, but with one major difference—the buyer gets the deed at closing! The buyer makes a downpayment, and signs a note for the loan at specified terms. The seller takes back a mortgage.

What happens in case of default? The seller must institute foreclosure proceedings. The seller cannot merely re-enter the property. The buyer will be given the right of redemption. Should the home sell at a public auction, the seller/lender would receive the unpaid balance of the loan, and the buyer would receive any surplus funds.

Use of Second Mortgages

A second mortgage is subordinated to the rights of the first mortgage holder who has properly recorded his interest.

Suppose you want to sell your $80,000 home. You have accepted an offer, and your buyer qualifies for an 80% conventional loan. As closing nears, your buyer informs you that he will be short $3,500 at closing. You could offer to pay $3,500 worth of his closing costs, or better yet make him a loan for $3,500. He can sign a promissory note to you, and you can get a second mortgage from him after closing. (That would give you a security interest in the property, should the buyer fail to pay off the $3,500 loan.) Your second mortgage is entitled to consideration in the event the buyer defaults on either loan, but only after the prior first mortgage of $64,000 is fully paid off to the lending institution.

Why would a seller do this? Because the offer may be the best or only offer he received! The seller doesn't wish to blow the sale just because he doesn't want to wait a while to receive a small portion of his proceeds.

Be creative in financing! Where there's a will there's a way! In certain situations a seller may even want to carry a second mortgage at 0% interest.

Buy-Downs

Have you ever browsed through the real estate section in the Sunday paper and spotted a builder's ad offering 8 percent* interest rates on financing? Your first reaction is, "This must be a mistake! Interest rates are 14 percent everywhere else!" Then you notice the asterisk and read a footnote explaining that the 8 percent interest is only for the first year of your loan. After that, your monthly payments increase to the usual amount necessary to amortize the loan at 14 percent. The home builder or seller offers what is known as an interest-rate "buy-down." The builder "buys-down" the interest rate from 14 to 8 percent by making up the difference in payment to the lender.

Suppose a buyer borrows $50,000 at 14 percent for thirty years, but the seller offers to buy-down the interest rate to 8 percent in the first year. The buyer's payments in that first year will be $366.89 a month, while the seller would pay $225.55 monthly to the lender. The lender would receive a total monthly payment of $592.44.

In effect, the seller partially "subsidizes" the buyer's monthly loan payments. This subsidy totals $2,706.60 for the first year. In the second year the buyer is on his own and makes the full monthly payments of $592.44 on the conventional loan. Why doesn't the seller just reduce the price of the home by $2,706.60? A price reduction would have little effect on the monthly payments and do little to solve the resulting affordability problem.

Are there any regulations on these buy-downs? How big can the buy-down be? Five percent? Ten percent? Fifteen percent? How many years can a buy-down be in effect? Five years or longer? Only the buyer and seller can answer these questions in a contract. In other words, these items are all open to negotiation. How nice for you!

VARIATIONS OF THE BASIC BUY-DOWN

Creative financing is a lot like making your own ice-cream sundae: the possibilities are endless! Consider these variations of the basic buy-down. If a buyer wants a $50,000 loan, but can't afford to pay the going market rate of 14 percent, a creative buy-down could be the answer. In the first year he pays 8 percent interest; in the second year he pays 10 percent; in the third year he pays 12 percent; and in the fourth year the subsidy ends, thus he makes full payments at 14 percent. This arrangement by the subsidizing seller would coincide with the buyer's escalating salary and financial ability to meet the full monthly payments.

A Repayable Buy-Down

Here's another scenario that may work for a buyer. Why not suggest to his parents (or consider yourself) a repayable buy-down loan? For a $50,000 loan at 14 percent, you could suggest a two-year buy-down to 8 percent. The total subsidy would be $5,413.20, while his monthly payments for two years would be $366.89

A Sleepy Buy-Down

When does he start repaying the subsidy? Stipulate in the note that he makes no payments on principal or interest until the beginning of the third year. This buy-down agreement would give him some financial breathing room. He could even give you (or the parents) a second mortgage to provide more security than just the note.

Balloon Mortgages

Any mortgage that requires the borrow to repay the entire debt before all the principal has been fully amortized is called a "balloon" mortgage. Suppose a buyer needs to borrow $80,000 to finance the purchase of a house. A savings and loan association will give him a loan of only $60,000 at 13 percent for thirty years, with monthly payments of $663.72.

You (the seller) agree to give the buyer a second mortgage for $20,000 at 13 percent, but only for three years, which would require monthly payments of $673.88. Payments on both loans would cost the buyer $1,337.60 a month—a figure he cannot afford. Do you have any alternatives?

You could tell the buyer that you will give him a loan of thirty years, not three years, but you will insert a clause in the note that says the entire loan is due and payable at the end of the third year. Monthly payments on this second mortgage would be $221.24, a sum much more affordable than $673.88! After the third year the buyer must either sell or refinance, because his final payment on the second loan swells (or "balloons") to the entire remaining principal balance.

INTEREST-ONLY BALLOONS

An interest-only balloon is a variation of the balloon mortgage, which calls for monthly payments that cover only the interest due on the loan, with no payment on the principal required until the final (balloon) payment is due. Interest-only balloon mortgages rarely exceed five years in term.

Legal Aid Is a Must!

Whenever you consider participating in the financing of the sale of your own home, be sure to discuss the matter with your lawyer. The credit history, work history, and personal background of your buyer(s) should be investigated and checked. Contracts should provide for your protection from buyer default, the destruction and waste of your property, and should shield you from liability for the buyer's actions.

13
Before You Count Your Cash, Let's Talk About Closing

The process by which the sale of real property is formally completed may be called the closing, settlement, or escrow. Regardless of its name, the object of the process is the same: to finalize and settle all financial matters between buyer, seller, and lender(s); and to transfer title via deed to the buyer.

Different areas of the country have developed various local customs regarding the nature of title closing. On the West Coast and in Florida, escrow closings are the custom. The parties to the transaction select a neutral escrow agent to gather, process, and disperse all relevant funds and documents to the right parties. This escrow agent may be the escrow department (a closing department) of a bank, savings and loan, or title insurance company. The escrow agent may also be an individual company. Attorneys may serve as escrow agents. Because the escrow agents have important legal and financial responsibilities they should be bonded. Most states license and regulate escrow agents.

The escrow agent is acting as an agent for the buyer and the seller, and owes each the fiduciary duties of loyalty, obedience, and disclosure. Since much of the escrow agent's work is conducted by mail and telephone, it is not uncommon to complete title closing without the buyer and the seller or their representatives meeting. Should a layman have an attorney if the closing is to be handled via escrow? Opinions differ on this issue, but my opinion is, yes! Unless you are knowledgeable in real estate law, who do you expect to advise you regarding the nature and consequences of documents you are asked to sign? Generally, lenders, real estate brokers, closers, escrow agents, and trust departments can prepare legal documents, but when they try to give legal advice, they may be practicing law without being licensed to do so. The only question you should be concerned with is how do I best protect myself.

If you live in the Midwest, East, or South, closing is usually conducted at a meeting where many people are present, such as: the buyer and his attorney and real estate broker; the seller and his attorney and real estate broker; the lender(s); the title insurance company; and the closer. The closer who runs the meeting may be an attorney, a representative from the title insurance company or the lending institution, or an independent closing company.

You probably already have some mental images of closing. Your concern now is probably how much it will cost, and will some hidden costs spring up. These are common concerns, and federal legislation aimed at correcting settlement abuses, such as channeling business to certain title companies or providers for a fee, was originally enacted in 1974.

RESPA

The Real Estate Settlement Procedures Act (RESPA) gives the consumer/ borrower protection from unethical practice, abuse, and surprise costs. It was enacted to regulate closings and to bring a significant degree of standardization to the process. RESPA was originally aimed at FHA and VA loans, as well as loans that were to be sold in the secondary mortgage market to FNMA, GNMA, and FHLMC. Today, virtually all lenders comply with RESPA's requirements.

At the time buyers apply for a loan, the lender is required under RESPA to provide a Good Faith Estimate of Settlement Charges (pages 98–99). Should the lender require the use of certain providers of settlement services (such as XYZ Title Insurance Company), the buyer must be given their identity and address, and any related business interests between the lender and provider must be disclosed. Many lenders go beyond the requirements and provide much more information than RESPA requires, including estimates of prepaid insurance and tax escrows, estimates of total monthly payment, and details of the financial transaction.

Another helpful item required by RESPA is a HUD information booklet on settlement costs. Upon loan application, the borrower must receive this booklet within three days. The booklet explains the rights of a borrower, and acquaints him or her with the terminology and process of closing.

RESPA also requires lenders to use the Uniform Settlement Statement (page 114) at closing. You have the right to examine the Uniform Settlement Statement one business day before closing is to be held, although it may not be complete.

Because you are curious (and rightfully so!), let's talk more about common closing costs that you-the-seller could be responsible for. First of all, understand that virtually all closing costs are a matter of negotiation between the borrower/buyer and the seller as to which party will pay certain costs. Some contracts provide that the seller will pay *all* closing costs. Other contracts provide that the buyer will pay *all* closing costs. Most contracts call for a division of costs, usually based upon local custom.

How successful can a borrower/buyer be in getting a seller to pay certain closing costs that customarily are the seller's responsibility in your town? The answer depends on the bargaining position of the borrower/buyer. Has the home been on the market for a long time? Is the seller anxious to sell?

For a list of the most common settlement charges, take a moment to refer to part L of the Uniform Settlement Statement (page 114). All of those items in the numbered series 700 through 1400 are potential costs to you. Look at that list. Seen enough? Let's get a better understanding of these items.

Loan Origination Fee

Lenders have fixed and variable costs in processing the loan, so they charge a fee to cover these costs. The fee varies among lenders and areas, and is normally a percentage of the loan amount (1% to 2% is common). Customarily, the borrower/buyer pays this fee.

Loan Discount

To raise the effective yield on the loan, lenders may demand a one-time-only lump sum payment. This loan discount is commonly called the points. One point equals 1 percent of the loan amount, one-half point equals ½ of 1% (or .005 in decimal form), and so on. Suppose you are getting a $90,000 loan, and the points are ¾%. The loan discount fee would be $90,000 x .0075, equaling a fee of $675. It is customary for the buyer to pay at least up to the first point. As stressed earlier, resolve this in your contract.

Appraisal Fee

The lender needs to know the value of the property, which is serving as the collateral (security) for the loan, in case of default. The appraisal may be done by the lender's staff or by an independent appraiser. The appraised value mainly depends on location, condition, and recent sales prices of comparable homes in the same area. It is customary for the buyer to pay this fee.

Credit Report

The lender is interested in the borrower(s)' past history of managing debt. Credit reporting agencies gather information about them from a variety of sources, and provide the lender with a composite picture. The fee for this service is usually paid by the buyer. If the borrowers think the credit report is in error, the Fair Credit Reporting Act entitles them to have access to a summary (not the exact report). Should they need to know more about their credit rights, contact the FTC for one of its information pamphlets.

Lender's Inspection Fee

Sometimes the lender or his representatives will further inspect the property, besides the examination by the appraiser. This is most likely with new or rehabilitated housing. The buyer is generally responsible for this fee.

Mortgage Insurance Application Fee

If mortgage insurance is being utilized, there is an application fee. Sometimes the fee covers the appraisal of the property also, so don't pay twice. Ask the lender questions. The buyer usually pays this fee.

Assumption Fee

When the buyer assumes the seller's existing loan, the lender will charge a fee to defray his expenses. FHA assumption fees are limited by law. Conventional loan assumption fees vary, and are set at the discretion of the lender. It is customary for the buyer to pay the assumption fee.

Prepaid Interest

Prepaid interest is the interest accumulated from the closing date until the end of the particular month in which the closing took place. For example, let us say the borrowers loan closed on June 15th. The prepaid interest would be fifteen days' worth, to cover the use of the lender's money for the last fifteen days of June. The first monthly payment is then due August 1st. (The first day of the month is usually the agreed-upon date.) So the borrower's first payment is made after the lender's money has been used. The interest prepayment is paid before the money is used, in order to adjust the payments to the day chosen for monthly payments to be made.

The prepaid interest amount is one month at the maximum. It is best to compute a full thirty days' interest, to avoid any surprises at closing. To compute this amount, use this formula:

1. Loan amount × interest rate = one year's interest; then,

2. One year's interest divided by twelve months = one month's interest.

Mortgage Insurance Premium

The purpose of mortgage insurance is to protect the lender should the homeowner default on his loan payments. It is not PMI. The premium is usually paid by the buyer.

A. **Settlement Statement**

U.S. Department of Housing
and Urban Development

OMB No. 2502-0265 (Exp. 12-31-86)

B. Type of Loan

1. ☐ FHA 2. ☐ FmHA 3. ☐ Conv. Unins.
4. ☐ VA 5. ☐ Conv. Ins.

6. File Number	7. Loan Number	8. Mortgage Insurance Case Number

C. Note: This form is furnished to give you a statement of actual settlement costs. Amounts paid to and by the settlement agent are shown. Items marked "(p.o.c.)" were paid outside the closing; they are shown here for informational purposes and are not included in the totals.

D. Name and Address of Borrower	E. Name and Address of Seller	F. Name and Address of Lender

G. Property Location	H. Settlement Agent	
	Place of Settlement	I. Settlement Date

J. Summary of Borrower's Transaction		K. Summary of Seller's Transaction	
100. Gross Amount Due From Borrower		**400. Gross Amount Due To Seller**	
101. Contract sales price		401. Contract sales price	
102. Personal property		402. Personal property	
103. Settlement charges to borrower (line 1400)		403.	
104.		404.	
105.		405.	
Adjustments for items paid by seller in advance		*Adjustments for items paid by seller in advance*	
106. City/town taxes to		406. City/town taxes to	
107. County taxes to		407. County taxes to	
108. Assessments to		408. Assessments to	
109.		409.	
110.		410.	
111.		411.	
112.		412.	
120. Gross Amount Due From Borrower		**420. Gross Amount Due To Seller**	
200. Amounts Paid By Or In Behalf Of Borrower		**500. Reductions In Amount Due To Seller**	
201. Deposit or earnest money		501. Excess deposit (see instructions)	
202. Principal amount of new loan(s)		502. Settlement charges to seller (line 1400)	
203. Existing loan(s) taken subject to		503. Existing loan(s) taken subject to	
204.		504. Payoff of first mortgage loan	
205.		505. Payoff of second mortgage loan	
206.		506.	
207.		507.	
208.		508.	
209.		509.	
Adjustments for items unpaid by seller		*Adjustments for items unpaid by seller*	
210. City/town taxes to		510. City/town taxes to	
211. County taxes to		511. County taxes to	
212. Assessments to		512. Assessments to	
213.		513.	
214.		514.	
215.		515.	
216.		516.	
217.		517.	
218.		518.	
219.		519.	
220. Total Paid By/For Borrower		**520. Total Reduction Amount Due Seller**	
300. Cash At Settlement From/To Borrower		**600. Cash At Settlement To/From Seller**	
301. Gross Amount due from borrower (line 120)		601. Gross amount due to seller (line 420)	
302. Less amounts paid by/for borrower (line 220)	( )	602. Less reductions in amt. due seller (line 520)	( )
303. Cash ☐ From ☐ To Borrower		603. Cash ☐ To ☐ From Seller	

L. Settlement Charges

700. Total sales/Broker's Commission based on price $ @ %=	paid from borrower's funds at settlement	paid from seller's funds at settlement
Division of Commission (line 700) as follows:		
701. $ to		
702. $ to		
703. Commission paid at Settlement		
704.		
800. Items Payable In Connection With Loan		
801. Loan Origination Fee %		
802. Loan Discount %		
803. Appraisal Fee to		
804. Credit Report to		
805. Lender's Inspection Fee		
806. Mortgage Insurance Application Fee to		
807. Assumption Fee		
808.		
809.		
810.		
811.		
900. Items Required By Lender To Be Paid In Advance		
901. Interest from to @$ /day		
902. Mortgage Insurance Premium for months to		
903. Hazard Insurance Premium for years to		
904. years to		
905.		
1000. Reserves Deposited With Lender		
1001. Hazard Insurance months@$ per month		
1002. Mortgage insurance months@$ per month		
1003. City property taxes months@$ per month		
1004. County property taxes months@$ per month		
1005. Annual assessments months@$ per month		
1006. months@$ per month		
1007. months@$ per month		
1008. months@$ per month		
1100. Title Charges		
1101. Settlement or closing fee to		
1102. Abstract or title search to		
1103. Title examination to		
1104. Title insurance binder to		
1105. Document preparation to		
1106. Notary fees to		
1107. Attorney's fees to		
(includes above items numbers:)		
1108. Title insurance to		
(includes above items numbers:)		
1109. Lender's coverage $		
1110. Owner's coverage $		
1111.		
1112.		
1113.		
1200. Government Recording and Transfer Charges		
1201. Recording fees: Deed $; Mortgage $; Releases $		
1202. City/county tax/stamps: Deed $; Mortgage $		
1203. State tax/stamps: Deed $; Mortgage $		
1204.		
1205.		
1300. Additional Settlement Charges		
1301. Survey to		
1302. Pest inspection to		
1303.		
1304.		
1305.		
1400. Total Settlement Charges (enter on lines 103, Section J and 502, Section K)		

Before You Count Your Cash, Let's Talk About Closing 115

Hazard Insurance Premium

Both buyer and lender want the property to be protected from damage caused by fire or weather-related events. (Protection against theft and personal liability is also desirable.) Lenders normally want the first year's premium to be paid at or before closing. Normally, the buyer pays the premium.

Reserves Deposited with Lenders

To be sure that the buyer has sufficient funds on hand to pay his hazard insurance, mortgage insurance, and various property taxes, lenders require buyers to fund reserve accounts also called "escrow accounts" or "impound accounts." Upon settlement, buyers normally make monthly payments to each escrow account. Once the buyer begins monthly escrow payment, he cannot be required to pay more than $\frac{1}{12}$ of the annual charges for each item, unless a deficit occurs in any account. (For example, deficits may occur if property taxes or insurance premiums are raised.) RESPA and state regulations are designed to limit the size of escrow accounts, and a few states (California is currently one) require that the buyer be paid interest on the funds in his escrow accounts. Ballpark figures for prepaid escrows are 14 months insurance, three months taxes, and two months PMI (if PMI is used). Again, the buyer pays these costs by custom. Custom can be contractually altered.

Title Charges

The items listed in the 1100 series of Part L. Settlement Charges on the Uniform Settlement Statement are those items that are most common nationwide, although practices vary from area to area. The basic idea behind securing title services is to be sure that the seller transfers a good and marketable title, free from liens and encumbrances, to the buyer. In some areas, a title search is conducted by a title company, which issues a preliminary title report (binder or commitment) prior to closing when a title insurance policy is issued. The purpose of title insurance is to protect the lender and/or buyer from unknown or undiscovered flaws in the title that the title examination did not uncover. In other areas, the title search process centers around abstracting. An abstract is a summary of recorded documents, in chronological order, that show an interest in real property that may affect title. It is customary for sellers to have the abstract brought up to date; then the buyer has the right to examine the chain of title and note his objections, if any. Normally, the buyer will hire an attorney to render a title opinion.

Government Recording and Transfer Charges

Certain documents are recorded in the county where the property is located. Among these documents may be a release of a previous mortgage when the old note is paid off. Also, the new mortgage is recorded, as well as the new deed. These are recording/filing fees. Another potential cost is that of state or local revenue/tax stamps. Normally, the fee is based upon the purchase price of the property. These revenue stamps for the "privilege" of transferring real estate are an expense paid by the seller in most areas.

Additional Settlement Charges

Many contracts call for the seller to provide a certificate showing that the premises are free from termite damage and infestation. Some contracts call for structural inspections by a licensed engineer. A survey of the property is necessary to show the exact location of the lot line, easements, and structures. Either buyer or seller might pay these fees, as per their contract.

Prorations

Certain items that are ongoing expenses are commonly prorated between buyer and seller. An obvious example would be property taxes. Various localities may bill property owners at the beginning, middle, or end of the tax year.

Example: Suppose the city of Yerington sends out their 1991 property tax in October of 1991, and payment is due by December 15, 1991. You are buying a home on July 1, 1991. How should the buyer and seller account for the 1991 property tax bill? Since each will live in the home 6 months of the year, they should split the tax bill. But closing is July 1, and the tax bill is not going to be issued until October. Such a scenario can be handled in one of two ways. First, the previous year's tax bill can be agreed upon as the basis for proration. If the previous year's bill was $600, the seller would owe the buyer $300 for the six months of accrued 1991 taxes that are not yet due. Buyer and seller may also contract to make any necessary adjustments after the 1991 tax bill is issued, in case taxes rise or fall.

Preparing to Close

Even though you have a well-drafted, signed contract for the sale of your house, you cannot celebrate until they have the deed and the keys and you have the money. This grand event is called closing or settlement. Between the time the contract is signed and the transaction finally is settled and closed, events can surface that may potentially kill the deal.

Buyer's Remorse

Buyers sometimes develop "cold feet" about the deal, and have second thoughts about going through with the purchase of your home. This psychological phenomenon is known as "buyer's remorse." It may be fueled by comments made to the buyers by friends, relatives, or anyone interested in real estate. Comments such as "you paid too much," "that's a neighborhood on the decline," and "there is a better buy over on Dwyer Street" all precipitate doubts that lead to buyer's remorse. Sometimes events can change rapidly in a buyer's life. An impending marriage may be canceled, a divorce may be filed, a buyer may be transferred to another city, or one of the buyers may be hospitalized or deceased. You'll be very grateful for having a good earnest-money deposit and a good attorney in these situations.

Contigencies Fail

Deals may also be potentially killed by various contingencies that are not fulfilled. Suppose your house does not appraise at a price high enough to support the buyer's requested loan amount? Suppose the buyer does not qualify for the type and amount of loan specified in the contract of sale of your home? What if the inspection of your property turns up serious problems? Suppose the buyers can't sell their home, and don't have the cash yet to close? What if you have clouds on your title?

Be Informed to Avoid Surprises

With all the paperwork and activity going on, someone must monitor the progress of the deal and report to you. Your agent, attorney, or escrow agent should help with this. You can assist by cooperating with requests for documents and information. You'll get calls from the buyers' representatives wanting to schedule a time for the inspection or survey. The buyers may want to show your home to their out-of-town relatives who are visiting this weekend. You will be talking with the movers. Stay on top of things, and keep in touch with all the key players in the game.

A well-drafted contract has spelled out the closing costs that each party will be responsible for. The only surprise should be the dollar amount of these costs. Arrange to get these figures for both the buyer and yourself a few days *before* closing/settlement to head off any glitches at the scheduled closing.

14
Tax Consequences of Your Sale

Now that you have decided to sell your home, let's consider what effect the income tax laws will have on your decision. Before you panic and break out in a cold sweat, relax! There is some good news in this chapter. Some basic knowledge of income tax fundamentals will get you started in the right direction.

The first step is to figure out how much capital gain or loss will result from the sale. You've probably heard the term "capital gain" before. When you sell property, the difference between your selling price and the "tax basis" of the property while in your hands equals the capital gain that you will have to report on your income tax return. What is tax basis? As a general rule, the tax basis of your home (for income tax purposes) is what you pay for it. You can also add to your original purchase price the cost of any permanent improvements that you make to the home itself, or to the grounds. A burglar alarm system, intercom system, tennis courts, and additions of new rooms are all examples of permanent improvements that add to the tax basis of your home. By contrast, ordinary repairs are not considered permanent improvements, and do not increase the basis.

Let's look at a common scenario to explain the concepts of "tax basis" and "capital gain." If Sally buys a home for $50,000 and makes $8,000 of permanent improvements to it, her basis in the property for income tax purposes is $58,000. If she then sells the home to Bob for $65,000, her capital gain from the sale is $7,000 ($65,000 minus $58,000).

You are required to report capital gains as taxable income on your income tax return, unless some other provision of the law gives you a break. In our example, Sally would have to report $7,000 of capital gain income on her next tax return. That could result in $1,960 in taxes for her! Fortunately, Congress has provided several income tax breaks for homeowners that can be utilized if certain qualifications are met.

One of the provisions allows you to defer the payment of income taxes on capital gains from the sale of your home. Let's call this the "tax deferral rule."

Basically, if you use the capital gains to buy a replacement home of greater value within two years either before or after the sale, you will qualify for this break. Another provision is available only for people who are fifty-five or older. This one excludes forever up to $125,000 of otherwise taxable capital gain. We'll refer to this provision as the "one-time exclusion rule."

It is possible for you to combine these two provisions during a lifetime of home ownership and completely avoid the payment of income taxes on capital gains! As your standard of living improves, you can move into more expensive homes without ever having to pay income taxes for the privilege. Of course, the tax laws might change. What the government gives, it may also take away. It is encouraging, though, that Congress has consistently provided income tax benefits such as these for homeowners.

What About Capital Losses?

You might be wondering, "If capital gains from the sale of my home can be taxable, it seems only fair that capital losses would be deductible." Well, it may be fair, but our lawmakers don't think so. Capital losses from the sale of your home are not deductible for income tax purposes. If your home drops in value, there is no income tax relief to soften the blow.

Going back to our example of Sally and Bob, if Sally sells her home (having a $58,000 income tax basis) to Bob for only $54,000, she will have a $4,000 capital loss. This loss won't help to reduce her tax bill, however, because her home is considered "personal use property." On the other hand, if Sally had moved out of the home and converted it into rental property, she would be entitled to deduct any capital losses due to declines in value after the time of conversion. She would also be allowed to deduct her expenses for mortgage interest, depreciation, and repairs relating to the rental property. A word of caution is appropriate: The conversion from personal use to rental property must be made in good faith and result in actual rental of the property, and not be just a maneuver to reduce taxes.

Deferring Income Taxes

As noted earlier, you can defer income taxes on capital gains from the sale of your home if you meet certain requirements. Now we'll look at this provision in a little more detail.

If you sell your principal residence at a gain and replace it within two years before or after the sale, the gain will only be taxed currently to the extent that the adjusted sales price of the old residence exceeds the cost of the new one. Essentially, this means that if the gain is reinvested in a new residence of greater value, taxation will be deferred.

Let's consider our first example in which Sally sold her residence to Bob for $65,000, resulting in a $7,000 capital gain. If Sally buys a replacement home within two years before or after the sale, she will defer taxes on the gain if the new residence costs her at least $65,000.

Now, we'll add a couple of new facts to make our example more realistic. Let's assume that Sally paid $3,900 in commissions to her real estate agent and also spent $1,000 to fix up her old residence in the process of selling it.

The sales commission will reduce her capital gain from $7,000 to $3,100. The "adjusted sales price" equals $60,100. ($65,000 minus the $3,900 sales commission; less the $1,000 of fix-up costs, as long as the costs were for work performed within ninety days before the sale contract and were paid within thirty days after the sale date.) If she buys a new home for at least $60,000 during the replacement period, she will be able to defer all of the tax on her capital gain.

Notice that the tax is "deferred" and not simply forgiven. What happens to the deferred capital gain income of $3,100? It reduces the tax basis of the replacement residence. If Sally buys a $70,000 replacement home, the income tax basis of the new home will be only $66,900. If home values keep increasing, you can see that there eventually could be a large build-up of deferred capital gain income. That could be a ticking tax time bomb for Sally, unless she is careful to not set it off. She (and you) can avoid an untimely tax explosion by staying within the tax deferral qualification rules.

First of all, both the old home that is sold and the replacement home must be used as the taxpayer's *primary* residence. No matter how many homes you may own, you may only have one primary residence at a time.

Generally speaking, you can only take advantage of these tax deferral benefits once every two years. The old residence must be replaced by a new one within two years before or after the sale of the old one. This replacement period can be extended to up to four years after the sale if either the taxpayer or his spouse is on extended active duty in the United States armed forces.

If you buy more than one new primary residence during the replacement period, this special tax deferral rule will apply only to the last one. Also, the rule applies to only one sale within the two year replacement period preceding the last sale. There is an important exception for job-related moves. As long as you meet the standards for moving expense deductions, the tax deferral rule will apply to all replacement homes bought as a result of these moves. If you are thinking of buying a new home and will not qualify for moving expense deductions, perhaps you should wait until the two year period is up to qualify for tax deferral.

If you end up exchanging an old residence for a new one, this transaction will be treated just like a sale for purposes of the tax deferral rule.

What if you have trouble selling your old residence and have to move into your new one before you get it sold? If you rent it out to tenants, will that cause you to lose the benefits of the tax deferral rule? Not necessarily. As long as the rental is temporary and subordinate to sales efforts, the old residence will still qualify for tax deferral benefits even though it has been rented out prior to sale. In such cases, you will still be allowed to deduct mortgage interest expense during the rental period, although the IRS may question deductions for repairs and depreciation expense.

We've already mentioned the "ticking tax time bomb" of deferred capital gain income. If you do a good job of using the tax deferral rule, you're likely to accumulate substantial deferred capital gains over the years. Later in life, if you decide to cut back on your lifestyle by purchasing a less expensive home, the income tax consequences could be devastating. What is the remedy that can help you avoid this tax trap and shelter capital gain income for good? The one-time exclusion rule.

The One-Time Exclusion Rule

Taxpayers who are fifty-five or over may elect to exclude up to $125,000 of capital gain income from the sale of a principal residence. This may be enough to shelter all of the capital gain build-up under the tax deferral rule. This exclusion is not merely a deferral. It completely eliminates forever the possibility of taxation on up to $125,000 of capital gain. One hitch: the property must have been used as a principal residence for at least three of the five years preceding the sale.

Such a valuable tax benefit must be used prudently. For instance, you may want to wait to make this election until the potential for tax savings is greatest (i.e., when the amount of capital gain is as close to $125,000 as possible, or greater).

For purposes of this rule, a husband and wife are treated as a single taxpayer. This election can only be made by a taxpayer once in a lifetime. If you are married and either your spouse or you has made this election before, then neither of you can take it again. If you join your spouse in making this election, you cannot ever take it again, even if you remarry. If one spouse makes the election, the other must join in for it to be valid.

A couple, both over fifty-five and both homeowners, who want to marry each other might be better off to both sell their homes and take this exclusion before they tie the knot if that would result in a combined exclusion of more than $125,000 for them. It's perfectly legal, and just good planning.

One more thing about this one-time election: If you make the election and later wish that you hadn't, the election can be revoked. You can do this by amending the return for the year when the election was made at any time within three years after the due date of the return.

Estate Planning Notes

Estate planning considerations can sometimes play a part in your decisions, too. A parent who owns a primary residence that has appreciated in value may want to give the property to his or her children. If you're in this position, it might be better for you to keep the property until death, unless that would create unnecessary estate taxes. Why? Because the tax basis for capital gain purposes would be lower if a lifetime gift is made than if the property is passed on at the time of your death, resulting in higher income taxes for your children. Using this same logic, it might be better to retain a residence until death, even if you have to rent it out, than to sell it and

Form **2119**	**Sale of Your Home** ▶ Attach to Form 1040 for year of sale. ▶ See Separate Instructions. ▶ Please print or type.	OMB No. 1545-0072 **1990** Attachment Sequence No. **20**
Department of the Treasury Internal Revenue Service		

Your first name and initial (If joint, also give spouse's name and initial.)   Last name | Your social security number

Fill in Your Address Only If You Are Filing This Form by Itself and Not With Your Tax Return	Present address (no., street, and apt. no., rural route, or P.O. box no. if mail is not delivered to street address)	Spouse's social security number
	City, town or post office, state, and ZIP code	

Part I General Information

1a Date your former main home was sold (month, day, year) . . . . ▶ ___ / ___ / ___

 b Enter the face amount of any mortgage, note (e.g., second trust), or other financial instrument on which you will receive periodic payments of principal or interest from this sale (see Instructions) . . | **1b**

2 Have you bought or built a new main home? . . . . ☐ Yes ☐ No

3 Is or was any part of either main home rented out or used for business? (If "Yes," see Instructions.) . . . . . . ☐ Yes ☐ No

Part II Gain on Sale (Do not include amounts you deduct as moving expenses.)

4 Selling price of home. (Do not include personal property items that you sold with your home.) . . . | **4**

5 Expense of sale. (Include sales commissions, advertising, legal, etc.) . . . . | **5**

6 Amount realized. Subtract line 5 from line 4 . . . . | **6**

7 Basis of home sold. (See Instructions.) . . . . | **7**

8a **Gain on sale.** Subtract line 7 from line 6 . . . . | **8a**

 • If line 8a is zero or less, stop here and attach this form to your return.

 • If you answered "Yes" on line 2, go to Part III or Part IV, whichever applies. Otherwise, go to line 8b.

 b If you haven't replaced your home, do you plan to do so within the replacement period (see Instructions)? . . . . ☐ Yes ☐ No

 • If "Yes," stop here, attach this form to your return, and see Instructions under **Additional Filing Requirements.**

 • If "No," go to Part III or Part IV, whichever applies.

Part III One-Time Exclusion of Gain for People Age 55 or Older (If you are not taking the exclusion, go to Part IV now.)

9a Were you 55 or older on date of sale? . . . . ☐ Yes ☐ No

 b Was your spouse 55 or older on date of sale? . . . . ☐ Yes ☐ No

 If you did not answer "Yes" on either line 9a or 9b, go to Part IV now.

 c Did the person who answered "Yes" on line 9a or 9b own and use the property as his or her main home for a total of at least 3 years (except for short absences) of the 5-year period before the sale? (If "No," go to Part IV now.) . . . . ☐ Yes ☐ No

 d **If you answered "Yes" on line 9c, do you elect to take the one-time exclusion?** (If "No," go to Part IV now.) . . ☐ Yes ☐ No

 e At time of sale, who owned the home? . . . . ☐ You   ☐ Your spouse   ☐ Both of you

 f Social security number of spouse at time of sale if you had a different spouse from the one above at time of sale. (Enter "None" if you were not married at time of sale.) . . . . ▶

 g **Exclusion.** Enter the **smaller** of line 8a or $125,000 ($62,500, if married filing separate return) . . | **9g**

Part IV Adjusted Sales Price, Taxable Gain, and Adjusted Basis of New Home

10 Subtract the amount on line 9g, if any, from the amount on line 8a . . . . . . | **10**

 • If line 10 is zero, stop here and attach this form to your return.

 • If you answered "Yes" on line 2, go to line 11 now.

 • If you are reporting this sale on the installment method, stop here and see line 1b Instructions.

 • All others, stop here and enter the amount from line 10 on Schedule D, line 3 or line 10.

11 Fixing-up expenses. (See Instructions for time limits.) . . . . | **11**

12 **Adjusted sales price.** Subtract line 11 from line 6 . . . . | **12**

13a Date you moved into new home (month, day, year) ▶ ___ / ___ / ___   **b** Cost of new home . | **13b**

14a Add the amount on line 9g, if any, and the amount on line 13b and enter the total . . . . . | **14a**

 b Subtract line 14a from line 12. If the result is zero or less, enter -0- . . . . | **14b**

 c **Taxable gain.** Enter the **smaller** of line 10 or line 14b . . . . | **14c**

 • If line 14c is zero, go to line 15 and attach this form to your return.

 • If you are reporting this sale on the installment method, see line 1b Instructions and go to line 15.

 • All others, enter the amount from line 14c on Schedule D, line 3 or line 10, and go to line 15.

15 Postponed gain. Subtract line 14c from line 10 . . . . | **15**

16 **Adjusted basis of new home.** Subtract line 15 from line 13b . . . . | **16**

Sign Here Only If You Are Filing This Form by Itself and Not With Your Tax Return	Under penalties of perjury, I declare that I have examined this form, including attachments, and to the best of my knowledge and belief, it is true, correct, and complete.
	Your signature Date Spouse's signature Date
	▶ (If a joint return, both must sign.)

For Paperwork Reduction Act Notice, see separate Instructions.   ★U.S.GPO:1990-0-265-165   Form **2119** (1990)

Tax Consequences of Your Sale 123

take the one-time exclusion. The reason is that the income tax basis of property that has appreciated in value is "written up" to fair market value at the time of death.

Consider the following example. A home that Sara paid $60,000 for is now worth $210,000. Sara is an elderly widow in poor health who has never taken the one-time $125,000 exclusion. She wants to give the property to her children, Greg and Nancy, and move into a retirement home. She will not incur estate tax upon death.

Sara would be better off to keep the property in her name and rent it out until she dies. At death, Greg and Nancy can sell it without any capital gain since the income tax basis will then be equal to its fair market value (now $210,000), which is about what they would sell it for.

One more point relating to estate planning deserves mention. With the increasing use of trusts in estate planning, you may be considering putting your primary residence into a trust, or perhaps you've already done so. There is a possibility that the IRS would deny the benefits of both the tax deferral rule and the one-time exclusion rule if you put the property into a trust rather than owned it individually. You should consult your attorney, CPA, or financial planner about this so that you don't lose these valuable tax benefits.

Reporting Your Gains

An information return must be filed with the IRS to report the proceeds from the sale of your residence. You are also required to report this information by filing Form 2119 with your income tax return, regardless of whether you replace the old residence. If you intend to buy a new home within the replacement period, but have not done so by the time you file your return, you do not have to pay tax on capital gain at that time. If it later turns out that you owe tax, however, you'll have to amend the prior year's return by filing Form 1040X and a revised Form 2119, plus you'll be required to pay interest on the tax liability.

Any capital gain that turns out to be taxable should be reported on Schedule D of Form 1040.

Form 2119 is reproduced for you on page 123.

Final Comment

Armed with this information, you should be able to understand the basics of income tax and estate planning consequences of buying and selling a home. This does not take the place of a professional advisor, though.

You should still consult a good attorney, CPA, or financial planner to help guide you through difficult decisions. They can help you to apply these tax and estate planning considerations to your unique circumstances. Then you'll be able to enjoy a lifetime of tax-wise home ownership.

15
To FISBO, or Not to FISBO: That Is the Question!

Depending on which studies and statistics you believe, an estimated 10 to 15% of all homes sold are sold by owners without using real estate brokers. The major reason some sellers opt for the FISBO For-Sale-By-Owner marketing option is they hope to save a 5% to 7% commission, and pocket that savings. Minor reasons may include seller perceptions that they can do a better job of selling a product they know best or a general dislike for amateurish real estate agents based on past experiences. Some sellers distrust agents and don't believe that they act in the seller's best interest, but instead act in their own best interest to facilitate a quick sale, even at a lowball price.

Agent or FISBO?

Certain basic tasks must be performed when selling a home. *Somebody* must 1) price the home; 2) advertise the home; 3) show the home; 4) negotiate the deal; and 5) guide the transaction to a successful closing. That somebody may be a FISBO seller, an agent, an attorney, an escrow or closing agent, or "somebody" may be a combination of all these somebodies. Regardless of who performs these tasks and services, they require knowledge, expertise, and time to be performed properly.

Agents and brokers will argue that a seller is emotionally and financially better off to market his or home through a broker. For those considering the FISBO route, or for those who are already FISBOs and getting calls from dozens of agents, I present the major arguments for using a broker, followed by short responses that FISBOs make.

Pricing the Home
Agents have access to relevant data on comparable sales and current listings and know the local market firsthand because they are in it daily. By using

a comparative (or competitive) market analysis (CMA), an agent can help the seller avoid the dangers of overpricing or underpricing. FISBO response: I can get that data on comparables from other sources, including an independent appraiser. Appraisers' fees are modest, and the appraisal is a great negotiating tool.

Selling at a Higher Price

Agents will point out that what is most important is not necessarily selling price, but how much cash the seller nets at closing after deducting all his expenses (advertisements, signs, flyers, appraiser, attorney, closing costs, etc.) from the sale price.

FISBO response: it's true that net proceeds are the important thing. But I'm betting that my expenses will be less than your 7% commission.

Agents point out that if the home does not sell, the owner is out all of those costs. Agents stress that they are more likely to produce more buyers, and that increases the odds of getting better offers.

FISBO response: probably true.

Agents believe that they can better justify the value of the home and its asking price by showing the buyers other comparable homes in the same price range, so that the buyer can get a firsthand look at the current market.

FISBO response: I can't show any house but mine. I can give the buyers the addresses of comparables, but I don't want to lose a prospective sale.

Agents may cite surveys "proving" that sellers actually netted more by using a broker to sell their home rather than going FISBO.

FISBO response: Show me a study of data for my price range and neighborhood for this year. Real estate markets are local in nature and change daily.

The Saved Commission

Agents point out that sellers do not save the 5–7% commission. Expenses may eat up half of the commission, then the seller may give away the other half (or more) to the buyer in the form of a price reduction. Why do you think buyers spend their own time (and gas money) looking for properties and then going through the hassles of negotiating and getting the financing and preparing for closing alone, when an agent will do all that and better for buyers and for free? The buyers expect to save the commission!

FISBO response: the buyer will settle for a 1–2% reduction on price because it still beats his other options through sellers with agents (no reduction).

Exposure to Buyers

The multiple listing service (MLS) that the agent's broker belongs to exposes a listed property to virtually all of the hundreds or thousands of real estate agents in the area. A listed property is showcased in an MLS book that prints a picture of the home and also gives pertinent information about the home. All the agents in town work with hundreds or thousands of buyers, and they will all be working to sell your home.

FISBO response: you've got me there! The MLS system is efficient and effective, and one of your best sales tools. As long as you don't run afoul of anti-trust laws, you brokers have a winning system.

Agents remind sellers that their brokerage firm belongs to a nationwide referral service that sends out-of-town buyers to the local firm.

FISBO response: how many of these relocation referrals resulted in a sale of a home in *my* price range this year?

Brokers run extensive advertising campaigns, all aimed at attracting more buyers. Brokers may advertise on billboards, signs, television, radio, in special magazines for homebuyers (such as those you see at the supermarket), daily newspapers, the MLS books, and other vehicles. Brokers go fishing for buyers with a big, wide net. FISBO sellers have a single line in the water. Brokers generate many buyers for homes in your price range, as well as others. In practice, buyers that think they are looking for a home priced around $90,000 may actually buy a home for $80,000 or, more likely, $100,000. Agents can convert lookers in different price ranges into a buyer in your price range. In practice, only one buyer in about 25 will buy the home they phone to visit. Selling is a numbers game, Mr. or Mrs. FISBO, and we pros have the numbers on our side!

FISBO response: you are right, your efforts to find buyers dwarf mine. What percentage of all qualified buyers who are currently looking for a home in my neighborhood and price range work with you or MLS brokers? You really do not know. Unlike listings, buyers are not subject to headcounts. Since buyers do not contract with brokers, they are a fickle bunch who will generally work with several agents as well as FISBOs. They are loyal to themselves. I'm betting that there are enough unattached buyers out there, and I'm aiming my ads at a specific, narrow target market.

Qualifying Prospects

Agents will qualify prospective buyers to be sure that they are financially able to afford the house for sale that they want to inspect. By qualifying the buyers ahead of time, only serious lookers will visit a listed home.

FISBO response: good agents qualify buyers. Some agents will show any looker any property. I can qualify prospects on the phone or in person because I have the knowledge and the moxie.

Showing the Home

Agents note that FISBO sellers are tied down to their home and their telephones. Also, the schedule of a prospect may not be conducive to the schedule of a FISBO owner to arrange a convenient appointment. Hot prospects want to see homes right away, not tomorrow. You can't sell 'em if you can't show 'em!

FISBO response: I have made plans to cover the phone at all times, and our showing schedule will be flexible and reasonable.

To FISBO or Not to FISBO: That Is the Question!   127

Agents point out that FISBO sellers have less time for shopping, visiting friends, golf, tennis, and leisure.

FISBO response: we think the trade-off is worth it. (Lost leisure vs. more cash at closing.) MLS agents use keyboxes to allow showings while the owners are at work or out.

FISBO response: that's a good idea.

Agents point out the potential risks, such as theft and assault, in showing your home to strangers.

FISBO response: we show by appointment only and screen the prospects. Valuables are removed, and we only show when two adults are present.

Agents concede that FISBOs know their own house better than any agent could, but argue that agents know the needs and wants of the buyers that they bring and therefore can show the home better.

FISBO response: you do know *your* buyers better, and may be able to show my home better to buyers you have worked with. But remember, not *all* buyers work with your or agents. Buyers are independent, and I hope to talk with many, discern their needs, and subrogate mine.

Agents argue that drive-by lookers who are not with agents rarely stop and get out of the car. Drive-bys with agents may be persuaded by the agent to go inside.

FISBO response: that's true.

Agents say that homes show better when the owner is absent because prospects find it easier to imagine themselves living in the home and enjoying its benefits and attributes.

FISBO response: Touché! To try to minimize "turf anxiety," I have de-personalized my home. When showing my home, I'll say and do certain things to encourage visualization of ownership in the buyer.

Agents Can Facilitate Negotiations as Middlemen

Agents develop a rapport with buyers, as well as credibility and trust. Buyers are more apt to talk freely with agents about concerns and worries. Agents can counter these objections with professional techniques and get the buyer's signature. Agents are not prone to react emotionally to negative comments about the home, whereas owners might. Owners are usually inexperienced in negotiating situations. Agents are useful in resolving a stalemate or impasse in negotiations. A FISBO seller weakens his position if he initiates contact after an impasse, but an agent is better able to follow up without making any price concessions. Buyers are more apt to reveal their motives to a middleman.

FISBO response: if a middleman is needed, my experienced real estate attorney has agreed to assist.

Agent reply: how expensive will that be?

Agents Can Keep the Deal on Track Until Closing

Buyers may need a nudge or assistance from time to time. Agents are well-versed in basic and creative financing. Agents may network with lenders, termite inspectors, and providers of various title and closing services that either the buyer or seller needs. The agent can help arrange the swiftest and most cost-effective services. Because the brokerage firm provides a high volume of customers to these related real estate service providers, an agent of the firm may be able to cut through red tape and delays and ask for favors.

FISBO response: my attorney and his/her firm are heavy hitters with very powerful networks.

Are You Cut Out to be a FISBO?

Should you become a FISBO? Advisors hold differing opinions on the question. Some say do it! In any given year, there may be 200,000 to 500,000 successful FISBOs. Being a FISBO can be exciting as well as rewarding. Some say do not do it! Leave it to the pros, they will do a faster job and get you a better net price with fewer headaches. Some say it is too complicated to be a FISBO, others say it's a piece of cake.

What do I say? Put me down as a maybe. It depends upon circumstances, character traits, and knowledge. If your market is currently a seller's market where buyers outnumber sellers, it's a good time for FISBOs. Check the average number of days that a home is on the market before it sells. If homes are moving in a month or less, that is a very good sign. If interest rates are relatively low, and lenders are eager to lend, this helps. If your location is desirable, that is a big plus. Finally, your home must be priced right.

I have sketched here a composite profile of a successful FISBO seller. FISBO sellers who succeed have the time to devote to marketing, showings, negotiations, and follow-up activities. They do not regret being tied to the home and the telephone, and are patient people. They are persistent, self-motivated, and have the mental toughness it takes to handle rejection and set-backs. They have good interpersonal skills and can handle themselves in negotiations without letting their emotions overcome them. Successful FISBO's usually have above-average knowledge (for laymen) of real estate financing, and they virtually all have a good real estate attorney to guide and assist them.

What's in It for You?

A FISBO may (notice I said may) save some of the commission. After paying for ads, an appraisal, and perhaps some legal fees that are not typical of a brokered sale, the FISBO seller may have to give away some of the commission to the buyer. What's left for you after your efforts? Some authors take the approach that you can calculate your gain by subtracting your costs from the commission you save. If you have a $100,000 home, and brokers charge a 6% commission in your area, you can subtract your marketing and legal expenses (let's say $1,000 for sake of example) from $6,000 to see what you saved. They carry it a step further and point out that if you spent a total of 50 hours of time being a FISBO, you made $5,000 ÷ 50 or $100 per hour. This type of analysis is somewhat helpful, but limited by its assumptions. Some of these are that the home sells at the same price, with or without a broker; that all of the time you spend on preparations (such as reading this book) is counted; and of course that the home sells.

I prefer to simply remind you of your opportunity costs, whatever they may be. How do you value lost leisure time? Remember also to concentrate on your net proceeds—the cash you will get a closing/settlement. Being a FISBO is a demanding part-time job in most instances. Your "pay" may work out to be $100 per hour, $20 per hour, $0 per hour, or maybe minus $20 per hour. Estimates suggest that roughly half of all FISBOs wind up listing with a broker within 4 weeks. I owe it to you to paint a realistic picture of FISBOs.

Agents Versus FISBO's

One of the most common surprises that FISBOs encounter in the first days of their selling efforts is the deluge of calls and visits from agents that they get. Typical comments from FISBOs are: "half of my calls were from agents"; "we were under siege"; "our house was like bait tossed into a pool of sharks"; "our ad said principals only—no brokers, yet we still got calls every day." Are you surprised? Recall what I said just a few seconds ago: half of all FISBOs will give up trying to sell it themselves in less than four weeks. No wonder training tapes teach agents to ignore ads and read a FISBO yard sign as really saying "Please help me, Mr. or Ms. Agent!"

Agents will contact you by mail, by telephone, and by ringing your door-bell. Most of the material that comes in the mail will be slick brochures or handouts that offer a few generic tips for FISBO sellers. There may be several follow-up letters letting you know what the XYZ firm can do to help you. Other mailouts purport to give you a helpful list of what-to-do's and what-items-you'll-need. Those items will contain some "real estatese" language (CMAs, CRVs, WRAP's, etc.) as well as some imposing sounding items about title insurance or financing, all aimed at reminding you that selling a home can be a complex affair.

The bell ringers get your address out of *crisscross* directories that match up addresses to phone numbers. They usually have something to give you, such as a complimentary For-Sale-By-Owner information package loaded with complicated legal forms or maybe even a For-Sale-By-Owner yard sign you can use or a photo of your home. The main objective of the bell-ringing agent is to get *inside* the home, where he or she can learn more about your motives for selling and expectations. The agent may "have a buyer looking for just this type of home in this neighborhood." Depending upon your strategy for handling agents, you may or may not admit him. Agents who telephone you will be discussed on pages 137 & 138.

FISBO Strategies

There are three basic FISBO strategies you may employ: you can be a FISBO for as long as it takes to make a sale; you can go it alone as a FISBO for X days as a "trial period"; and you can be a FISBO, but invite brokers to participate at a reduced 3% commission.

The first strategy requires that you be able to work under no moving deadlines or time constraints. You basically ignore market conditions and fluctuations, because time is on your side. Most sellers face some time pressures that may be precipitated by events or deadlines. (We want to be settled before the new school year starts; we want to be in the new home before the baby is born; I have to be there by July 15th to begin work, etc.)

The second strategy is to give yourself X days to sell the home as a FISBO, so if that fails you still have enough time to turn the house over to the pros to sell so you can move in time to satisfy your plans. How long should your trial period be? That depends upon your local market conditions and the average current selling time for homes in your price range. Give yourself at least 30 days, and sometimes 90 days or more may be justified. During this trial period, you will *not* allow brokers to participate, despite their claims that they have a buyer who is just right for your home.

Not allowing immediate broker participation, even at a reduced 3% commission, is based upon the premise that serious prospective buyers that are out there right now looking for a home to buy should be given a couple of weeks to see your ads or signs or hear about you. If they don't find you in 30 days, they will never find you by themselves. So before you give them a reasonable time to find out that your home is For Sale By Owner, why compete against your own advertising efforts and dollars by letting an agent in on the sale just now?

Because guidelines are so general, I hesitate to give one. Nonetheless, readers always ask how long the trial period should be and expect a response. Try 150% of the average days on market. If the average time it takes to sell a home priced in your range is 30 days in your area, your trial period should be 45 days (1.5 × 30 = 45). If the pros take 30 days to sell, even with their MLS system and many buyer networks, you must be a little more patient.

You can opt for strategy three, and invite any broker or agent to help sell your home from day one, provided that they accept a 3% commission. This approach will get you more buyer exposure than the first two strategies, but less than a full commission MLS listing would.

Strategy three is the 3% solution. Right now, return to chapter 5 and review the sections on the "open listing" and "commission fees." Your attorney can provide you with an open-listing agreement to utilize. He or she will include contingencies and conditions that terminate the listing, such as if you list your home exclusively with a broker; you sell it; an agent sells it at 3%; or you withdraw the home from the market. You may even have several forms drawn up to provide for a one-time-only showing or a showing for a specifically named buyer. Even though an oral listing contract may be valid in some states, avoid it.

Your ads should note "brokers invited at 3%." Every agent who phones you should be mailed a fact sheet and a 3% open-listing agreement. Most agents will balk at your 3% commission. Their brokers generally tell them to never even think about it! You'll hear reasons such as "my broker doesn't allow it" and "we can't make money at 3%—our ads and overhead cost that much or more." You can counter with "how can you survive and prosper taking a 3% split commission on co-brokered MLS deals? If you are happy to split a commission with another broker, why not with me?" (Of course, the answer to that is that if these 3% FISBOs are successful, there will be even more FISBOs. Also brokers sometimes sell a home "in-house" and don't split a 6 or 7% commission.)

If you adopt the 3% strategy, be sure that any agent who crosses your threshold with a buyer has signed an agreement. You should be very friendly with all of your 3% sales force and even phone them periodically and say "how come you haven't brought me any buyers yet? I thought your firm worked with hundreds of them?" This turning of the tables can be fun and effective. If your FISBO fizzles, the agents all know the odds are good that you'll list with one of them, so they'll be nice to you.

It is also possible that you may combine strategies. You may decide to go strictly FISBO for 30 days; then from days 31 to 90 invite brokers to participate at 3%; and after 90 days list the property with a discount or full-commission broker. Until you contract with someone, nothing is binding about your strategy and you may decide to alter it due to changing family or market conditions.

If you are going to try the FISBO route, the next few chapters contain tips just for you.

16
Telephone Tips for FISBOs

The telephone is your critical link to prospective buyers. Real estate professionals know this and try to keep an agent on floor and phone duty from early morning until 9 P.M. or later. Agents are given extensive training in proper telephone techniques. Why all the fuss about a telephone call? To answer that question, let's examine the behavior of a prospective buyer.

Brian and Kathy McKeough are newlyweds living in an apartment complex. They want to begin looking for a starter home. Kathy circles a few ads in the *Sunday Gazette*. Your ad is the first one she calls, but you are not home. She leaves a message on your answering machine. It's just 11 A.M. Sunday morning, and you are at brunch with the relatives after attending an early church service. Kathy talks to the owners who placed the second advertisement, and is told to come by their open house between 1 P.M. to 5 P.M. On the third call, Kathy reaches Susan Accettura, who is a real estate sales agent with the Lorenz World of Homes firm. Susan, a young widow with three children knows how important answering the phone is, because to her it is her livelihood. You can bet that Susan will be over in her car to pick up the McKeoughs in no time flat. She will show them the home that was advertised, then she'll show them pictures of dozens of more starter homes in her MLS book or on the walls at the swank Lorenz offices. Susan will qualify them, and help the buyers understand some of the complexities of financing. She does this at no cost to the buyers! So, where does that leave you? You are out in the cold. You return the McKeough's phone call, but now they are not home. They are with an agent who will show them dozens of comparable homes, none of which is yours. Now, back to the original questions: why all the fuss about a telephone call? There are two good reasons to fuss over every phone call: first, hundreds and hundreds of sellers and agents are competing for each and every buyer; and second, buyers are on *their* schedule, not yours.

Answer the Phone!

Lesson number one is to have your phone answered at all times, preferably by you or your spouse. Answering machines are better than a ringing phone that no one picks up, but just barely. Many people will hang up on an answering machine, and some people will not leave their phone number on some stranger's machine. If you must use an answering machine, your best bet is to record a message for callers that gives them more information than the ad, but teases them just enough to make them want to leave their name and number or try calling you back. Answering services may be helpful, especially if they do more than just take messages. If the service can read a prepared statement and answer a few questions, you might consider utilizing their service. Call forwarding is another option to investigate. Your ad can specify to call between noon and 8 P.M. You may want to list your work number also. (Be sure to clear that with your boss!) While we are talking about ads, I should remind you to synchronize your telephone coverage with the days your ad will run in the paper.

Before you run your first ad, decide who will answer the phone and what the order of preference is. For example, Mom answers first, then Dad, 16 year old Jamie is third in line, and none of the other kids should ever answer the phone for any reason. You need to establish a few rules. Between 9 A.M. and 8 P.M. any personal calls should be limited to 2 or 3 minutes. After 8 P.M. is best for personal calls but try not to tie up the phone.

Handling the Calls

When you receive a call from a prospective buyer, your inflection and tone should connote warmth, friendliness, and enthusiasm for your product. Eliminate any background noises in your home that can distract the buyer. What sort of noises can occur? Babies may be crying or drumming on their plates with a spoon; dishwashers, radios, televisions, and washers and dryers may be noisy; kids may be playing with toy machine guns or talking robots; and the dog may be barking at the kids or the mailman. You should be well organized and have your fact sheet, notes, directions, notepad, and pens right next to the telephone(s) you plan to use.

There are four major objectives you hope to accomplish when speaking with a telephone caller who is interested in your home.

1. Give the caller the information he or she wants. (Answer his or her questions, be specific. Your fact sheet will help you.)

2. Learn about the caller's real estate needs. (Does the caller have a move-in deadline? Is eating space in the kitchen a must, or will a dining room be OK?)

3. Qualify the caller financially. (Does the caller have the income to qualify for the loan needed to buy your home?)

4. Coax the qualified callers into seeing your home. (If they won't visit, they won't buy!)

Accomplishing your major objectives can be very difficult, even if you're a seasoned real estate pro. It takes two to converse, and the caller has his own objectives. The caller wants to get certain information and perhaps get an appointment. The caller does not want to divulge any personal information. If you let the caller ask all the questions, he or she will control the conversation and you will never accomplish your objectives. Let's eavesdrop on a telephone conversation that a seller handles very well.

Telephone rings

Seller: Hello

Prospect: Hi, I'm calling about your ad in the paper, and . . .

Seller: Yes, I'm glad you called. I'm the owner, my name is Chuck Claus. What's yours?

Prospect: My name is Kerry Ann Gennuso.

Seller: What would you like to know about the property, Kerry Ann?

Prospect: How big are the bedrooms?

Seller: The master bedroom is 16 feet x 20 feet, and the two other bedrooms are each 12 feet x 15 feet. They are very comfortable for the five of us. How many do you have in your family?

Prospect: We have two teenage boys.

Seller: That's nice. Each boy could have his own room, or the boys could room together, and you could use the extra room for something else. Where do the boys go to school?

Prospect: They go to Saint Cajetan High School. What schools are near your home?

Seller: Saint Kevin Jerome is only one mile from us, and the public high school, Adam Smith, is three blocks away. Both schools have excellent academic reputations, and strong extracurricular activities for the kids. I've got all sorts of information about the schools, and when you come to visit the home I can give you a set of photocopied materials. Would you like to come by?

Prospect: Well, maybe. I'll have to check with my husband, Walt.

Seller: That's great, we'd love to show you both our home. It sounds like we may have what you have been looking for. I know looking for a new house can be a hassle. We've been through it three times. It saves a lot of time to be sure you have the financing lined up right. Now, I'm not being nosey, Kerry Ann, but I need to ask you a few questions so you don't waste your time. Do you or your husband work?

Prospect: Yes, my husband works for General Electric. I'm a homemaker.

Seller: That's nice! What is your husband's salary?

Prospect: I think it is around $40,000 per year.

Seller: Terrific. You folks should have no problem getting a good loan. Are you selling your current home?

Prospect: No, we rent a two bedroom house. We've only been in town a few months.

Seller: Do you have a deadline to move?

Prospect:	We want to be out of here in 2 months when our lease expires.
Seller:	I see. You don't have much time to waste. Let's get moving on this. Why don't we set up an appointment for tomorrow night at 7:30 P.M. That will give you time to arrange things with your husband. You can call me back if there is a problem. How does that sound?
Prospect:	That's a good idea.
Seller:	OK, we're all set for 7:30 tomorrow night. Let me have your home phone and work phone. If the house sells before tomorrow, I'll call you to save you a trip.
Prospect:	Our home number is 634-5789, my husband's work number is 321-1000.
Seller:	Got it. Let me tell you the best directions to get here. What is your address over there?
Prospect:	8201 Trainum Drive.
Seller:	OK, take Trainum south to Bishop Ave. Then go right about two miles on Bishop until you come to the Nunn expressway. That's Highway 24. Go south on the expressway for four miles, and exit at Moore Street. Turn right onto Moore, and go to the second stoplight, which is Morrow. Turn right on Morrow and drive about two and a half blocks to our home. We will be on the right side of the street, our address is 322 Morrow. It's a red brick home. OK? Repeat it back to me.
Prospect:	(repeats directions)
Seller:	That's perfect, Kerry Ann. We look forward to meeting you and your husband tomorrow night at 7:30. I'll call you tomorrow to confirm it. Goodbye.

Go back and read the conversation again. How does the seller control the conversation? By asking questions! Is the seller upbeat and positive? Does the seller accomplish his objectives?

More Telephone Tips

When you give directions, send the prospective buyers over the route with the fewest complications or turns. Also try to make it the most scenic route. Some callers don't want to make an appointment, but want the address to drive by first and look over the home and neighborhood. Try to get them inside your home. Be sure to tell them the open house hours. Remind them that except during open house hours, you will not admit visitors without appointments. Also remind them that the best way to know the market is to see lots of homes, so the viewing will be beneficial even if they don't like the house. Mail these "wafflers," as well as everyone you talk to, one of your fact sheets. Keep a good supply of fact sheets, envelopes, and stamps on hand. Mail the information promptly.

When setting up a showing appointment, try to get all the decision makers to come. (Both spouses, the single buyer and her parents, the young couple and their expert friend, etc.) Schedule appointments 30 to 40 minutes apart. This is enough time for a showing, and waiting buyers can sometimes give a buyer on the brink a push over the edge to make an offer. Appointments should be at exact times. Never tell someone to drop by "sometime this evening." Tie them down. For safety's sake, get every visitor's name, address, and phone number before they come. You can look in the phone book to verify this data, or call them back to confirm the appointment. Always have two adults present. (Neighbors are very understanding, and can be of much help.) Don't get involved in negotiations on the phone. Tell callers you will consider all written offers upon consultation with your attorney.

Agents Will Call

FISBO ads attract real estate agents. Their training manuals suggest that a For Sale By Owner sign is really a "Help Wanted" sign. Agents are carefully coached in handling phone calls to FISBOs. The ace up your sleeve is that an agent must disclose the fact that they are licensed agents. Early in your conversation, bring the question to the forefront. Agents will try to control the conversation and ask *you* the questions. Here's how: "Hello, I'm calling about your ad. Does the house have a detached garage?" (If not a garage, the agent will ask about another feature.) Your reply should be "Yes it does. Let me introduce myself first. I'm Miles Minkmann, the owner. What is your name, and are you a principal or agent?" If the caller is an agent, she or he must identify himself as such. The agent will identify himself and ask you another question in the same breath. You can ignore the question, and simply state "You are tieing up my phone, Mr. Agent, and that's very rude. Goodbye." (click) Or, you may want to work with agents, and you may wish to talk. If the caller is not an agent, just play it off with a quick explanation: "the phone is ringing off the hook with buyers and agents. This home is hot, and it's priced right."

Just to prepare you a bit for the deluge of phone calls from agents, here are examples of three of the more popular pitches to FISBOs that you may hear. Pitch #1: "I have a buyer" works like this:

Agent: Hello, is this the two-bedroom home advertised?
FISBO: Yes . . .
Agent: (cuts in quickly) Does the home have a basement? (If not a basement, some other feature that is fairly common in your area.)
FISBO: Yes, we do . . .
Agent: That's great! I have a buyer who is looking for a home in your area with a basement. I'd like to help you in selling your home. I'm Paula Bush with Happy Homes, can I come by this afternoon to see the home at 3 P.M., or would 4 P.M. be better?

Pitch #2: "Let's trade buyers" operates this way:

Agent: (after introductory chatter) I work with dozens of buyers, and can't always find each one the perfect house. If I cannot match my buyers with our homes, is it OK if I send them to you, free of any commission at all?

FISBO: Sure, go ahead!

Agent: I'm hoping that if I send you buyers I cannot satisfy, you will reciprocate and send me all the buyers that aren't interested in buying your house. Now, I'll have to see your home so I know exactly what features and extras you have. I'm free at 10 A.M. or noon.

Pitch #3: "I could be a principal" goes this way:

Agent: (after introduction) I saw your "no agents" (or "principals only") notice in the ad. I sometimes invest in single family homes myself. Would it be OK if I came by to see your home?

The objective of all agents who telephone is to make an appointment to see the house. Once inside, they can gain your trust and perhaps get a listing. Once you have talked with them or they have visited, the follow-up calls and the "I'll stop by's" just keep on coming. Each follow-up action usually follows this format: the agent "gives" the FISBO something, (information about a change in mortgage rates or points, or maybe some legal forms such as binders or earnest-money deposit forms) and asks if the FISBO has had any nibbles from buyers. (Aw, gee. Too bad, but I'm sure you'll do well. Our office wrote seven contracts this weekend. The buyers are hot!) Agents always promise to drop by again, to give you those new mortgage rate sheets or legal forms or whatever. Their objective is more personal contact with the FISBO.

Exactly how you should handle the agent calls and bell ringers depends upon your overall FISBO strategy (see pages 77 & 78). You may invite them to your open house, you may have a special agent open house and pass out your 3% open-listing forms, or you may tell them no agents will cross the threshold during a 60-day trial period.

17
A Guide to FISBO Showings

Your home is in good condition, you have set the stage inside your home for a great showing, and the buyers are coming in 15 minutes. Now is the perfect time to mentally prepare yourself for the showing process. I want you to put yourself in the buyer's shoes, and try to remember what was going on in your mind when you bought this house. Buyers may look at dozens of homes before finding the right one. Buyers are filled with excitement, adventure, stress, worry, and disappointment. Buyers are in search of a big part of their American dream. Purchasing a high-priced item (auto, house) is a complicated decision that creates distorted perceptions in buyers. It is smart to keep several basic thoughts in mind:

1. We are not sure why people "fall in love" with one house and not another. There are many emotional and rational factors involved. Expect only 5%–10% of your prospects to like your home.

2. Real estate is a numbers game. You may talk to hundreds of people; show the home to dozens of people; and negotiate with a few before you find a serious buyer. The lesson is: Be patient!

3. Be affable and polite. Do not take objections and negative comments about your house personally. Keep your cool.

4. Be nice to every looker! They may not seem hot to buy today, yet they may call again for another showing. If they do not call again, they may mention your home to another prospective buyer.

5. Dress conservatively, neat, and in a style that speaks well of your neighborhood.

This mental recap has put you in the proper frame of mind to greet the prospects. Be sure you meet the guests at the front door, even if your family never uses the front door. Your front entrance was designed to be the gateway to the floor plan and should help create a more dramatic first impression of your home's interior. Greet your visitors cordially, and complete the introductions.

Is There a Guide in the House?

FISBO sellers must decide whether to escort the prospects on a guided tour of the home, or to first let the prospective buyers wander and browse on their own. Both viewpoints have staunch advocates. Those who advocate a guided tour point out the following merits: 1) a guided tour allows you to show the best rooms initially to create a strong first impression; 2) a guided tour allows you to point out features that a buyer may not notice on his own; 3) a guided tour allows you to converse more with the buyers to ascertain their needs, wants and objections; and 4) a guided tour allows the seller to keep an eye on the buyers to prevent pilferage.

Those who advocate an unguided tour note that the buyers will not "psychologically buy" the home and imagine themselves living there if the seller is hovering nearby. Buyers do not converse as openly with owners present because they may be afraid of tipping their hand too early, or of offending the sellers with negative comments. Sellers can be too abrupt in a tour, and fail to give the home a chance to work its magic on the buyers. The unguided tour advocates also point out that most buyers know within several minutes whether or not they want to continue seeing the home, or if they just want to get out of there and move on to look at other comparables. The unguided tour saves time and energy, because no amount of sales talk will help if the buyers have an initially negative reaction to a home.

There are a few hybrid approaches that try to combine the benefits of both the guided and unguided tour. We have already discussed the "tag the features" approach when we covered the "Open House" in Chapter 8. Others advocate the "Five Minute Tour," where the FISBO seller leads the buyers through the home in a rapid manner, and points out certain features as they go. ("Those are triple-insulated storm windows, which is why the baby's room is draft-free and toasty warm.") Before the five minute tour begins, the seller explains that "this will be a fast, five minute run-through, just to show you the layout and a few hidden surprises and features. Then I'll get out of your way, and you can wander and inspect things for yourself."

Unescorted buyers should be armed with a fact sheet. This is a big help, because they can see the exact dimensions of the master bedroom and mentally "see" if their bed and furniture will fit comfortably. The fact sheet is also packed with comments about features such as "oak floor beneath carpeting" that help the buyers learn about invisible or less visible features. (To review information about fact sheets, see Chapter 8.)

The Tour Agenda

If you decide to guide the tour, you should begin the tour in your best room or area. This gives the buyer a strong first impression of your home. Your best area may be your yard, complete with lush landscaping and a beautiful pool. Or your best spot may be your high-tech kitchen. If you have talked with the buyers previously on the telephone, you may know what turns them on. If they told you on the phone that they were especially interested in your large family room or big basement or workshop or library, then show that area first. The tour agenda can be customized for different buyers. Try to start with your "best" spot, and finish with your second best area.

You should rehearse your tour. That's right—I said you should practice your tour. Try it out on your family or friends. Concentrate on the hidden features of each room. If need be, hang a tag on certain items, or tape an index card on the door, just as we discussed in the earlier section on holding an Open House. Suppose you were going to show your second bedroom. Your index card may contain several memory joggers such as: 256 cubic feet of storage in closet; 3-speed ceiling fan w/ 7 year warranty; oak hardwood floor; five electrical outlets; special storm windows.

Suppose you can't remember all these things about the room. So what?! When you show bedroom #2 to a prospective buyer, handle things this way: "I don't know much about giving a sales pitch, Mr. and Mrs. Bishop, but I do know a lot about the house we have lived in for five years. I jotted down a few reminders on this index card so I will not forget to tell you about some nice features here. There is a beautiful hardwood floor under this carpet. We put the carpet in for the baby to crawl on. It's nice to know you folks could have it either way, isn't it?" After you have rehearsed a few times, you'll be confident and ready to work with prospective buyers.

Sizing Up Buyer Needs

Plan to have two adults home when you are going to show your home. There is more safety in numbers. When your prospective buyers arrive, one of you should greet them at the front door, and usher them inside. Smile and be cordial. Introduce yourself, and then your spouse. "Mr. and Mrs. Crooms, I'd like you to meet my wife, Krystal." After introductions, get the conversation started. "Krystal and I sure are going to miss this house. We have lived here for six years. We love our house and we love our neighborhood, but our new baby has precipitated a search for a bigger house." (You have volunteered some personal information, and told them your motive for selling; now it is their turn. You have two good leading questions.) "Do you live in this neighborhood, Mr. and Mrs. Crooms?" What you hope to do by asking the right questions is to learn the housing needs of the buyers; which attributes are important to them (good schools for the kids? proximity to work? a big family room?), and how soon the buyers must find a new residence. Follow-up questions can help you. "How old are your children? Are they in school? Which one? Is it a good school?" (That last one is really loaded, and will give you a chance to *listen* to the buyer. A passionate response should tell you that schools *are* one important attribute the buyers are seeking. You can stress how good your Milton Friedman school district is, and tell them about some innovative programs that are offered. If they do not live in the neighborhood, ask "I'm curious, Mr. and Mrs. Crooms, what factors led you to pick our neighborhood to buy a home in?" Listen carefully! They may mention anything: mature trees, good schools, rapid appreciation, close to work, good shopping, nice parks, big lots, lots of kids to play with theirs, etc. They are telling you what benefits are important. Make a mental note, and emphasize how your home and neighborhood supply those benefits to fit their needs. This introductory conversation should be relaxed, yet purposeful.

Keep your talk very brief. Remember, put yourself in the buyers' shoes. Their house-hunting search can be exciting or dull, exhilarating or disappointing. They are on an emotional roller coaster. (So are you, the seller!) Be upbeat and enthusiastic about your home and your neighborhood. It is contagious. The buyers are anxious to see your home, so get them started soon after they enter your home.

Hold Your Tongue

If you have decided to accompany the prospective buyers while they inspect your home, you must control your natural impulse to speak. You must give your home a chance to speak for itself. It will do most of the talking; you must be comfortable with the silence. The buyers are seeing your living room for the first time. Their imaginations are running wild. She wonders how to arrange *their* furniture in *your* living room. He can see a great housewarming party taking place in this room. Family, friends and associates from work will all be here, congratulating me on a good buy. You must shut up! If you blather on, you break their vivid imagery. Watch their eyes to see how involved they are. Some pros claim they watch the size of the pupils. Watch their lips for a hint of a smile or expression of satisfaction. Watch their body language when they turn to face you. They are saying "my mind is finished imagining" or "I've seen enough." Your talk should be aimed at one objective: calling the buyer's attention to a feature they may have missed. Let me remind you again—do not overtalk!

Space, Pace, and Touching

Another type of behavior to avoid is encroaching on another's physical space. Don't crowd people, and do not stand around them. You will make them feel uneasy and hurried. Don't even *enter* a small room with prospects, just remain in the doorway so you do not make a small room seem even smaller.

Let the prospective buyers set the pace of the tour. If the buyers do not like your home, they will move through it at a fast pace. If the buyers are interested in your home, they will move at a slower pace, lingering here, pausing there.

Buyers may be reluctant to touch *your* things while you are escorting them. You must figure out some way to get them to physically interact with the home. Sometimes suggestions and commands can be helpful. Try using action verbs and commands. "Open that closet door. There are 256 cubic feet of space in there." "Feel this fine workmanship on these custom-built cabinets." "Let me show you how to operate the attic fan."

Objections Are Good Signs

While you are touring, buyers may voice objections. That is a good sign, because they are seriously involved in considering your home and its attributes. Do not argue with a prospect; you may win the argument but you almost never win a sale. Be cordial, and agree with the buyer. You can address the thrust of the objection in a tactful way. "Yes, this closet is small. We're lucky we have a total of six closets in the house, and lots of storage space in the basement, attic, and garage." "You're right, the highway is pretty noisy, especially right now during rush hour. It quiets down after dinner. It's one of the trade-offs for the fantastic convenience it offers us when we go to work, school, or shopping." (Here you have agreed with their objection, qualified it somewhat, and then countered the objection with a positive benefit such as convenient access.) In every short conversation you have, try to mention the best benefits of your home and neighborhood. You are selling lifestyle, and your home is part of the bundle of attributes.

Are the Buyers Getting Warm?

During the tour, the buyers may give you some verbal or physical cues to evidence their interest in your home. If you are having trouble reading their interest level, there are a few questions you can ask to take their pulse. After you have shown the home, ask them "would you like to go outside and examine the backyard?" (you can substitute "garage," "attic," or "basement" for backyard when appropriate.) Hot buyers and those who are getting warm will say yes. The mere lookers have probably seen enough.

Another way to determine their interest level is to say "would you like me to leave you two alone for awhile, so that you can talk?" An alternative approach is this question: "did we go too fast? Is there something you'd like to see again?"

IF THEY SEEM INTERESTED

Suppose the buyers have completed the tour and show continued interest in your home. Then what?! Ask them "would you like me to share some information with you about our utility bills or our warranties or inspections?"

When the buyers say yes, it is time to move to your best or most pleasing room. (That could be your den with a fireplace, or it might be your attractive kitchen.) Simply say to the buyers "come with me, I have those materials in the den." Seat them in the best chairs with the scenic view, and offer them something to drink. Be relaxed. Don't be pushy or try to oversell. Stick closely to the business at hand—remember, you are trying to sell your house, you are not trying to make new friends at a church social function.

IF THEY ARE NOT INTERESTED—GET FEEDBACK

If the buyers have no further interest in your home, be cordial and thank them for visiting and say something empathetic like "We know how hard it can be to find the house that is just right for you. It took us three months to find our first (or next, or this) home. You never seem to find 100% of perfection, but you'll find something that is close. Was there something in particular that worried you or turned you off about this house?" This gives you a chance to get some feedback about your home. Buyers may object to location, room size, only one bathroom, price, condition of the home, or a number of things. If the objection cannot be overcome, continue to remain cordial, give them a fact sheet and ask them to pass it on to one of their friends who may be house hunting.

Other Sales Tools

You should maintain seven (7) files to assist you in the marketing process. I suggest you get the big folders with pockets, and color code them or label them conspicuously. File number one would be labelled "Home Info." In this file, put your previous twelve months' utility bills. If each utility company does not furnish you a cumulative list, you should construct one, so the buyers can see at a glance your trends and averages. (You may wish to create the form for your own use.) If the buyers wish to verify the numbers on your utility payment record sheet, your bills should be arranged in separate envelopes for the buyer's perusal.

This file should also contain a copy of any inspection reports you have. You should have a termite inspection done by a professional exterminator, and get a certificate showing that your home is free from visible termite infestation and also damage. If you have also had the house treated or sprayed for other bugs and pests, include your receipt in the folder. Perhaps you have a continuing service with an exterminator who visits regularly. Display your paperwork, it will impress the buyers, especially the females who tend to hate insects and bugs more vehemently than males. You can have your home inspected by professional services that inspect the electrical, mechanical, plumbing, and structural components of your home. These are most impressive and reassuring to the buyers, because they are not experts in these matters and worry about buying a home that needs a new furnace two months after closing/settlement. These inspections are reasonable in cost, and well worth the price. To find a local inspector, ask a lender or try the yellow pages under "Home Inspection Services." Some services will sell you a one-year maintenance agreement covering your electrical, mechanical, and plumbing components. Buyers really love that!

If your home is newish, it may be protected by a builder's warranty, or the major components (such as your heating and cooling system) may still be under warranty protection. If appropriate, include these documents in the file. Any blueprints or floor plans you have are helpful, as is a survey of your property. If you can't find your survey, your lender or title insurance company will probably send you a copy. Your property tax bills should also be in this file.

File number two could be labelled "Neighborhood." You should photocopy a local map, enlarging your area and neighborhood. On this blown-up map, you can clearly mark points of interest, such as the local schools, parks, grocery stores, shopping malls, hospitals, police and fire stations, public transportation, etc. Don't forget to circle or star your home on the map.

You can also include in this file any handouts you can get from the school district, the bus and transit system, local chamber of commerce, and other civic groups that promote your area. Buyers who are strangers to your neighborhood appreciate this input.

File number three is the "Financing" file. We have discussed this topic in great detail in Chapter 12. File number four should be your "Fact sheet" file. Five number five is the "Appraisal" file. As mentioned previously in Chapter 12, the appraisal of your home by an independent expert adds credibility to your asking price. It also helps reassure buyers that the home will appraise properly when they go through the loan application process. A formal, written appraisal is one of the most dramatic and effective sales tools that a FISBO seller can use. I highly recommend that every FISBO seller strongly consider getting one.

File number six should be labelled "Personal Property" and contain a list of all the personal property items that you may consider transferring to a purchaser. You should list each item and briefly describe its features and any warranties. Include original sales price information and any repair history. When you start seriously negotiating with a buyer, these personal property items may be useful bargaining chips. (Review personal property again on page 45.)

File number seven is your "Legal" file, and you should have blank binders, contract-to-purchase forms, and anything else your attorney recommends.

Using These Files

Now that you have an interested prospect sitting with you, you can proceed to go over the information in files one through four (home, neighborhood, financing, and fact sheet.) These first four files are what I call "Post-Tour

Sales Talk" files, whereas the final three files (appraisal, personal property, and legal) are "Negotiating" files. Present all the material in files one through four, and then pause and relax for a moment. The buyers may make the first move, and ask "would you drop your price by $2,000?" Or the buyers may say nothing, and expect you to take charge. You can take charge by saying "Well, Mr. and Mrs. Buyer, where do we go from here? Do you want to make an offer to buy this house?" As soon as one party mentions price or making an offer, negotiations have begun. Sometimes buyers want to talk price and negotiate while you are still in the process of showing and touring. What should you do? Stay cool, and be upbeat. Answer this way: "We will consider any written offer with our attorney. There are other details besides price we must have in writing, such as an earnest-money deposit, downpayment, what type of financing you will get, closing date, and other contingencies." You can call their bluff or see their serious intent with one simple phrase: "let's go in the den right now and you can fill out a written offer."

18
Understanding the Buyer's Financing: A Review for FISBO Sellers

If you are a FISBO seller you must "qualify" your prospective buyers. This means that you must assess the financial position of your prospects to determine if they can realistically expect to be approved by a lender to get a home loan in the amount necessary to buy your home. You don't want to waste valuable time negotiating with someone who will never make it to the closing table, nor do you want to take your home off the market and lose valuable selling time because you signed a contract with a buyer who has no hope of getting the right loan.

How do you as a seller qualify a prospect? Whenever a prospect evidences a serious interest in your home (perhaps during or after a showing) you should qualify the prospect before you do any negotiating. Some sellers are a little squeamish about digging for financial information from the prospective buyers. Try these approaches. "Have you talked with any lenders yet about getting a mortgage and home loan?" "Are you selling your own home now, or do you rent?" "Before we even talk about possible negotiations, we better be sure we're on the right path. Have you thought about what size downpayment you could afford?" These words will turn the discussion to the topic of the buyer's finances. You can show them your prepared information on what monthly payments would be for several types of loans that are most likely to be used. (FHA? Conventional loan with 10% or 20% down?) If you are dealing with first-time buyers, you can ask "do you know how lenders figure out how much of a loan you can get?" Prospects who are currently homeowners are probably aware of loan qualification procedures, but you need to check. "Let's be sure we all understand what it would take financially to buy this home. You should have a monthly gross income of $XYZ . . ." Another good phrase is "If you buy this house or another like it in the same price range, how do you plan to finance it?"

You do not have to have the knowledge of a loan closer, but you need to understand the basics of qualifying and the various financing alternatives your buyer might seek. All you need to do is to be sure that your prospective buyer is in the right ballpark financially. Your attorney and the lenders can take it from there. Now is a good time to review the basics, so you can help nudge interested buyers towards a contract.

Conventional Loans

As the word suggests, "conventional" loans are normal, everyday home loans. A conventional loan is not a government-insured loan (FHA), nor a government-guaranteed loan (VA). For conventional loans, the lender's only security is the property; therefore, the lender will usually require a 20% or 25% downpayment. This sizeable initial investment by the buyer minimizes the risk for lenders.

QUALIFYING RATIOS

To qualify for a conventional loan, the borrower/buyer must meet two criteria: 1) monthly housing expenses (including principal, interest, taxes, and insurance) cannot exceed 25% to 28% (depending on your area) of the borrower/buyer's monthly gross income; and 2) the borrower/buyer's long-term debt cannot exceed 33% to 36% of monthly gross income (including housing costs). Long-term debts are more than six months in length (auto loans, student loans, and the like). These guidelines are slightly flexible, as each loan applicant is considered individually by each lender.

Insured Conventional Loans

There is a type of conventional loan that features a lower downpayment, called the insured conventional loan. A private insurer guarantees the lender that the top 20 percent of the loan will be repaid in the event of a default by the borrower. The private insurer sells the borrower Private Mortgage Insurance, known as PMI.

Private Mortgage Insurance

PMI is not a new concept but is often confused with other forms of mortgage protection. Mortgage-credit life insurance insures the borrower that if he dies, his mortgage will be paid off. Mortgage accident or health insurance insures the borrower that if he is unable to work because of disability, his mortgage payments will be made for some contractual period. These forms of protection insure the borrower/buyer, whereas PMI insures the lender against loan default.

PMI makes everyone happy. The lending institution is happy because the private insurer has guaranteed the top 20 percent, which is the risky part of the loan. The bottom, or remaining 80 percent of the loan is usually safely secured by the property itself. The buyer is happy, because his initial costs are reduced! Instead of a 20 percent downpayment, the buyer may only need 5 percent, for example. (A 20 percent downpayment on an $80,000 home is $16,000. But a 5 percent downpayment is only $4,000! That saves the buyer $12,000 in cash that would be due at closing.) And of course the private insurer is happy, because he's making money by charging a fee for his service.

TYPICAL PMI COSTS

There are about a dozen major providers of PMI, and their fees naturally vary somewhat with risk factors such as percent of downpayment, age of property, strength of borrower, etc. Here are some pricing guidelines for you. Expect to pay an initial fee of ½% to 1% of the loan. In succeeding years, the normal renewal fee is ¼%. These numbers are a pleasant surprise compared to what you pay for government insurance (MIP) on FHA loans. (Currently FHA charges 3.8% due at closing in one lump sum.)

QUALIFYING FOR PMI

Buyers (as well as real estate salespersons) need to understand that both the property and the borrower must qualify for PMI. PMI qualifying criteria are generally more stringent than FHA criteria, but are in line with conventional mortgage lenders. Current qualification guidelines require that total housing expenses not exceed 25% to 28% of the borrower's gross income, and total fixed payments (debt) cannot exceed 33% to 36% of gross income.

HOW LONG DOES A BUYER PAY PREMIUMS?

Each lender will set his own rules about how long a borrower must carry PMI. Most lenders will allow cancellation of PMI when the loan balance drops below 80% of the purchase price. Some lenders believe that a seven-year term provides adequate protection.

FHA Loans Are Attractive

Several features of the FHA loan make it attractive to borrowers. First, FHA loans require low downpayments; for owner-occupied property is is 5% or less! (Investor properties require 15% down.) Second, FHA loans made before December 1, 1986 can be assumed at their original interest rate and term without any restrictions on the buyer. This can be important when you sell your home. A prospective purchaser can assume your loan at its original interest rate (say 9%), when market rates have climbed to 11%. This makes your home more desirable than its competitors. However, there are some restrictions on FHA loans made between December 1, 1986 and December

14, 1989. FHA loans on owner-occupied properties can be assumed without the new borrower qualifying, provided the FHA loan is more than one year old. If the loan is less than one year old, the new borrower must qualify. (For investor-owned properties, loans that are more than two years old are fully assumable without qualification.) Lenders may charge the new borrower a very small assumption fee. A buyer who wants to assume an FHA loan made after December 14, 1989 must be credit-worthy. A third advantage of FHA loans is that they contain no prepayment penalties. The borrower can prepay additional principal amounts, or pay off the entire principal balance without incurring any fees.

LIMITATIONS OF FHA LOANS

You may be wondering why everybody doesn't have an FHA loan. FHA loans do have some limitations or disadvantages. The major limitation of the FHA loan is that maximum loan amounts are set for different regions. These maximum amounts are set at levels that cover "modestly" priced housing. Some areas have lots of modestly priced homes for sale, other areas have few.

These maximum loan amounts do vary from region to region. To find out the current limits for your area, phone a local lender of your FHA office. (FHA is part of the Department of Housing and Urban Development (HUD), and may be listed in your phone book under HUD.)

The property itself must also qualify. Properties that are structurally damaged or below building code specifications must be repaired and corrected prior to loan approval.

FHA-REQUIRED REPAIRS

Before the loan is finalized, an FHA inspector visits the house and appraises its condition. A list of things that need repairs or improvements is made. FHA standards are the measuring stick. The requirements must be met in order for the loan to be approved.

Who pays for these requirements? The basic answer is that you must look to the provisions of your contract for sale. Most contracts state a maximum dollar amount that both the buyer and seller are willing to pay.

What happens when the requirements will cost more than the contracting parties agreed to be responsible for? If this happened, either party could cancel the entire deal, or both parties could arrive at a new supplementary agreement to the contract, fixing responsibility for these costs in a new manner.

Contracts sometimes are written in a manner providing for low maximum amounts for the parties to pay for requirements. Why? First, it gives either party an out, if they want it. Second, some real estate salespeople do not want to argue with the parties until a later date. At this later date, both parties have psychologically committed themselves to the sale and purchase of "their home." They'll grumble, but almost always go through with the deal.

To beat this mind-game, a seller may have an FHA appraisal done ahead of time, before he puts his home on the market. This must be done through a lender, who will then tell the seller that if a qualified buyer is found in 60 or 90 days and the requirements are met, the lender will finance the deal based on the appraised value.

MORTGAGE INSURANCE PREMIUM

The FHA insures loans. So, where do they get the pool of reserve funds to pay out in case a borrower defaults? The FHA collects insurance premiums from borrowers. Prior to September of 1983, borrowers paid their insurance premiums in small chunks as part of their monthly payments. The annual insurance premium was about one half of one percent of the principal balance. Should a buyer assume an FHA loan that was made prior to September of 1983, the monthly payments will include the insurance premium.

FHA loans made after September 1, 1983, require payments of a lump-sum mortgage insurance premium (MIP) that is payable by the borrower at closing. As of early 1991, this up front payment is equal to 3.8% of the loan on a mortgage of 25 years or more. (For 20 year loans it is 3% and for 15 year loans it is 2.4%.) For example, on a 30-year FHA loan of $101,250, the MIP would be $3,847.50, due at closing.

As of July 1, 1991, FHA borrowers will also pay (in addition to the MIP) a yearly premium of 0.5% of the loan amount. This annual premium will be paid by the borrower for a period of five to ten years, depending upon the size of the borrower's downpayment. If these additional premiums put the troubled FHA Mutual Mortgage Insurance Fund (the pool of reserve funds) on sound financial footing, then FHA plans to lower the upfront lump sum MIP payment in 1993 and 1994 from 3.8% to 3%. After October 1, 1994, plans call for dropping the MIP to 2.25%.

Few borrowers realize that when they pay off their FHA loan, they may be entitled to a refund of part of their insurance premiums. This amount will depend on actual defaults on loans within the pool of mortgages to which the borrower's loan was assigned. Ask parents or friends who have paid off a previous FHA loan if they received an insurance refund. They may wish to contact their lender or HUD/FHA Distributive Funds to check this out.

FHA QUALIFICATION RATIOS

Qualifying for an FHA loan is a bit different from qualifying for a conventional loan. The major difference is that whereas gross income figures are used for conventional loans, net income is used for FHA qualification. There are two basic FHA qualification rules.

1) Total housing expenses cannot be more than 38 percent of net income. For purposes of calculation, housing expenses include: total proposed mort-

gage payments, including principal, interest, taxes, and insurance; utilities; and maintenance expenses. Net income is gross income minus federal income tax.

2) Total fixed payments cannot be more than 53 percent of net income. Total fixed payments include total housing expenses; alimony and child support payments; state and local tax obligations; social security/retirement obligations; and long-term debt, such as auto, boat, or student loans.

DOWNPAYMENT NEEDED

The required downpayment fluctuates with the loan amount you desire. If the appraised value of the home is below $50,000, the downpayment is 3% of the appraised value, plus 5 percent of the amount above $25,000. For homes valued above $50,000, the downpayment is generally 5%.

CLOSING COSTS

FHA determines the closing costs, sets the fees and publishes them in a schedule. FHA does this to prevent lenders from padding their costs with extras or additional fees for the buyer.

Items typically included in the scheduled closing costs are the title insurance, loan origination fee, abstracting and recording fees, escrow fees, and credit report fees.

Each FHA office has its own allowable closing cost schedule, and costs vary from region to region due to different supply and demand factors. To be sure of current costs in your area, phone a local lender or FHA.

VA or GI Loans

Veterans who meet eligibility standards may seek a VA loan. The Veterans Administration (VA) loan is backed by a government guarantee to the lender to honor your note should you default. Some people refer to the VA loan as a "GI home loan."

ADVANTAGES OF THE VA LOAN

The downpayment is a matter for the lender and the GI buyer to negotiate. It may be zero! Loan closing costs, including the prepaid escrow items, may be paid in whole or in part by the seller. The GI could conceivably move in virtually free! Lenders, as a practice, will negotiate some minimum downpayment, as they feel it is desirable for the buyers to have something at stake.

VA QUALIFYING

Qualifying for a VA loan is not as precise as qualifying for an FHA or conventional loan. Remember, the purpose of the Veterans Administration is to help the veteran and his or her family. Criteria include past financial and credit management, cash reserves to handle emergencies, as well as sufficient income to meet monthly payments and expenses.

The maximum VA loan amount a buyer can get is reviewed periodically, but tends to be in the same range as the FHA limit. Interested parties can call the local VA or a mortgage lender. The property will be appraised, and the VA will issue a certificate of reasonable value (CRV). In some areas, an FHA appraisal may be substituted for the CRV.

From the seller's perspective, your home may be priced in the range that attracts buyers who are likely to utilize FHA or VA financing. These types of loans make it easier for prospective buyers to afford your home. On the negative side, there is more paperwork involved, as well as more parties. This usually means loan approval takes more time than conventional loans. Another problem area might be the inspection and any required repairs.

Adjustable-Rate Mortgages

The adjustable-rate mortgage (ARM) is a generic name that describes a variety of loans that feature interest rate adjustments (and therefore monthly payment adjustments) in contractually specified amounts and intervals. Unlike a fixed-rate mortgage (FRM), the borrower's mortgage interest rate fluctuates as general interest rates fluctuate. Interest rates are a function of supply and demand factors and inflation. Generally, as inflation rises, so do interest rates. The reverse is also generally true.

The ARM was developed to cope with the inflation of the late 1970s and 1980s, and the corresponding volatility of interest rates. Thrift institutions had been bearing the lion's share of the risk of inflation, due to the nature of their business. Thrifts held long-term assets (mortgages) that yielded fixed returns that were being eroded in terms of decreased purchasing power caused by inflation. ARMs are designed to shift the risk of inflation from the lender to the borrower. Lenders like that!

ADVANTAGES OF ARMS

What features of the ARM attract borrowers? First, ARMs offer lower initial interest rates than fixed-rate mortgages (FRMs). How much lower? Typically, about 150 basis points, or interest rates that are 1.5% less than FRMs.

The second advantage of ARMs is that the lower initial interest rates lead to smaller monthly payments, thereby making it easier for more borrowers to qualify for loans. It should come as no surprise that ARMs tend to be more popular with borrowers as interest rates rise. Ease of qualification explains much of this correlation.

A third feature of ARMs that borrowers find advantageous is that virtually all ARMs are assumable and have little or no prepayment penalties.

This can be important to borrowers when they face the prospect of selling their home in the future. Almost all FRMs are not assumable.

If interest rates do drop, it is possible that the borrower's monthly payments will be lowered, thus another advantage of ARMs. Contrast that possibility with monthly payments for FRMs which do not change. Of course, if interest rates rise, ARMs borrowers will have higher monthly payments, while FRM borrowers do NOT.

A fifth advantage of ARMs is that recent regulations give increased protection to ARM borrowers. Also, the development of convertible ARMs which allow the borrower to convert his ARM to an FRM is perceived by consumers as a desirable feature.

It is not within the scope of this book to explain the complexities of ARMs. If you need a good primer, a book such as *How to Buy a Home While You Can Still Afford To* (by Michael C. Murphy, Sterling Publishing Co.) will help a lot.

Assumption of Existing Loan

Assuming your existing loan may be a financing possibility that the buyer should explore, especially if your loan is a low-interest-rate loan that can be assumed without the buyer qualifying via the normal test ratios for income and debt.

Understand that whether or not a loan can be assumed is to be judged by the terms of the original loan. To find out this information, you have to phone the lender. The lender will tell you if the loan may be assumed and what the policy is on assumption. Is the interest rate the same, or can the lender adjust it? Is there a fee for this assumption or loan transfer? Must the buyer "qualify" and meet certain requirements of the lender? Does the lender require the buyer to have enough money to pay the owner without additional loans being incurred? The only way to find out all the answers is to ask the lender.

We have noted earlier that FHA and VA loans typically have few or no restrictions on assumptions. Virtually all conventional loans made since the mid-1970s *cannot* be assumed, because the loan agreement specifies that the outstanding loan balance is "due-on-sale." On the other hand, many of the recent Adjustable-Rate Mortgages (ARMs) may be assumed, but the new borrower must qualify. The most attractive assumption situations for buyers involve owners with low equity in the home, or owners who will take a note and finance the equity via an owner-carry second mortgage.

A seller/owner should be aware of some potential problems when a buyer assumes the existing mortgage. What happens if the buyer defaults on his loan payments? The lender may foreclose, and sell the property. If the sale price does not produce enough money to pay off the loan balance, the interest that is in arrears, and all the foreclosure costs and attorneys' fees, then the note holder can sue *you*, the original maker of the note for any deficiency amount.

Another disturbing development in recent years is the fraudulent practice known as "equity skimming." The typical con job works this way: a buyer offers to assume your non-qualifying FHA or VA loan, and gives you little or no cash for your equity (or promises to pay you for your equity at a later date.) The market is soft or depressed in your area, so you agree. The buyer takes possession at closing, and then never makes any payments to the lender. In most states, it will take six to nine months to get the non-paying buyer out of the property. (You better hope they haven't trashed the place!) A slicker variation of the game has the buyer not living in the house, but renting it to someone else. The assuming buyer collects rent every month, but never makes any of the mortgage loan payments he promised to. Guess where that leaves you? You guessed it—still liable on the original note you signed.

The moral of the story: try to get as much money down as you can in assumptions, and investigate the background of the buyer as thoroughly as possible. Check on the status of the original loan periodically, as well as the condition of your house.

Equity Sharing

Potential homebuyers who do not have enough money to make the necessary downpayment and/or lack the earnings capacity to meet the monthly payments may ask a third party for help.

This third-party investor could pay some or all of the initial costs as well as the monthly expenses. In return for this financial aid, the investor will share in some percentage of the equity and appreciation. The investor normally is the co-owner of the home, and his or her name may also appear on the mortgage and note held by the lender. Tax advantages similar to those for landlords flow to the investor.

Who are some investors likely to help the buyer out? Why not ask the buyer to approach his parents or relatives with a sound financial proposal that benefits both him and them?

I recommend that two clauses be inserted in any partnership agreement with the investor: 1) a clause that states that the resident/partner(s) must sell or refinance the loan before "x" years (3–5 years?); and 2) a clause that gives the resident/partner(s) the preemptive right to buy out the investor/partner(s) before the date requiring refinancing.

Shared Appreciation Mortgages

Private lenders have received good response to programs that offer homebuyers a significantly reduced interest rate in return for a share in the future appreciation of the home.

Suppose your buyer makes $22,000 a year, has $10,000 to put down on a

BIROS
REALTORS

9501 SOUTH HAMLIN AVENUE • EVERGREEN PARK, ILLINOIS 60642 • (312) 422-0011

BUYER QUALIFICATION FORM

NAME _____   NAME _____

ADDRESS _____   ADDRESS (IF DIFFERENT) _____

HOME PHONE _____   HOME PHONE (IF DIFFERENT) ____

AGE _____   AGE _____

EMPLOYER _____   EMPLOYER _____

BUSINESS PHONE _____   BUSINESS PHONE _____

POSITION _____   POSITION _____

LENGTH OF SERVICE _____   LENGTH OF SERVICE _____

ANNUAL INCOME _____   ANNUAL INCOME _____

OTHER INCOME _____   OTHER INCOME _____

BANKING-Checking_____

       Savings_____ Balance_____

AUTO LOAN_____ Months Remaining_____

OUTSTANDING DEBTS (over $500.00) _____

_____

_____

NUMBER OF DEPENDANTS_____ ALIMONY AND/OR CHILD SUPPORT_____

PREVIOUSLY FILED BANKRUPTCY _____(YEAR)

VETERAN_____._____

$60,000 home, and current interest rates are 15%. Monthly payments on a $50,000 loan for thirty years at 15% would be $632. Your buyer would need a gross income of $2,528 a month (or $30,336 a year) to qualify for such a loan. Since the buyer only makes $22,000 a year, he can't qualify!

What if a lender were to give him a 10% interest rate (a full third less) if he in turn promises the lender one-third of the future appreciation of the home? Sound good? Let's check the arithmetic. At 10% a $50,000 loan requires monthly payments of $439, and a monthly gross income of $1,756 ($21,072 a year) to qualify. So, his monthly payments would be almost $200 lower, and he could qualify with $9,000 less in salary.

Is the trade-off worth it? That's the buyer's decision. Considering our above example, I'd say it's better to have two-thirds of something than all of nothing!

Special Low-Interest Loans

Many cities and counties sponsor low-interest-rate home loan programs. Where does the money come from? It is raised by the sale of tax-exempt revenue bonds. Let's suppose that the interest rate on these bonds is 8½%, compared to the 15% prevailing in the market. This tax-free status induces investors to buy the bonds, borrower/buyers get cheap rates, and politicians becomes heroes.

How does a buyer get this cheap money? Check with your Housing Authority area office and ask if they have such a program, or are planning one. Now, let me scare you—the demand for these loans is incredible! A buyer must be persistent and well-informed.

Is it worth the effort? Consider this: A $50,000 loan for thirty years at 15% means $632 in monthly payments on the principal and interest. But at, say 8½%, monthly payments would be $384.

Lease with an Option to Purchase

Sometimes sellers encounter depressed markets and near impossible conditions for selling their homes. If the seller can wait out the downturn in the real estate cycle without taking a big bath financially, it may be wise to consider a lease arrangement with the option to purchase. A seller may rent the home to interested prospective buyers for a specified period (12 to 18 months, for example), and give the prospective buyer the option to purchase the home on or before a certain date. Obviously the seller will not be turning his equity into cash just yet. (Although he may borrow against it.) The seller/owner retains title, and the renters/buyers get more time to save money, get another job, line up financing, and hope for lower interest rates.

CONTRACTUAL CONSIDERATIONS

Let's talk about some practical considerations. First, how much should the rent be? Obviously, the owner must cover the mortgage payments and upkeep expenses. A guideline that is still valid in many areas is that monthly rent should be 1 percent of the market value of the home. For example, a $50,000 home should rent for $500. Also, because the owner may not be too keen on the idea initially, the buyer may have to offer a premium rental amount or a large option fee.

Second, an option offer or contract must be supported by consideration to be legally valid. A buyer may have to pay some option money to the seller, if the option agreement is separate from the rental agreement. Will this option money apply to an eventual purchase? Not unless your contract says so!

Third, decide on a purchase price in the option agreement that would allow the renter to buy. I suggest a clause calling for an independent appraisal by a professional selected by both parties be included in the contract. This could be important because a buyer's ability to get maximum financing on the home will depend upon the lender's appraised value, as well as his earnings capacity.

A situation could develop where the seller insists on $55,000 for the home, but the lender's appraisal is only $50,000. If the lender will loan the buyer a maximum of 90 percent of appraised value, his maximum loan will be $45,000. This means he needs $10,000 down, not just $5,000! That could put an end to your deal.

Be sure to utilize the skills of professionals when drafting a lease-purchase option agreement.

Monthly Mortgage Payment

The following tables show you the monthly payments necessary to amortize (or fully pay) a given loan amount at a given interest rate, for a period of years. The monthly payment is one sum that includes repayment on the principal loan amount, plus interest payment.

Let's work an example together. If you borrow $30,000 at 14 percent for thirty years, what will your monthly payments be?

Look at the following pages, and find 14 percent. Then locate the loan amount—$30,000. The corresponding figure under the thirty-year column is $355.46. That $355.46 is your monthly payment on principal and interest to the lender. These tables do not include monthly charges for taxes and insurance; you learned how to calculate these in the Financing chapters.

O.K., let's try one more, to be *sure* you know how to use these tables. What are the monthly payments for a $43,550 loan at 13 percent for thirty years? First, locate the 13 percent page and thirty-year column.

(1) Find the monthly payment for $40,000	=	$442.48
(2) Find the monthly payment for $3,000	=	33.19
(3) Find the monthly payment for $500	=	5.53
(4) Find the monthly payment for $50	=	.55
(5) Total		$481.75

Get the idea? If not, go over it again!

YEARLY INTEREST RATE = 8.00%

LOAN LIFE IN YEARS

PRINCIPAL	10	15	20	25	30
			MONTHLY PAYMENTS		
$ 25.00	$ .30	$ .24	$ .21	$ .19	$ .18
$ 50.00	$ .61	$ .48	$ .42	$ .39	$ .37
$ 100.00	$ 1.21	$ .96	$ .84	$ .77	$ .73
$ 200.00	$ 2.43	$ 1.91	$ 1.67	$ 1.54	$ 1.47
$ 300.00	$ 3.64	$ 2.87	$ 2.51	$ 2.32	$ 2.20
$ 400.00	$ 4.85	$ 3.82	$ 3.35	$ 3.09	$ 2.94
$ 500.00	$ 6.07	$ 4.78	$ 4.18	$ 3.86	$ 3.67
$ 1000.00	$ 12.13	$ 9.56	$ 8.36	$ 7.72	$ 7.34
$ 2000.00	$ 24.27	$ 19.11	$ 16.73	$ 15.44	$ 14.68
$ 3000.00	$ 36.40	$ 28.67	$ 25.09	$ 23.15	$ 22.01
$ 4000.00	$ 48.53	$ 38.23	$ 33.46	$ 30.87	$ 29.35
$ 5000.00	$ 60.66	$ 47.78	$ 41.82	$ 38.59	$ 36.69
$ 10000.00	$ 121.33	$ 95.57	$ 83.64	$ 77.18	$ 73.38
$ 15000.00	$ 181.99	$ 143.35	$ 125.47	$ 115.77	$ 110.06
$ 20000.00	$ 242.66	$ 191.13	$ 167.29	$ 154.36	$ 146.75
$ 25000.00	$ 303.32	$ 238.91	$ 209.11	$ 192.95	$ 183.44
$ 30000.00	$ 363.98	$ 286.70	$ 250.93	$ 231.54	$ 220.13
$ 35000.00	$ 424.65	$ 334.48	$ 292.75	$ 270.14	$ 256.82
$ 40000.00	$ 485.31	$ 382.26	$ 334.58	$ 308.73	$ 293.51
$ 45000.00	$ 545.97	$ 430.04	$ 376.40	$ 347.32	$ 330.19
$ 50000.00	$ 606.64	$ 477.83	$ 418.22	$ 385.91	$ 366.88
$ 55000.00	$ 667.30	$ 525.61	$ 460.04	$ 424.50	$ 403.57
$ 60000.00	$ 727.97	$ 573.39	$ 501.86	$ 463.09	$ 440.26
$ 65000.00	$ 788.63	$ 621.17	$ 543.69	$ 501.68	$ 476.95
$ 70000.00	$ 849.29	$ 668.96	$ 585.51	$ 540.27	$ 513.64
$ 75000.00	$ 909.96	$ 716.74	$ 627.33	$ 578.86	$ 550.32
$ 80000.00	$ 970.62	$ 764.52	$ 669.15	$ 617.45	$ 587.01
$ 85000.00	$1031.28	$ 812.30	$ 710.97	$ 656.04	$ 623.70
$ 90000.00	$1091.95	$ 860.09	$ 752.80	$ 694.63	$ 660.39
$ 95000.00	$1152.61	$ 907.87	$ 794.62	$ 733.23	$ 697.08
$100000.00	$1213.28	$ 955.65	$ 836.44	$ 771.82	$ 733.76
$125000.00	$1516.59	$1194.56	$1045.55	$ 964.77	$ 917.21
$150000.00	$1819.91	$1433.48	$1254.66	$1157.72	$1100.65

YEARLY INTEREST RATE = 8.25%

LOAN LIFE IN YEARS

PRINCIPAL	10	15	20	25	30
			MONTHLY PAYMENTS		
$ 25.00	$ .31	$ .24	$ .21	$ .20	$ .19
$ 50.00	$ .61	$ .49	$ .43	$ .39	$ .38
$ 100.00	$ 1.23	$ .97	$ .85	$ .79	$ .75
$ 200.00	$ 2.45	$ 1.94	$ 1.70	$ 1.58	$ 1.50
$ 300.00	$ 3.68	$ 2.91	$ 2.56	$ 2.37	$ 2.25
$ 400.00	$ 4.91	$ 3.88	$ 3.41	$ 3.15	$ 3.01
$ 500.00	$ 6.13	$ 4.85	$ 4.26	$ 3.94	$ 3.76
$ 1000.00	$ 12.27	$ 9.70	$ 8.52	$ 7.88	$ 7.51
$ 2000.00	$ 24.53	$ 19.40	$ 17.04	$ 15.77	$ 15.03
$ 3000.00	$ 36.80	$ 29.10	$ 25.56	$ 23.65	$ 22.54
$ 4000.00	$ 49.06	$ 38.81	$ 34.08	$ 31.54	$ 30.05
$ 5000.00	$ 61.33	$ 48.51	$ 42.60	$ 39.42	$ 37.56
$ 10000.00	$ 122.65	$ 97.01	$ 85.21	$ 78.85	$ 75.13
$ 15000.00	$ 183.98	$ 145.52	$ 127.81	$ 118.27	$ 112.69
$ 20000.00	$ 245.31	$ 194.03	$ 170.41	$ 157.69	$ 150.25
$ 25000.00	$ 306.63	$ 242.54	$ 213.02	$ 197.11	$ 187.82
$ 30000.00	$ 367.96	$ 291.04	$ 255.62	$ 236.54	$ 225.38
$ 35000.00	$ 429.28	$ 339.55	$ 298.22	$ 275.96	$ 262.94
$ 40000.00	$ 490.61	$ 388.06	$ 340.83	$ 315.38	$ 300.51
$ 45000.00	$ 551.94	$ 436.56	$ 383.43	$ 354.80	$ 338.07
$ 50000.00	$ 613.26	$ 485.07	$ 426.03	$ 394.23	$ 375.63
$ 55000.00	$ 674.59	$ 533.58	$ 468.64	$ 433.65	$ 413.20
$ 60000.00	$ 735.92	$ 582.08	$ 511.24	$ 473.07	$ 450.76
$ 65000.00	$ 797.24	$ 630.59	$ 553.84	$ 512.49	$ 488.32
$ 70000.00	$ 858.57	$ 679.10	$ 596.45	$ 551.92	$ 525.89
$ 75000.00	$ 919.89	$ 727.61	$ 639.05	$ 591.34	$ 563.45
$ 80000.00	$ 981.22	$ 776.11	$ 681.65	$ 630.76	$ 601.01
$ 85000.00	$1042.55	$ 824.62	$ 724.26	$ 670.18	$ 638.58
$ 90000.00	$1103.87	$ 873.13	$ 766.86	$ 709.61	$ 676.14
$ 95000.00	$1165.20	$ 921.63	$ 809.46	$ 749.03	$ 713.70
$100000.00	$1226.53	$ 970.14	$ 852.07	$ 788.45	$ 751.27
$125000.00	$1533.16	$1212.68	$1065.08	$ 985.56	$ 939.08
$150000.00	$1839.79	$1455.21	$1278.10	$1182.68	$1126.90

YEARLY INTEREST RATE = 8.50%

LOAN LIFE IN YEARS
MONTHLY PAYMENTS

PRINCIPAL	10	15	20	25	30
$ 25.00	$ .31	$ .25	$ .22	$ .20	$ .19
$ 50.00	$ .62	$ .49	$ .43	$ .40	$ .38
$ 100.00	$ 1.24	$ .98	$ .87	$ .81	$ .77
$ 200.00	$ 2.48	$ 1.97	$ 1.74	$ 1.61	$ 1.54
$ 300.00	$ 3.72	$ 2.95	$ 2.60	$ 2.42	$ 2.31
$ 400.00	$ 4.96	$ 3.94	$ 3.47	$ 3.22	$ 3.08
$ 500.00	$ 6.20	$ 4.92	$ 4.34	$ 4.03	$ 3.84
$ 1000.00	$ 12.40	$ 9.85	$ 8.68	$ 8.05	$ 7.69
$ 2000.00	$ 24.80	$ 19.69	$ 17.36	$ 16.10	$ 15.38
$ 3000.00	$ 37.20	$ 29.54	$ 26.03	$ 24.16	$ 23.07
$ 4000.00	$ 49.59	$ 39.39	$ 34.71	$ 32.21	$ 30.76
$ 5000.00	$ 61.99	$ 49.24	$ 43.39	$ 40.26	$ 38.45
$ 10000.00	$ 123.99	$ 98.47	$ 86.78	$ 80.52	$ 76.89
$ 15000.00	$ 185.98	$ 147.71	$ 130.17	$ 120.78	$ 115.34
$ 20000.00	$ 247.97	$ 196.95	$ 173.56	$ 161.05	$ 153.78
$ 25000.00	$ 309.96	$ 246.18	$ 216.96	$ 201.31	$ 192.23
$ 30000.00	$ 371.96	$ 295.42	$ 260.35	$ 241.57	$ 230.67
$ 35000.00	$ 433.95	$ 344.66	$ 303.74	$ 281.83	$ 269.12
$ 40000.00	$ 495.94	$ 393.90	$ 347.13	$ 322.09	$ 307.57
$ 45000.00	$ 557.94	$ 443.13	$ 390.52	$ 362.35	$ 346.01
$ 50000.00	$ 619.93	$ 492.37	$ 433.91	$ 402.61	$ 384.46
$ 55000.00	$ 681.92	$ 541.61	$ 477.30	$ 442.87	$ 422.90
$ 60000.00	$ 743.91	$ 590.84	$ 520.69	$ 483.14	$ 461.35
$ 65000.00	$ 805.91	$ 640.08	$ 564.09	$ 523.40	$ 499.79
$ 70000.00	$ 867.90	$ 689.32	$ 607.48	$ 563.66	$ 538.24
$ 75000.00	$ 929.89	$ 738.55	$ 650.87	$ 603.92	$ 576.68
$ 80000.00	$ 991.89	$ 787.79	$ 694.26	$ 644.18	$ 615.13
$ 85000.00	$1053.88	$ 837.03	$ 737.65	$ 684.44	$ 653.58
$ 90000.00	$1115.87	$ 886.27	$ 781.04	$ 724.70	$ 692.02
$ 95000.00	$1177.86	$ 935.50	$ 824.43	$ 764.97	$ 730.47
$100000.00	$1239.86	$ 984.74	$ 867.82	$ 805.23	$ 768.91
$125000.00	$1549.82	$1230.92	$1084.78	$1006.53	$ 961.14
$150000.00	$1859.79	$1477.11	$1301.73	$1207.84	$1153.37

YEARLY INTEREST RATE = 8.75%

LOAN LIFE IN YEARS
MONTHLY PAYMENTS

PRINCIPAL	10	15	20	25	30
$ 25.00	$ .31	$ .25	$ .22	$ .21	$ .20
$ 50.00	$ .63	$ .50	$ .44	$ .41	$ .39
$ 100.00	$ 1.25	$ 1.00	$ .88	$ .82	$ .79
$ 200.00	$ 2.51	$ 2.00	$ 1.77	$ 1.64	$ 1.57
$ 300.00	$ 3.76	$ 3.00	$ 2.65	$ 2.47	$ 2.36
$ 400.00	$ 5.01	$ 4.00	$ 3.53	$ 3.29	$ 3.15
$ 500.00	$ 6.27	$ 5.00	$ 4.42	$ 4.11	$ 3.93
$ 1000.00	$ 12.53	$ 9.99	$ 8.84	$ 8.22	$ 7.87
$ 2000.00	$ 25.07	$ 19.99	$ 17.67	$ 16.44	$ 15.73
$ 3000.00	$ 37.60	$ 29.98	$ 26.51	$ 24.66	$ 23.60
$ 4000.00	$ 50.13	$ 39.98	$ 35.35	$ 32.89	$ 31.47
$ 5000.00	$ 62.66	$ 49.97	$ 44.19	$ 41.11	$ 39.34
$ 10000.00	$ 125.33	$ 99.94	$ 88.37	$ 82.21	$ 78.67
$ 15000.00	$ 187.99	$ 149.92	$ 132.56	$ 123.32	$ 118.01
$ 20000.00	$ 250.65	$ 199.89	$ 176.74	$ 164.43	$ 157.34
$ 25000.00	$ 313.32	$ 249.86	$ 220.93	$ 205.54	$ 196.68
$ 30000.00	$ 375.98	$ 299.83	$ 265.11	$ 246.64	$ 236.01
$ 35000.00	$ 438.64	$ 349.81	$ 309.30	$ 287.75	$ 275.35
$ 40000.00	$ 501.31	$ 399.78	$ 353.48	$ 328.86	$ 314.68
$ 45000.00	$ 563.97	$ 449.75	$ 397.67	$ 369.96	$ 354.02
$ 50000.00	$ 626.63	$ 499.72	$ 441.86	$ 411.07	$ 393.35
$ 55000.00	$ 689.30	$ 549.70	$ 486.04	$ 452.18	$ 432.69
$ 60000.00	$ 751.96	$ 599.67	$ 530.23	$ 493.29	$ 472.02
$ 65000.00	$ 814.62	$ 649.64	$ 574.41	$ 534.39	$ 511.36
$ 70000.00	$ 877.29	$ 699.61	$ 618.60	$ 575.50	$ 550.69
$ 75000.00	$ 939.95	$ 749.59	$ 662.78	$ 616.61	$ 590.03
$ 80000.00	$1002.61	$ 799.56	$ 706.97	$ 657.71	$ 629.36
$ 85000.00	$1065.28	$ 849.53	$ 751.15	$ 698.82	$ 668.70
$ 90000.00	$1127.94	$ 899.50	$ 795.34	$ 739.93	$ 708.03
$ 95000.00	$1190.60	$ 949.48	$ 839.53	$ 781.04	$ 747.37
$100000.00	$1253.27	$ 999.45	$ 883.71	$ 822.14	$ 786.70
$125000.00	$1566.58	$1249.31	$1104.64	$1027.68	$ 983.38
$150000.00	$1879.90	$1499.17	$1325.57	$1233.22	$1180.05

Monthly Mortgage Payment 161

YEARLY INTEREST RATE = 9.00%

LOAN LIFE IN YEARS

	PRINCIPAL	10	15	20	25	30
			MONTHLY PAYMENTS			
$	25.00	$ .32	$ .25	$ .22	$ .21	$ .20
$	50.00	$ .63	$ .51	$ .45	$ .42	$ .40
$	100.00	$ 1.27	$ 1.01	$ .90	$ .84	$ .80
$	200.00	$ 2.53	$ 2.03	$ 1.80	$ 1.68	$ 1.61
$	300.00	$ 3.80	$ 3.04	$ 2.70	$ 2.52	$ 2.41
$	400.00	$ 5.07	$ 4.06	$ 3.60	$ 3.36	$ 3.22
$	500.00	$ 6.33	$ 5.07	$ 4.50	$ 4.20	$ 4.02
$	1000.00	$ 12.67	$ 10.14	$ 9.00	$ 8.39	$ 8.05
$	2000.00	$ 25.34	$ 20.29	$ 17.99	$ 16.78	$ 16.09
$	3000.00	$ 38.00	$ 30.43	$ 26.99	$ 25.18	$ 24.14
$	4000.00	$ 50.67	$ 40.57	$ 35.99	$ 33.57	$ 32.18
$	5000.00	$ 63.34	$ 50.71	$ 44.99	$ 41.96	$ 40.23
$	10000.00	$ 126.68	$ 101.43	$ 89.97	$ 83.92	$ 80.46
$	15000.00	$ 190.01	$ 152.14	$ 134.96	$ 125.88	$ 120.69
$	20000.00	$ 253.35	$ 202.85	$ 179.95	$ 167.84	$ 160.92
$	25000.00	$ 316.69	$ 253.57	$ 224.93	$ 209.80	$ 201.16
$	30000.00	$ 380.03	$ 304.28	$ 269.92	$ 251.76	$ 241.39
$	35000.00	$ 443.37	$ 354.99	$ 314.90	$ 293.72	$ 281.62
$	40000.00	$ 506.70	$ 405.71	$ 359.89	$ 335.68	$ 321.85
$	45000.00	$ 570.04	$ 456.42	$ 404.88	$ 377.64	$ 362.08
$	50000.00	$ 633.38	$ 507.13	$ 449.86	$ 419.60	$ 402.31
$	55000.00	$ 696.72	$ 557.85	$ 494.85	$ 461.56	$ 442.54
$	60000.00	$ 760.05	$ 608.56	$ 539.84	$ 503.52	$ 482.77
$	65000.00	$ 823.39	$ 659.27	$ 584.82	$ 545.48	$ 523.00
$	70000.00	$ 886.73	$ 709.99	$ 629.81	$ 587.44	$ 563.24
$	75000.00	$ 950.07	$ 760.70	$ 674.79	$ 629.40	$ 603.47
$	80000.00	$1013.41	$ 811.41	$ 719.78	$ 671.36	$ 643.70
$	85000.00	$1076.74	$ 862.13	$ 764.77	$ 713.32	$ 683.93
$	90000.00	$1140.08	$ 912.84	$ 809.75	$ 755.28	$ 724.16
$	95000.00	$1203.42	$ 963.55	$ 854.74	$ 797.24	$ 764.39
$100000.00		$1266.76	$1014.27	$ 899.73	$ 839.20	$ 804.62
$125000.00		$1583.45	$1267.83	$1124.66	$1049.00	$1005.78
$150000.00		$1900.14	$1521.40	$1349.59	$1258.79	$1206.93

YEARLY INTEREST RATE = 9.25%

LOAN LIFE IN YEARS

	PRINCIPAL	10	15	20	25	30
			MONTHLY PAYMENTS			
$	25.00	$ .32	$ .26	$ .23	$ .21	$ .21
$	50.00	$ .64	$ .51	$ .46	$ .43	$ .41
$	100.00	$ 1.28	$ 1.03	$ .92	$ .86	$ .82
$	200.00	$ 2.56	$ 2.06	$ 1.83	$ 1.71	$ 1.65
$	300.00	$ 3.84	$ 3.09	$ 2.75	$ 2.57	$ 2.47
$	400.00	$ 5.12	$ 4.12	$ 3.66	$ 3.43	$ 3.29
$	500.00	$ 6.40	$ 5.15	$ 4.58	$ 4.28	$ 4.11
$	1000.00	$ 12.80	$ 10.29	$ 9.16	$ 8.56	$ 8.23
$	2000.00	$ 25.61	$ 20.58	$ 18.32	$ 17.13	$ 16.45
$	3000.00	$ 38.41	$ 30.88	$ 27.48	$ 25.69	$ 24.68
$	4000.00	$ 51.21	$ 41.17	$ 36.63	$ 34.26	$ 32.91
$	5000.00	$ 64.02	$ 51.46	$ 45.79	$ 42.82	$ 41.13
$	10000.00	$ 128.03	$ 102.92	$ 91.59	$ 85.64	$ 82.27
$	15000.00	$ 192.05	$ 154.38	$ 137.38	$ 128.46	$ 123.40
$	20000.00	$ 256.07	$ 205.84	$ 183.17	$ 171.28	$ 164.54
$	25000.00	$ 320.08	$ 257.30	$ 228.97	$ 214.10	$ 205.67
$	30000.00	$ 384.10	$ 308.76	$ 274.76	$ 256.91	$ 246.80
$	35000.00	$ 448.11	$ 360.22	$ 320.55	$ 299.73	$ 287.94
$	40000.00	$ 512.13	$ 411.68	$ 366.35	$ 342.55	$ 329.07
$	45000.00	$ 576.15	$ 463.14	$ 412.14	$ 385.37	$ 370.20
$	50000.00	$ 640.16	$ 514.60	$ 457.93	$ 428.19	$ 411.34
$	55000.00	$ 704.18	$ 566.06	$ 503.73	$ 471.01	$ 452.47
$	60000.00	$ 768.20	$ 617.52	$ 549.52	$ 513.83	$ 493.61
$	65000.00	$ 832.21	$ 668.97	$ 595.31	$ 556.65	$ 534.74
$	70000.00	$ 896.23	$ 720.43	$ 641.11	$ 599.47	$ 575.87
$	75000.00	$ 960.25	$ 771.89	$ 686.90	$ 642.29	$ 617.01
$	80000.00	$1024.26	$ 823.35	$ 732.69	$ 685.11	$ 658.14
$	85000.00	$1088.28	$ 874.81	$ 778.49	$ 727.92	$ 699.27
$	90000.00	$1152.29	$ 926.27	$ 824.28	$ 770.74	$ 740.41
$	95000.00	$1216.31	$ 977.73	$ 870.07	$ 813.56	$ 781.54
$100000.00		$1280.33	$1029.19	$ 915.87	$ 856.38	$ 822.68
$125000.00		$1600.41	$1286.49	$1144.83	$1070.48	$1028.34
$150000.00		$1920.49	$1543.79	$1373.80	$1284.57	$1234.01

YEARLY INTEREST RATE = 9.50%

LOAN LIFE IN YEARS

PRINCIPAL	10	15	20	25	30
			MONTHLY PAYMENTS		
$ 25.00	$ .32	$ .26	$ .23	$ .22	$ .21
$ 50.00	$ .65	$ .52	$ .47	$ .44	$ .42
$ 100.00	$ 1.29	$ 1.04	$ .93	$ .87	$ .84
$ 200.00	$ 2.59	$ 2.09	$ 1.86	$ 1.75	$ 1.68
$ 300.00	$ 3.88	$ 3.13	$ 2.80	$ 2.62	$ 2.52
$ 400.00	$ 5.18	$ 4.18	$ 3.73	$ 3.49	$ 3.36
$ 500.00	$ 6.47	$ 5.22	$ 4.66	$ 4.37	$ 4.20
$ 1000.00	$ 12.94	$ 10.44	$ 9.32	$ 8.74	$ 8.41
$ 2000.00	$ 25.88	$ 20.88	$ 18.64	$ 17.47	$ 16.82
$ 3000.00	$ 38.82	$ 31.33	$ 27.96	$ 26.21	$ 25.23
$ 4000.00	$ 51.76	$ 41.77	$ 37.29	$ 34.95	$ 33.63
$ 5000.00	$ 64.70	$ 52.21	$ 46.61	$ 43.68	$ 42.04
$ 10000.00	$ 129.40	$ 104.42	$ 93.21	$ 87.37	$ 84.09
$ 15000.00	$ 194.10	$ 156.63	$ 139.82	$ 131.05	$ 126.13
$ 20000.00	$ 258.80	$ 208.84	$ 186.43	$ 174.74	$ 168.17
$ 25000.00	$ 323.49	$ 261.06	$ 233.03	$ 218.42	$ 210.21
$ 30000.00	$ 388.19	$ 313.27	$ 279.64	$ 262.11	$ 252.26
$ 35000.00	$ 452.89	$ 365.48	$ 326.25	$ 305.79	$ 294.30
$ 40000.00	$ 517.59	$ 417.69	$ 372.85	$ 349.48	$ 336.34
$ 45000.00	$ 582.29	$ 469.90	$ 419.46	$ 393.16	$ 378.38
$ 50000.00	$ 646.99	$ 522.11	$ 466.07	$ 436.85	$ 420.43
$ 55000.00	$ 711.69	$ 574.32	$ 512.67	$ 480.53	$ 462.47
$ 60000.00	$ 776.39	$ 626.53	$ 559.28	$ 524.22	$ 504.51
$ 65000.00	$ 841.08	$ 678.75	$ 605.89	$ 567.90	$ 546.56
$ 70000.00	$ 905.78	$ 730.96	$ 652.49	$ 611.59	$ 588.60
$ 75000.00	$ 970.48	$ 783.17	$ 699.10	$ 655.27	$ 630.64
$ 80000.00	$1035.18	$ 835.38	$ 745.70	$ 698.96	$ 672.68
$ 85000.00	$1099.88	$ 887.59	$ 792.31	$ 742.64	$ 714.73
$ 90000.00	$1164.58	$ 939.80	$ 838.92	$ 786.33	$ 756.77
$ 95000.00	$1229.28	$ 992.01	$ 885.52	$ 830.01	$ 798.81
$100000.00	$1293.98	$1044.22	$ 932.13	$ 873.70	$ 840.85
$125000.00	$1617.47	$1305.28	$1165.16	$1092.12	$1051.07
$150000.00	$1940.96	$1566.34	$1398.20	$1310.54	$1261.28

YEARLY INTEREST RATE = 9.75%

LOAN LIFE IN YEARS

PRINCIPAL	10	15	20	25	30
			MONTHLY PAYMENTS		
$ 25.00	$ .33	$ .26	$ .24	$ .22	$ .21
$ 50.00	$ .65	$ .53	$ .47	$ .45	$ .43
$ 100.00	$ 1.31	$ 1.06	$ .95	$ .89	$ .86
$ 200.00	$ 2.62	$ 2.12	$ 1.90	$ 1.78	$ 1.72
$ 300.00	$ 3.92	$ 3.18	$ 2.85	$ 2.67	$ 2.58
$ 400.00	$ 5.23	$ 4.24	$ 3.79	$ 3.56	$ 3.44
$ 500.00	$ 6.54	$ 5.30	$ 4.74	$ 4.46	$ 4.30
$ 1000.00	$ 13.08	$ 10.59	$ 9.49	$ 8.91	$ 8.59
$ 2000.00	$ 26.15	$ 21.19	$ 18.97	$ 17.82	$ 17.18
$ 3000.00	$ 39.23	$ 31.78	$ 28.46	$ 26.73	$ 25.77
$ 4000.00	$ 52.31	$ 42.37	$ 37.94	$ 35.65	$ 34.37
$ 5000.00	$ 65.39	$ 52.97	$ 47.43	$ 44.56	$ 42.96
$ 10000.00	$ 130.77	$ 105.94	$ 94.85	$ 89.11	$ 85.92
$ 15000.00	$ 196.16	$ 158.90	$ 142.28	$ 133.67	$ 128.87
$ 20000.00	$ 261.54	$ 211.87	$ 189.70	$ 178.23	$ 171.83
$ 25000.00	$ 326.93	$ 264.84	$ 237.13	$ 222.78	$ 214.79
$ 30000.00	$ 392.31	$ 317.81	$ 284.55	$ 267.34	$ 257.75
$ 35000.00	$ 457.70	$ 370.78	$ 331.98	$ 311.90	$ 300.70
$ 40000.00	$ 523.08	$ 423.74	$ 379.41	$ 356.45	$ 343.66
$ 45000.00	$ 588.47	$ 476.71	$ 426.83	$ 401.01	$ 386.62
$ 50000.00	$ 653.85	$ 529.68	$ 474.26	$ 445.57	$ 429.58
$ 55000.00	$ 719.24	$ 582.65	$ 521.68	$ 490.13	$ 472.53
$ 60000.00	$ 784.62	$ 635.62	$ 569.11	$ 534.68	$ 515.49
$ 65000.00	$ 850.01	$ 688.59	$ 616.54	$ 579.24	$ 558.45
$ 70000.00	$ 915.39	$ 741.55	$ 663.96	$ 623.80	$ 601.41
$ 75000.00	$ 980.78	$ 794.52	$ 711.39	$ 668.35	$ 644.37
$ 80000.00	$1046.16	$ 847.49	$ 758.81	$ 712.91	$ 687.32
$ 85000.00	$1111.55	$ 900.46	$ 806.24	$ 757.47	$ 730.28
$ 90000.00	$1176.93	$ 953.43	$ 853.66	$ 802.02	$ 773.24
$ 95000.00	$1242.32	$1006.39	$ 901.09	$ 846.58	$ 816.20
$100000.00	$1307.70	$1059.36	$ 948.52	$ 891.14	$ 859.15
$125000.00	$1634.63	$1324.20	$1185.65	$1113.92	$1073.94
$150000.00	$1961.55	$1589.04	$1422.77	$1336.71	$1288.73

YEARLY INTEREST RATE = 10.00%

LOAN LIFE IN YEARS

PRINCIPAL	10	15	20	25	30
			MONTHLY PAYMENTS		
$ 25.00	$ .33	$ .27	$ .24	$ .23	$ .22
$ 50.00	.66	.54	.48	.45	.44
$ 100.00	$ 1.32	$ 1.07	.97	.91	.88
$ 200.00	$ 2.64	2.15	1.93	1.82	1.76
$ 300.00	3.96	3.22	2.90	2.73	2.63
$ 400.00	$ 5.29	4.30	3.86	3.63	3.51
$ 500.00	6.61	5.37	4.83	4.54	4.39
$ 1000.00	$ 13.22	$ 10.75	$ 9.65	9.09	8.78
$ 2000.00	26.43	21.49	19.30	18.17	17.55
$ 3000.00	39.65	32.24	28.95	27.26	26.33
$ 4000.00	52.86	42.98	38.60	36.35	35.10
$ 5000.00	66.08	53.73	48.25	45.44	43.88
$ 10000.00	$ 132.15	$ 107.46	$ 96.50	90.87	$ 87.76
$ 15000.00	198.23	161.19	144.75	136.31	131.64
$ 20000.00	264.30	214.92	193.00	181.74	175.51
$ 25000.00	330.38	268.65	241.26	227.18	219.39
$ 30000.00	396.45	322.38	289.51	272.61	263.27
$ 35000.00	462.53	376.11	337.76	318.05	307.15
$ 40000.00	$ 528.60	429.84	386.01	363.48	351.03
$ 45000.00	$ 594.68	483.57	434.26	408.92	394.91
$ 50000.00	$ 660.75	537.30	482.51	454.35	438.79
$ 55000.00	$ 726.83	591.03	530.76	499.79	482.66
$ 60000.00	$ 792.90	644.76	579.01	545.22	526.54
$ 65000.00	$ 858.98	698.49	627.26	590.66	570.42
$ 70000.00	$ 925.06	752.22	675.51	636.09	614.30
$ 75000.00	$ 991.13	805.95	723.77	681.53	658.18
$ 80000.00	$1057.21	859.68	772.02	726.96	702.06
$ 85000.00	$1123.28	913.41	820.27	772.40	745.94
$ 90000.00	$1189.36	967.14	868.52	817.83	789.81
$ 95000.00	$1255.43	$1020.87	916.77	863.27	833.69
$100000.00	$1321.51	$1074.60	965.02	908.70	877.57
$125000.00	$1651.88	$1343.26	$1206.28	$1135.88	$1096.96
$150000.00	$1982.26	$1611.91	$1447.53	$1363.05	$1316.36

YEARLY INTEREST RATE = 10.25%

LOAN LIFE IN YEARS

PRINCIPAL	10	15	20	25	30
			MONTHLY PAYMENTS		
$ 25.00	$ .33	$ .27	$ .25	$ .23	$ .22
$ 50.00	.67	.54	.49	.46	.45
$ 100.00	$ 1.34	$ 1.09	.98	.93	.90
$ 200.00	$ 2.67	2.18	1.96	1.85	1.79
$ 300.00	4.01	3.27	2.94	2.78	2.69
$ 400.00	$ 5.34	4.36	3.93	3.71	3.58
$ 500.00	6.68	5.45	4.91	4.63	4.48
$ 1000.00	$ 13.35	$ 10.90	$ 9.82	9.26	8.96
$ 2000.00	26.71	21.80	19.63	18.53	17.92
$ 3000.00	40.06	32.70	29.45	27.79	26.88
$ 4000.00	53.42	43.60	39.27	37.06	35.84
$ 5000.00	66.77	54.50	49.08	46.32	44.81
$ 10000.00	$ 133.54	$ 109.00	$ 98.16	92.64	$ 89.61
$ 15000.00	200.31	163.49	147.25	138.96	134.42
$ 20000.00	267.08	217.99	196.33	185.28	179.22
$ 25000.00	333.85	272.49	245.41	231.60	224.03
$ 30000.00	400.62	326.99	294.49	277.91	268.83
$ 35000.00	467.39	381.48	343.58	324.23	313.64
$ 40000.00	$ 534.16	435.98	392.66	370.55	358.44
$ 45000.00	$ 600.93	490.48	441.74	416.87	403.25
$ 50000.00	$ 667.69	544.98	490.82	463.19	448.05
$ 55000.00	$ 734.46	599.47	539.90	509.51	492.86
$ 60000.00	$ 801.23	653.97	588.99	555.83	537.66
$ 65000.00	$ 868.00	708.47	638.07	602.15	582.47
$ 70000.00	$ 934.77	762.97	687.15	648.47	627.27
$ 75000.00	$1001.54	817.46	736.23	694.79	672.08
$ 80000.00	$1068.31	871.96	785.31	741.11	716.88
$ 85000.00	$1135.08	926.46	834.40	787.43	761.69
$ 90000.00	$1201.85	980.96	883.48	833.74	806.49
$ 95000.00	$1268.62	$1035.45	932.56	880.06	851.30
$100000.00	$1335.39	$1089.95	981.64	926.38	896.10
$125000.00	$1669.24	$1362.44	$1227.05	$1157.98	$1120.13
$150000.00	$2003.08	$1634.93	$1472.46	$1389.57	$1344.15

YEARLY INTEREST RATE = 10.50%

LOAN LIFE IN YEARS

PRINCIPAL	10	15	20	25	30
			MONTHLY PAYMENTS		
$ 25.00	$ .34	$ .28	$ .25	$ .24	$ .23
$ 50.00	$ .67	$ .55	$ .50	$ .47	$ .46
$ 100.00	$ 1.35	$ 1.11	$ 1.00	$ .94	$ .91
$ 200.00	$ 2.70	$ 2.21	$ 2.00	$ 1.89	$ 1.83
$ 300.00	$ 4.05	$ 3.32	$ 3.00	$ 2.83	$ 2.74
$ 400.00	$ 5.40	$ 4.42	$ 3.99	$ 3.78	$ 3.66
$ 500.00	$ 6.75	$ 5.53	$ 4.99	$ 4.72	$ 4.57
$ 1000.00	$ 13.49	$ 11.05	$ 9.98	$ 9.44	$ 9.15
$ 2000.00	$ 26.99	$ 22.11	$ 19.97	$ 18.88	$ 18.29
$ 3000.00	$ 40.48	$ 33.16	$ 29.95	$ 28.33	$ 27.44
$ 4000.00	$ 53.97	$ 44.22	$ 39.94	$ 37.77	$ 36.59
$ 5000.00	$ 67.47	$ 55.27	$ 49.92	$ 47.21	$ 45.74
$ 10000.00	$ 134.93	$ 110.54	$ 99.84	$ 94.42	$ 91.47
$ 15000.00	$ 202.40	$ 165.81	$ 149.76	$ 141.63	$ 137.21
$ 20000.00	$ 269.87	$ 221.08	$ 199.68	$ 188.84	$ 182.95
$ 25000.00	$ 337.34	$ 276.35	$ 249.59	$ 236.05	$ 228.68
$ 30000.00	$ 404.80	$ 331.62	$ 299.51	$ 283.25	$ 274.42
$ 35000.00	$ 472.27	$ 386.89	$ 349.43	$ 330.46	$ 320.16
$ 40000.00	$ 539.74	$ 442.16	$ 399.35	$ 377.67	$ 365.90
$ 45000.00	$ 607.21	$ 497.43	$ 449.27	$ 424.88	$ 411.63
$ 50000.00	$ 674.67	$ 552.70	$ 499.19	$ 472.09	$ 457.37
$ 55000.00	$ 742.14	$ 607.97	$ 549.11	$ 519.30	$ 503.11
$ 60000.00	$ 809.61	$ 663.24	$ 599.03	$ 566.51	$ 548.84
$ 65000.00	$ 877.08	$ 718.51	$ 648.95	$ 613.72	$ 594.58
$ 70000.00	$ 944.54	$ 773.78	$ 698.87	$ 660.93	$ 640.32
$ 75000.00	$1012.01	$ 829.05	$ 748.78	$ 708.14	$ 686.05
$ 80000.00	$1079.48	$ 884.32	$ 798.70	$ 755.35	$ 731.79
$ 85000.00	$1146.95	$ 939.59	$ 848.62	$ 802.55	$ 777.53
$ 90000.00	$1214.41	$ 994.86	$ 898.54	$ 849.76	$ 823.27
$ 95000.00	$1281.88	$1050.13	$ 948.46	$ 896.97	$ 869.00
$100000.00	$1349.35	$1105.40	$ 998.38	$ 944.18	$ 914.74
$125000.00	$1686.69	$1381.75	$1247.97	$1180.23	$1143.42
$150000.00	$2024.02	$1658.10	$1497.57	$1416.27	$1372.11

YEARLY INTEREST RATE = 10.75%

LOAN LIFE IN YEARS

PRINCIPAL	10	15	20	25	30
			MONTHLY PAYMENTS		
$ 25.00	$ .34	$ .28	$ .25	$ .24	$ .23
$ 50.00	$ .68	$ .56	$ .51	$ .48	$ .47
$ 100.00	$ 1.36	$ 1.12	$ 1.02	$ .96	$ .93
$ 200.00	$ 2.73	$ 2.24	$ 2.03	$ 1.92	$ 1.87
$ 300.00	$ 4.09	$ 3.36	$ 3.05	$ 2.89	$ 2.80
$ 400.00	$ 5.45	$ 4.48	$ 4.06	$ 3.85	$ 3.73
$ 500.00	$ 6.82	$ 5.60	$ 5.08	$ 4.81	$ 4.67
$ 1000.00	$ 13.63	$ 11.21	$ 10.15	$ 9.62	$ 9.33
$ 2000.00	$ 27.27	$ 22.42	$ 20.30	$ 19.24	$ 18.67
$ 3000.00	$ 40.90	$ 33.63	$ 30.46	$ 28.86	$ 28.00
$ 4000.00	$ 54.54	$ 44.84	$ 40.61	$ 38.48	$ 37.34
$ 5000.00	$ 68.17	$ 56.05	$ 50.76	$ 48.10	$ 46.67
$ 10000.00	$ 136.34	$ 112.09	$ 101.52	$ 96.21	$ 93.35
$ 15000.00	$ 204.51	$ 168.14	$ 152.28	$ 144.31	$ 140.02
$ 20000.00	$ 272.68	$ 224.19	$ 203.05	$ 192.42	$ 186.70
$ 25000.00	$ 340.85	$ 280.24	$ 253.81	$ 240.52	$ 233.37
$ 30000.00	$ 409.02	$ 336.28	$ 304.57	$ 288.63	$ 280.04
$ 35000.00	$ 477.19	$ 392.33	$ 355.33	$ 336.73	$ 326.72
$ 40000.00	$ 545.35	$ 448.38	$ 406.09	$ 384.84	$ 373.39
$ 45000.00	$ 613.52	$ 504.43	$ 456.85	$ 432.94	$ 420.07
$ 50000.00	$ 681.69	$ 560.47	$ 507.61	$ 481.05	$ 466.74
$ 55000.00	$ 749.86	$ 616.52	$ 558.38	$ 529.15	$ 513.41
$ 60000.00	$ 818.03	$ 672.57	$ 609.14	$ 577.26	$ 560.09
$ 65000.00	$ 886.20	$ 728.62	$ 659.90	$ 625.36	$ 606.76
$ 70000.00	$ 954.37	$ 784.66	$ 710.66	$ 673.46	$ 653.44
$ 75000.00	$1022.54	$ 840.71	$ 761.42	$ 721.57	$ 700.11
$ 80000.00	$1090.71	$ 896.76	$ 812.18	$ 769.67	$ 746.78
$ 85000.00	$1158.88	$ 952.81	$ 862.94	$ 817.78	$ 793.46
$ 90000.00	$1227.05	$1008.85	$ 913.71	$ 865.88	$ 840.13
$ 95000.00	$1295.22	$1064.90	$ 964.47	$ 913.99	$ 886.81
$100000.00	$1363.39	$1120.95	$1015.23	$ 962.09	$ 933.48
$125000.00	$1704.23	$1401.18	$1269.04	$1202.62	$1166.85
$150000.00	$2045.08	$1681.42	$1522.84	$1443.14	$1400.22

Monthly Mortgage Payment

YEARLY INTEREST RATE = 11.00%

LOAN LIFE IN YEARS
MONTHLY PAYMENTS

PRINCIPAL	10	15	20	25	30
$ 25.00	$ .34	$ .28	$ .26	$ .25	$ .24
$ 50.00	$ .69	$ .57	$ .52	$ .49	$ .48
$ 100.00	$ 1.38	$ 1.14	$ 1.03	$ .98	$ .95
$ 200.00	$ 2.75	$ 2.27	$ 2.06	$ 1.96	$ 1.90
$ 300.00	$ 4.13	$ 3.41	$ 3.10	$ 2.94	$ 2.86
$ 400.00	$ 5.51	$ 4.55	$ 4.13	$ 3.92	$ 3.81
$ 500.00	$ 6.89	$ 5.68	$ 5.16	$ 4.90	$ 4.76
$ 1000.00	$ 13.77	$ 11.37	$ 10.32	$ 9.80	$ 9.52
$ 2000.00	$ 27.55	$ 22.73	$ 20.64	$ 19.60	$ 19.05
$ 3000.00	$ 41.32	$ 34.10	$ 30.97	$ 29.40	$ 28.57
$ 4000.00	$ 55.10	$ 45.46	$ 41.29	$ 39.20	$ 38.09
$ 5000.00	$ 68.87	$ 56.83	$ 51.61	$ 49.01	$ 47.62
$ 10000.00	$ 137.75	$ 113.66	$ 103.22	$ 98.01	$ 95.23
$ 15000.00	$ 206.62	$ 170.49	$ 154.83	$ 147.02	$ 142.85
$ 20000.00	$ 275.50	$ 227.32	$ 206.44	$ 196.02	$ 190.46
$ 25000.00	$ 344.37	$ 284.15	$ 258.05	$ 245.03	$ 238.08
$ 30000.00	$ 413.25	$ 340.98	$ 309.66	$ 294.03	$ 285.70
$ 35000.00	$ 482.12	$ 397.81	$ 361.27	$ 343.04	$ 333.31
$ 40000.00	$ 551.00	$ 454.64	$ 412.88	$ 392.05	$ 380.93
$ 45000.00	$ 619.87	$ 511.47	$ 464.48	$ 441.05	$ 428.55
$ 50000.00	$ 688.75	$ 568.30	$ 516.09	$ 490.06	$ 476.16
$ 55000.00	$ 757.62	$ 625.13	$ 567.70	$ 539.06	$ 523.78
$ 60000.00	$ 826.50	$ 681.96	$ 619.31	$ 588.07	$ 571.39
$ 65000.00	$ 895.37	$ 738.79	$ 670.92	$ 637.07	$ 619.01
$ 70000.00	$ 964.25	$ 795.62	$ 722.53	$ 686.08	$ 666.63
$ 75000.00	$ 1033.12	$ 852.45	$ 774.14	$ 735.08	$ 714.24
$ 80000.00	$ 1102.00	$ 909.28	$ 825.75	$ 784.09	$ 761.86
$ 85000.00	$ 1170.87	$ 966.11	$ 877.36	$ 833.10	$ 809.47
$ 90000.00	$ 1239.75	$ 1022.94	$ 928.97	$ 882.10	$ 857.09
$ 95000.00	$ 1308.62	$ 1079.77	$ 980.58	$ 931.11	$ 904.71
$ 100000.00	$ 1377.50	$ 1136.60	$ 1032.19	$ 980.11	$ 952.32
$ 125000.00	$ 1721.87	$ 1420.75	$ 1290.24	$ 1225.14	$ 1190.40
$ 150000.00	$ 2066.25	$ 1704.89	$ 1548.28	$ 1470.17	$ 1428.48

YEARLY INTEREST RATE = 11.25%

LOAN LIFE IN YEARS
MONTHLY PAYMENTS

PRINCIPAL	10	15	20	25	30
$ 25.00	$ .35	$ .29	$ .26	$ .25	$ .24
$ 50.00	$ .70	$ .58	$ .52	$ .50	$ .49
$ 100.00	$ 1.39	$ 1.15	$ 1.05	$ 1.00	$ .97
$ 200.00	$ 2.78	$ 2.30	$ 2.10	$ 2.00	$ 1.94
$ 300.00	$ 4.18	$ 3.46	$ 3.15	$ 2.99	$ 2.91
$ 400.00	$ 5.57	$ 4.61	$ 4.20	$ 3.99	$ 3.89
$ 500.00	$ 6.96	$ 5.76	$ 5.25	$ 4.99	$ 4.86
$ 1000.00	$ 13.92	$ 11.52	$ 10.49	$ 9.98	$ 9.71
$ 2000.00	$ 27.83	$ 23.05	$ 20.99	$ 19.96	$ 19.43
$ 3000.00	$ 41.75	$ 34.57	$ 31.48	$ 29.95	$ 29.14
$ 4000.00	$ 55.67	$ 46.09	$ 41.97	$ 39.93	$ 38.85
$ 5000.00	$ 69.58	$ 57.62	$ 52.46	$ 49.91	$ 48.56
$ 10000.00	$ 139.17	$ 115.23	$ 104.93	$ 99.82	$ 97.13
$ 15000.00	$ 208.75	$ 172.85	$ 157.39	$ 149.74	$ 145.69
$ 20000.00	$ 278.34	$ 230.47	$ 209.85	$ 199.65	$ 194.25
$ 25000.00	$ 347.92	$ 288.09	$ 262.31	$ 249.56	$ 242.82
$ 30000.00	$ 417.51	$ 345.70	$ 314.78	$ 299.47	$ 291.38
$ 35000.00	$ 487.09	$ 403.32	$ 367.24	$ 349.38	$ 339.94
$ 40000.00	$ 556.68	$ 460.94	$ 419.70	$ 399.30	$ 388.50
$ 45000.00	$ 626.26	$ 518.55	$ 472.17	$ 449.21	$ 437.07
$ 50000.00	$ 695.84	$ 576.17	$ 524.63	$ 499.12	$ 485.63
$ 55000.00	$ 765.43	$ 633.79	$ 577.09	$ 549.03	$ 534.19
$ 60000.00	$ 835.01	$ 691.41	$ 629.55	$ 598.94	$ 582.76
$ 65000.00	$ 904.60	$ 749.02	$ 682.02	$ 648.86	$ 631.32
$ 70000.00	$ 974.18	$ 806.64	$ 734.48	$ 698.77	$ 679.88
$ 75000.00	$ 1043.77	$ 864.26	$ 786.94	$ 748.68	$ 728.45
$ 80000.00	$ 1113.35	$ 921.88	$ 839.40	$ 798.59	$ 777.01
$ 85000.00	$ 1182.94	$ 979.49	$ 891.87	$ 848.50	$ 825.57
$ 90000.00	$ 1252.52	$ 1037.11	$ 944.33	$ 898.42	$ 874.13
$ 95000.00	$ 1322.10	$ 1094.73	$ 996.79	$ 948.33	$ 922.70
$ 100000.00	$ 1391.69	$ 1152.34	$ 1049.26	$ 998.24	$ 971.26
$ 125000.00	$ 1739.61	$ 1440.43	$ 1311.57	$ 1247.80	$ 1214.08
$ 150000.00	$ 2087.53	$ 1728.52	$ 1573.88	$ 1497.36	$ 1456.89

YEARLY INTEREST RATE = 11.50%

LOAN LIFE IN YEARS

PRINCIPAL	10	15	20	25	30
			MONTHLY PAYMENTS		
$ 25.00	$ .35	$ .29	$ .27	$ .25	$ .25
$ 50.00	$ .70	$ .58	$ .53	$ .51	$ .50
$ 100.00	$ 1.41	$ 1.17	$ 1.07	$ 1.02	$ .99
$ 200.00	$ 2.81	$ 2.34	$ 2.13	$ 2.03	$ 1.98
$ 300.00	$ 4.22	$ 3.50	$ 3.20	$ 3.05	$ 2.97
$ 400.00	$ 5.62	$ 4.67	$ 4.27	$ 4.07	$ 3.96
$ 500.00	$ 7.03	$ 5.84	$ 5.33	$ 5.08	$ 4.95
$ 1000.00	$ 14.06	$ 11.68	$ 10.66	$ 10.16	$ 9.90
$ 2000.00	$ 28.12	$ 23.36	$ 21.33	$ 20.33	$ 19.81
$ 3000.00	$ 42.18	$ 35.05	$ 31.99	$ 30.49	$ 29.71
$ 4000.00	$ 56.24	$ 46.73	$ 42.66	$ 40.66	$ 39.61
$ 5000.00	$ 70.30	$ 58.41	$ 53.32	$ 50.82	$ 49.51
$ 10000.00	$ 140.60	$ 116.82	$ 106.64	$ 101.65	$ 99.03
$ 15000.00	$ 210.89	$ 175.23	$ 159.96	$ 152.47	$ 148.54
$ 20000.00	$ 281.19	$ 233.64	$ 213.29	$ 203.29	$ 198.06
$ 25000.00	$ 351.49	$ 292.05	$ 266.61	$ 254.12	$ 247.57
$ 30000.00	$ 421.79	$ 350.46	$ 319.93	$ 304.94	$ 297.09
$ 35000.00	$ 492.08	$ 408.87	$ 373.25	$ 355.76	$ 346.60
$ 40000.00	$ 562.38	$ 467.28	$ 426.57	$ 406.59	$ 396.12
$ 45000.00	$ 632.68	$ 525.09	$ 479.89	$ 457.41	$ 445.63
$ 50000.00	$ 702.98	$ 584.09	$ 533.21	$ 508.23	$ 495.15
$ 55000.00	$ 773.27	$ 642.50	$ 586.54	$ 559.06	$ 544.66
$ 60000.00	$ 843.57	$ 700.91	$ 639.86	$ 609.88	$ 594.17
$ 65000.00	$ 913.87	$ 759.32	$ 693.18	$ 660.70	$ 643.69
$ 70000.00	$ 984.17	$ 817.73	$ 746.50	$ 711.53	$ 693.20
$ 75000.00	$1054.47	$ 876.14	$ 799.82	$ 762.35	$ 742.72
$ 80000.00	$1124.76	$ 934.55	$ 853.14	$ 813.17	$ 792.23
$ 85000.00	$1195.06	$ 992.96	$ 906.46	$ 864.00	$ 841.75
$ 90000.00	$1265.36	$1051.37	$ 959.79	$ 914.82	$ 891.26
$ 95000.00	$1335.66	$1109.78	$1013.11	$ 965.65	$ 940.78
$100000.00	$1405.95	$1168.19	$1066.43	$1016.47	$ 990.29
$125000.00	$1757.44	$1460.24	$1333.04	$1270.59	$1237.86
$150000.00	$2108.93	$1752.28	$1599.64	$1524.70	$1485.44

YEARLY INTEREST RATE = 11.75%

LOAN LIFE IN YEARS

PRINCIPAL	10	15	20	25	30
			MONTHLY PAYMENTS		
$ 25.00	$ .36	$ .30	$ .27	$ .26	$ .25
$ 50.00	$ .71	$ .59	$ .54	$ .52	$ .50
$ 100.00	$ 1.42	$ 1.18	$ 1.08	$ 1.03	$ 1.01
$ 200.00	$ 2.84	$ 2.37	$ 2.17	$ 2.07	$ 2.02
$ 300.00	$ 4.26	$ 3.55	$ 3.25	$ 3.10	$ 3.03
$ 400.00	$ 5.68	$ 4.74	$ 4.33	$ 4.14	$ 4.04
$ 500.00	$ 7.10	$ 5.92	$ 5.42	$ 5.17	$ 5.05
$ 1000.00	$ 14.20	$ 11.84	$ 10.84	$ 10.35	$ 10.09
$ 2000.00	$ 28.41	$ 23.68	$ 21.67	$ 20.70	$ 20.19
$ 3000.00	$ 42.61	$ 35.52	$ 32.51	$ 31.04	$ 30.28
$ 4000.00	$ 56.81	$ 47.37	$ 43.35	$ 41.39	$ 40.38
$ 5000.00	$ 71.01	$ 59.21	$ 54.19	$ 51.74	$ 50.47
$ 10000.00	$ 142.03	$ 118.41	$ 108.37	$ 103.48	$ 100.94
$ 15000.00	$ 213.04	$ 177.62	$ 162.56	$ 155.22	$ 151.41
$ 20000.00	$ 284.06	$ 236.83	$ 216.74	$ 206.96	$ 201.88
$ 25000.00	$ 355.07	$ 296.03	$ 270.93	$ 258.70	$ 252.35
$ 30000.00	$ 426.09	$ 355.24	$ 325.11	$ 310.44	$ 302.82
$ 35000.00	$ 497.10	$ 414.45	$ 379.30	$ 362.18	$ 353.29
$ 40000.00	$ 568.12	$ 473.65	$ 433.48	$ 413.92	$ 403.76
$ 45000.00	$ 639.13	$ 532.86	$ 487.67	$ 465.66	$ 454.23
$ 50000.00	$ 710.15	$ 592.07	$ 541.85	$ 517.40	$ 504.70
$ 55000.00	$ 781.16	$ 651.27	$ 596.04	$ 569.14	$ 555.18
$ 60000.00	$ 852.18	$ 710.48	$ 650.22	$ 620.88	$ 605.65
$ 65000.00	$ 923.19	$ 769.69	$ 704.41	$ 672.62	$ 656.12
$ 70000.00	$ 994.21	$ 828.89	$ 758.59	$ 724.36	$ 706.59
$ 75000.00	$1065.22	$ 888.10	$ 812.78	$ 776.10	$ 757.06
$ 80000.00	$1136.24	$ 947.30	$ 866.97	$ 827.84	$ 807.53
$ 85000.00	$1207.25	$1006.51	$ 921.15	$ 879.58	$ 858.00
$ 90000.00	$1278.26	$1065.72	$ 975.34	$ 931.32	$ 908.47
$ 95000.00	$1349.28	$1124.92	$1029.52	$ 983.06	$ 958.94
$100000.00	$1420.29	$1184.13	$1083.71	$1034.80	$1009.41
$125000.00	$1775.37	$1480.16	$1354.63	$1293.50	$1261.76
$150000.00	$2130.44	$1776.20	$1625.56	$1552.20	$1514.11

YEARLY INTEREST RATE = 12.00%

LOAN LIFE IN YEARS

MONTHLY PAYMENTS

PRINCIPAL	10	15	20	25	30
$ 25.00	$ .36	$ .30	$ .28	$ .26	$ .26
$ 50.00	$ .72	$ .60	$ .55	$ .53	$ .51
$ 100.00	$ 1.43	$ 1.20	$ 1.10	$ 1.05	$ 1.03
$ 200.00	$ 2.87	$ 2.40	$ 2.20	$ 2.11	$ 2.06
$ 300.00	$ 4.30	$ 3.60	$ 3.30	$ 3.16	$ 3.09
$ 400.00	$ 5.74	$ 4.80	$ 4.40	$ 4.21	$ 4.11
$ 500.00	$ 7.17	$ 6.00	$ 5.51	$ 5.27	$ 5.14
$ 1000.00	$ 14.35	$ 12.00	$ 11.01	$ 10.53	$ 10.29
$ 2000.00	$ 28.69	$ 24.00	$ 22.02	$ 21.06	$ 20.57
$ 3000.00	$ 43.04	$ 36.01	$ 33.03	$ 31.60	$ 30.86
$ 4000.00	$ 57.39	$ 48.01	$ 44.04	$ 42.13	$ 41.14
$ 5000.00	$ 71.74	$ 60.01	$ 55.05	$ 52.66	$ 51.43
$ 10000.00	$ 143.47	$ 120.02	$ 110.11	$ 105.32	$ 102.86
$ 15000.00	$ 215.21	$ 180.03	$ 165.16	$ 157.98	$ 154.29
$ 20000.00	$ 286.94	$ 240.03	$ 220.22	$ 210.64	$ 205.72
$ 25000.00	$ 358.68	$ 300.04	$ 275.27	$ 263.31	$ 257.15
$ 30000.00	$ 430.41	$ 360.05	$ 330.33	$ 315.97	$ 308.58
$ 35000.00	$ 502.15	$ 420.06	$ 385.38	$ 368.63	$ 360.01
$ 40000.00	$ 573.88	$ 480.07	$ 440.43	$ 421.29	$ 411.44
$ 45000.00	$ 645.62	$ 540.08	$ 495.49	$ 473.95	$ 462.88
$ 50000.00	$ 717.35	$ 600.08	$ 550.54	$ 526.61	$ 514.31
$ 55000.00	$ 789.09	$ 660.09	$ 605.60	$ 579.27	$ 565.74
$ 60000.00	$ 860.83	$ 720.10	$ 660.65	$ 631.93	$ 617.17
$ 65000.00	$ 932.56	$ 780.11	$ 715.71	$ 684.60	$ 668.60
$ 70000.00	$ 1004.30	$ 840.12	$ 770.76	$ 737.26	$ 720.03
$ 75000.00	$ 1076.03	$ 900.13	$ 825.81	$ 789.92	$ 771.46
$ 80000.00	$ 1147.77	$ 960.13	$ 880.87	$ 842.58	$ 822.89
$ 85000.00	$ 1219.50	$ 1020.14	$ 935.92	$ 895.24	$ 874.32
$ 90000.00	$ 1291.24	$ 1080.15	$ 990.98	$ 947.90	$ 925.75
$ 95000.00	$ 1362.97	$ 1140.16	$ 1046.03	$ 1000.56	$ 977.18
$100000.00	$ 1434.71	$ 1200.17	$ 1101.09	$ 1053.22	$ 1028.61
$125000.00	$ 1793.39	$ 1500.21	$ 1376.36	$ 1316.53	$ 1285.77
$150000.00	$ 2152.06	$ 1800.25	$ 1651.63	$ 1579.84	$ 1542.92

YEARLY INTEREST RATE = 12.25%

LOAN LIFE IN YEARS

MONTHLY PAYMENTS

PRINCIPAL	10	15	20	25	30
$ 25.00	$ .36	$ .30	$ .28	$ .27	$ .26
$ 50.00	$ .72	$ .61	$ .56	$ .54	$ .52
$ 100.00	$ 1.45	$ 1.22	$ 1.12	$ 1.07	$ 1.05
$ 200.00	$ 2.90	$ 2.43	$ 2.24	$ 2.14	$ 2.10
$ 300.00	$ 4.35	$ 3.65	$ 3.36	$ 3.22	$ 3.14
$ 400.00	$ 5.80	$ 4.87	$ 4.47	$ 4.29	$ 4.19
$ 500.00	$ 7.25	$ 6.08	$ 5.59	$ 5.36	$ 5.24
$ 1000.00	$ 14.49	$ 12.16	$ 11.19	$ 10.72	$ 10.48
$ 2000.00	$ 28.98	$ 24.33	$ 22.37	$ 21.43	$ 20.96
$ 3000.00	$ 43.48	$ 36.49	$ 33.56	$ 32.15	$ 31.44
$ 4000.00	$ 57.97	$ 48.65	$ 44.74	$ 42.87	$ 41.92
$ 5000.00	$ 72.46	$ 60.81	$ 55.93	$ 53.59	$ 52.39
$ 10000.00	$ 144.92	$ 121.63	$ 111.86	$ 107.17	$ 104.79
$ 15000.00	$ 217.38	$ 182.44	$ 167.78	$ 160.76	$ 157.18
$ 20000.00	$ 289.84	$ 243.26	$ 223.71	$ 214.35	$ 209.58
$ 25000.00	$ 362.30	$ 304.07	$ 279.64	$ 267.94	$ 261.97
$ 30000.00	$ 434.76	$ 364.89	$ 335.57	$ 321.52	$ 314.37
$ 35000.00	$ 507.22	$ 425.70	$ 391.50	$ 375.11	$ 366.76
$ 40000.00	$ 579.68	$ 486.52	$ 447.43	$ 428.70	$ 419.16
$ 45000.00	$ 652.14	$ 547.33	$ 503.35	$ 482.28	$ 471.55
$ 50000.00	$ 724.60	$ 608.15	$ 559.28	$ 535.87	$ 523.95
$ 55000.00	$ 797.06	$ 668.96	$ 615.21	$ 589.46	$ 576.34
$ 60000.00	$ 869.52	$ 729.78	$ 671.14	$ 643.05	$ 628.74
$ 65000.00	$ 941.98	$ 790.59	$ 727.07	$ 696.63	$ 681.13
$ 70000.00	$ 1014.44	$ 851.41	$ 782.99	$ 750.22	$ 733.53
$ 75000.00	$ 1086.90	$ 912.22	$ 838.92	$ 803.81	$ 785.92
$ 80000.00	$ 1159.36	$ 973.04	$ 894.85	$ 857.39	$ 838.32
$ 85000.00	$ 1231.82	$ 1033.85	$ 950.78	$ 910.98	$ 890.71
$ 90000.00	$ 1304.28	$ 1094.67	$ 1006.71	$ 964.57	$ 943.11
$ 95000.00	$ 1376.74	$ 1155.48	$ 1062.64	$ 1018.16	$ 995.50
$100000.00	$ 1449.20	$ 1216.30	$ 1118.56	$ 1071.74	$ 1047.90
$125000.00	$ 1811.50	$ 1520.37	$ 1398.21	$ 1339.68	$ 1309.87
$150000.00	$ 2173.80	$ 1824.45	$ 1677.85	$ 1607.62	$ 1571.84

YEARLY INTEREST RATE = 12.50%

		LOAN LIFE IN YEARS			
	10	15	20	25	30
PRINCIPAL		MONTHLY PAYMENTS			
$ 25.00	$ .37	$ .31	$ .28	$ .27	$ .27
$ 50.00	$ .73	$ .62	$ .57	$ .55	$ .53
$ 100.00	$ 1.46	$ 1.23	$ 1.14	$ 1.09	$ 1.07
$ 200.00	$ 2.93	$ 2.47	$ 2.27	$ 2.18	$ 2.13
$ 300.00	$ 4.39	$ 3.70	$ 3.41	$ 3.27	$ 3.20
$ 400.00	$ 5.86	$ 4.93	$ 4.54	$ 4.36	$ 4.27
$ 500.00	$ 7.32	$ 6.16	$ 5.68	$ 5.45	$ 5.34
$ 1000.00	$ 14.64	$ 12.33	$ 11.36	$ 10.90	$ 10.67
$ 2000.00	$ 29.28	$ 24.65	$ 22.72	$ 21.81	$ 21.35
$ 3000.00	$ 43.91	$ 36.98	$ 34.08	$ 32.71	$ 32.02
$ 4000.00	$ 58.55	$ 49.30	$ 45.45	$ 43.61	$ 42.69
$ 5000.00	$ 73.19	$ 61.63	$ 56.81	$ 54.52	$ 53.36
$ 10000.00	$ 146.38	$ 123.25	$ 113.61	$ 109.04	$ 106.73
$ 15000.00	$ 219.56	$ 184.88	$ 170.42	$ 163.55	$ 160.09
$ 20000.00	$ 292.75	$ 246.50	$ 227.23	$ 218.07	$ 213.45
$ 25000.00	$ 365.94	$ 308.13	$ 284.04	$ 272.59	$ 266.81
$ 30000.00	$ 439.13	$ 369.76	$ 340.84	$ 327.11	$ 320.18
$ 35000.00	$ 512.32	$ 431.38	$ 397.65	$ 381.62	$ 373.54
$ 40000.00	$ 585.50	$ 493.01	$ 454.46	$ 436.14	$ 426.90
$ 45000.00	$ 658.69	$ 554.63	$ 511.26	$ 490.66	$ 480.27
$ 50000.00	$ 731.88	$ 616.26	$ 568.07	$ 545.18	$ 533.63
$ 55000.00	$ 805.07	$ 677.89	$ 624.88	$ 599.69	$ 586.99
$ 60000.00	$ 878.26	$ 739.51	$ 681.68	$ 654.21	$ 640.35
$ 65000.00	$ 951.44	$ 801.14	$ 738.49	$ 708.73	$ 693.72
$ 70000.00	$1024.63	$ 862.77	$ 795.30	$ 763.25	$ 747.08
$ 75000.00	$1097.82	$ 924.39	$ 852.11	$ 817.77	$ 800.44
$ 80000.00	$1171.01	$ 986.02	$ 908.91	$ 872.28	$ 853.81
$ 85000.00	$1244.20	$1047.64	$ 965.72	$ 926.80	$ 907.17
$ 90000.00	$1317.39	$1109.27	$1022.53	$ 981.32	$ 960.53
$ 95000.00	$1390.57	$1170.90	$1079.33	$1035.84	$1013.89
$100000.00	$1463.76	$1232.52	$1136.14	$1090.35	$1067.26
$125000.00	$1829.70	$1540.65	$1420.18	$1362.94	$1334.07
$150000.00	$2195.64	$1848.78	$1704.21	$1635.53	$1600.89

YEARLY INTEREST RATE = 12.75%

		LOAN LIFE IN YEARS			
	10	15	20	25	30
PRINCIPAL		MONTHLY PAYMENTS			
$ 25.00	$ .37	$ .31	$ .29	$ .28	$ .27
$ 50.00	$ .74	$ .62	$ .58	$ .55	$ .54
$ 100.00	$ 1.48	$ 1.25	$ 1.15	$ 1.11	$ 1.09
$ 200.00	$ 2.96	$ 2.50	$ 2.31	$ 2.22	$ 2.17
$ 300.00	$ 4.44	$ 3.75	$ 3.46	$ 3.33	$ 3.26
$ 400.00	$ 5.91	$ 5.00	$ 4.62	$ 4.44	$ 4.35
$ 500.00	$ 7.39	$ 6.24	$ 5.77	$ 5.55	$ 5.43
$ 1000.00	$ 14.78	$ 12.49	$ 11.54	$ 11.09	$ 10.87
$ 2000.00	$ 29.57	$ 24.98	$ 23.08	$ 22.18	$ 21.73
$ 3000.00	$ 44.35	$ 37.47	$ 34.61	$ 33.27	$ 32.60
$ 4000.00	$ 59.14	$ 49.95	$ 46.15	$ 44.36	$ 43.47
$ 5000.00	$ 73.92	$ 62.44	$ 57.69	$ 55.45	$ 54.33
$ 10000.00	$ 147.84	$ 124.88	$ 115.38	$ 110.91	$ 108.67
$ 15000.00	$ 221.76	$ 187.33	$ 173.07	$ 166.36	$ 163.00
$ 20000.00	$ 295.68	$ 249.77	$ 230.76	$ 221.81	$ 217.34
$ 25000.00	$ 369.60	$ 312.21	$ 288.45	$ 277.26	$ 271.67
$ 30000.00	$ 443.52	$ 374.65	$ 346.14	$ 332.72	$ 326.01
$ 35000.00	$ 517.44	$ 437.09	$ 403.83	$ 388.17	$ 380.34
$ 40000.00	$ 591.36	$ 499.53	$ 461.52	$ 443.62	$ 434.68
$ 45000.00	$ 665.28	$ 561.98	$ 519.22	$ 499.07	$ 489.01
$ 50000.00	$ 739.20	$ 624.42	$ 576.91	$ 554.53	$ 543.35
$ 55000.00	$ 813.12	$ 686.86	$ 634.60	$ 609.98	$ 597.68
$ 60000.00	$ 887.04	$ 749.30	$ 692.29	$ 665.43	$ 652.02
$ 65000.00	$ 960.96	$ 811.74	$ 749.98	$ 720.88	$ 706.35
$ 70000.00	$1034.88	$ 874.19	$ 807.67	$ 776.34	$ 760.68
$ 75000.00	$1108.80	$ 936.63	$ 865.36	$ 831.79	$ 815.02
$ 80000.00	$1182.72	$ 999.07	$ 923.05	$ 887.24	$ 869.35
$ 85000.00	$1256.64	$1061.51	$ 980.74	$ 942.69	$ 923.69
$ 90000.00	$1330.56	$1123.95	$1038.43	$ 998.15	$ 978.02
$ 95000.00	$1404.48	$1186.39	$1096.12	$1053.60	$1032.36
$100000.00	$1478.40	$1248.84	$1153.81	$1109.05	$1086.69
$125000.00	$1848.00	$1561.05	$1442.26	$1386.31	$1358.37
$150000.00	$2217.60	$1873.25	$1730.72	$1663.58	$1630.04

YEARLY INTEREST RATE = 13.00%

LOAN LIFE IN YEARS

PRINCIPAL	10	15	20	25	30
			MONTHLY PAYMENTS		
$ 25.00	$ .37	$ .32	$ .29	$ .28	$ .28
$ 50.00	$ .75	$ .63	$ .59	$ .56	$ .55
$ 100.00	$ 1.49	$ 1.27	$ 1.17	$ 1.13	$ 1.11
$ 200.00	$ 2.99	$ 2.53	$ 2.34	$ 2.26	$ 2.21
$ 300.00	$ 4.48	$ 3.80	$ 3.51	$ 3.38	$ 3.32
$ 400.00	$ 5.97	$ 5.06	$ 4.69	$ 4.51	$ 4.42
$ 500.00	$ 7.47	$ 6.33	$ 5.86	$ 5.64	$ 5.53
$ 1000.00	$ 14.93	$ 12.65	$ 11.72	$ 11.28	$ 11.06
$ 2000.00	$ 29.86	$ 25.30	$ 23.43	$ 22.56	$ 22.12
$ 3000.00	$ 44.79	$ 37.96	$ 35.15	$ 33.84	$ 33.19
$ 4000.00	$ 59.72	$ 50.61	$ 46.86	$ 45.11	$ 44.25
$ 5000.00	$ 74.66	$ 63.26	$ 58.58	$ 56.39	$ 55.31
$ 10000.00	$ 149.31	$ 126.52	$ 117.16	$ 112.78	$ 110.62
$ 15000.00	$ 223.97	$ 189.79	$ 175.74	$ 169.18	$ 165.93
$ 20000.00	$ 298.62	$ 253.05	$ 234.32	$ 225.57	$ 221.24
$ 25000.00	$ 373.28	$ 316.31	$ 292.89	$ 281.96	$ 276.55
$ 30000.00	$ 447.93	$ 379.57	$ 351.47	$ 338.35	$ 331.86
$ 35000.00	$ 522.59	$ 442.83	$ 410.05	$ 394.74	$ 387.17
$ 40000.00	$ 597.24	$ 506.10	$ 468.63	$ 451.13	$ 442.48
$ 45000.00	$ 671.90	$ 569.36	$ 527.21	$ 507.53	$ 497.79
$ 50000.00	$ 746.55	$ 632.62	$ 585.79	$ 563.92	$ 553.10
$ 55000.00	$ 821.21	$ 695.88	$ 644.37	$ 620.31	$ 608.41
$ 60000.00	$ 895.86	$ 759.15	$ 702.95	$ 676.70	$ 663.72
$ 65000.00	$ 970.52	$ 822.41	$ 761.52	$ 733.09	$ 719.03
$ 70000.00	$1045.17	$ 885.67	$ 820.10	$ 789.48	$ 774.34
$ 75000.00	$1119.83	$ 948.93	$ 878.68	$ 845.88	$ 829.65
$ 80000.00	$1194.49	$1012.19	$ 937.26	$ 902.27	$ 884.96
$ 85000.00	$1269.14	$1075.46	$ 995.84	$ 958.66	$ 940.27
$ 90000.00	$1343.80	$1138.72	$1054.42	$1015.05	$ 995.58
$ 95000.00	$1418.45	$1201.98	$1113.00	$1071.44	$1050.89
$100000.00	$1493.11	$1265.24	$1171.58	$1127.83	$1106.20
$125000.00	$1866.38	$1581.55	$1464.47	$1409.79	$1382.75
$150000.00	$2239.66	$1897.86	$1757.36	$1691.75	$1659.30

YEARLY INTEREST RATE = 13.25%

LOAN LIFE IN YEARS

PRINCIPAL	10	15	20	25	30
			MONTHLY PAYMENTS		
$ 25.00	$ .38	$ .32	$ .30	$ .29	$ .28
$ 50.00	$ .75	$ .64	$ .59	$ .57	$ .56
$ 100.00	$ 1.51	$ 1.28	$ 1.19	$ 1.15	$ 1.13
$ 200.00	$ 3.02	$ 2.56	$ 2.38	$ 2.29	$ 2.25
$ 300.00	$ 4.52	$ 3.85	$ 3.57	$ 3.44	$ 3.38
$ 400.00	$ 6.03	$ 5.13	$ 4.76	$ 4.59	$ 4.50
$ 500.00	$ 7.54	$ 6.41	$ 5.95	$ 5.73	$ 5.63
$ 1000.00	$ 15.08	$ 12.82	$ 11.89	$ 11.47	$ 11.26
$ 2000.00	$ 30.16	$ 25.63	$ 23.79	$ 22.93	$ 22.52
$ 3000.00	$ 45.24	$ 38.45	$ 35.68	$ 34.40	$ 33.77
$ 4000.00	$ 60.32	$ 51.27	$ 47.58	$ 45.87	$ 45.03
$ 5000.00	$ 75.39	$ 64.09	$ 59.47	$ 57.33	$ 56.29
$ 10000.00	$ 150.79	$ 128.17	$ 118.94	$ 114.67	$ 112.58
$ 15000.00	$ 226.18	$ 192.26	$ 178.41	$ 172.00	$ 168.87
$ 20000.00	$ 301.58	$ 256.35	$ 237.89	$ 229.34	$ 225.15
$ 25000.00	$ 376.97	$ 320.43	$ 297.36	$ 286.67	$ 281.44
$ 30000.00	$ 452.37	$ 384.52	$ 356.83	$ 344.01	$ 337.73
$ 35000.00	$ 527.76	$ 448.61	$ 416.30	$ 401.34	$ 394.02
$ 40000.00	$ 603.16	$ 512.69	$ 475.77	$ 458.68	$ 450.31
$ 45000.00	$ 678.55	$ 576.78	$ 535.24	$ 516.01	$ 506.60
$ 50000.00	$ 753.94	$ 640.87	$ 594.72	$ 573.35	$ 562.89
$ 55000.00	$ 829.34	$ 704.95	$ 654.19	$ 630.68	$ 619.18
$ 60000.00	$ 904.73	$ 769.04	$ 713.66	$ 688.02	$ 675.46
$ 65000.00	$ 980.13	$ 833.13	$ 773.13	$ 745.35	$ 731.75
$ 70000.00	$1055.52	$ 897.22	$ 832.60	$ 802.69	$ 788.04
$ 75000.00	$1130.92	$ 961.30	$ 892.07	$ 860.02	$ 844.33
$ 80000.00	$1206.31	$1025.39	$ 951.54	$ 917.36	$ 900.62
$ 85000.00	$1281.71	$1089.48	$1011.02	$ 974.69	$ 956.91
$ 90000.00	$1357.10	$1153.56	$1070.49	$1032.03	$1013.20
$ 95000.00	$1432.49	$1217.65	$1129.96	$1089.36	$1069.48
$100000.00	$1507.89	$1281.74	$1189.43	$1146.70	$1125.77
$125000.00	$1884.86	$1602.17	$1486.79	$1433.37	$1407.22
$150000.00	$2261.83	$1922.60	$1784.15	$1720.05	$1688.66

Index